THE MAKING OF MARTIN LUTHER KING AND THE CIVIL RIGHTS MOVEMENT

The Making of Martin Luther King and the Civil Rights Movement

Edited by

Brian Ward
Lecturer in American History
University of Newcastle upon Tyne

and

Tony Badger
Paul Mellon Professor of American History
University of Cambridge

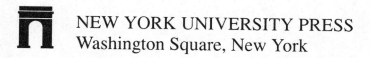 **NEW YORK UNIVERSITY PRESS**
Washington Square, New York

First published in the U.S.A. in 1996 by
NEW YORK UNIVERSITY PRESS
Washington Square
New York, N.Y. 10003

Library of Congress Cataloging-in-Publication Data
The making of Martin Luther King and the civil rights movement /
edited by Brian Ward and Tony Badger.
p.   cm.
Papers selected from the Martin Luther King, Jr. Memorial
Conference on Civil Rights and Race Relations held between 21 and 24
October, 1993 at the University of Newcastle upon Tyne.
Includes index.
ISBN 0–8147–9295–2. — ISBN 0–8147–9296–0 (pbk.)
1. King, Martin Luther, Jr., 1929–1968—Congresses.   2. Civil
rights movements—United States—History—20th century—Congresses.
3. Afro-Americans—Civil rights—Congresses.   4. United States—Race
relations—Congresses.   I. Ward, Brian, 1961–   .   II. Badger,
Tony.   III. Martin Luther King, Jr., Memorial Conference on Civil
Rights and Race Relations (1993 : University of Newcastle upon Tyne)
E185.97.K5M255   1996
323'.092—dc20   95–14667
[B]   CIP

Printed in Great Britain

Contents

PART III: REPRESENTATIONS

PART IV: COMPARISONS

Acknowledgements

On 13 November 1967, the University of Newcastle upon Tyne became the only institution in Britain to award Martin Luther King Jr an Honorary Doctorate, when it conferred upon the civil rights leader the degree of Doctor of Civil Law. Between 21 and 24 October 1993, in the twenty-fifth year since King's death, the University paid tribute to his memory, achievements and legacy by staging the Martin Luther King Jr Memorial Conference on Civil Rights and Race Relations, from which the twelve chapters of this book have been drawn.

While the essays contained in the volume testify to the scholarly excellence of the Conference, they tell only part of the story of those memorable few days in Newcastle. Three superb public lectures by cartoonist Doug Marlette, civil rights activist, author and politician Julian Bond, and former Mayor of Cincinnati and former US Ambassador to the UN Commission on Human Rights J. Kenneth Blackwell, drew large and appreciative audiences. So, too, did the performances of Claudia Menza and Charles Frye in 'The Claudia and Charles Show' – a compelling and revealing meditation on inter-racial relationships – and singer-writer Sandi Russell, in her enthralling celebration of African-American women's writings, 'Render Me My Song'. These performances were supplemented by a season of African-American films at the Tyneside Cinema, while the People's Gallery hosted a triple bill of related art exhibitions, comprising the first British showing of Doug Marlette's drawings on 'Race In America', a moving exhibition of photo-journalism depicting Martin Luther King and the civil rights movement, and a photographic exhibition recording the lives of Newcastle's own minority population. These public lectures, performances and exhibitions, coupled with extensive press coverage, helped to make the Conference a genuinely public affair, engaging a far wider audience than is usually associated with an academic conference and, hopefully, encouraging a greater awareness of the issues of race, racism and resistance to oppression which the 'academic' Conference and this volume address.

Inevitably, in the course of organizing such a diverse event, one is indebted to many individuals and institutions and this is a welcome opportunity for me, as Conference Director as well as co-editor, to express my personal thanks to the following individuals without whom neither the Conference nor this volume would have been possible. John Derry, Judie Newman and David Saunders served on the Conference Committee alongside Jerry Paterson, then Dean of Arts at the University of Newcastle upon Tyne. Jerry's constant enthusiasm for the Conference and recognition of the efforts of those who were struggling to make it happen, were absolutely crucial to its success. My thanks also go to Mr James Wright, the Vice-Chancellor of the University, who recognized the potential and significance of the project and responded with generous financial support and personal encouragement. Elsewhere in the University, Tony Rylance and Melanie Reed offered important help and advice concerning publicity, as did Margaret Lewis, whose general interest and assistance in all aspects of the proceedings was very much appreciated. In various ways Derek Bradford, Dorothy Croyden, Clare Hagan, Derek Nicholson and Mick Sharp also made vital contributions to the Conference.

Beyond the University, Nadeem Ahmad and Colin Mussett provided excellent links with the Newcastle upon Tyne City Council and the Lord Mayor's Office respectively and were instrumental in making the event a genuinely public affair. The same could be said of Gina Barron of the People's Gallery and Briony Hanson of the Tyneside Cinema, while Julie Bonner dealt with complicated – and endlessly changing – hotel requirements with good humour and great efficiency. William Armbruster, US Deputy Cultural Attaché in London, Nicholas Luddington and John Sears of the Roosevelt Center in New York, were good friends to the Conference from its inception.

I should also thank Tony Badger, my predecessor at the University of Newcastle upon Tyne and co-editor of this work, and Richard King, then chairman of the British Association for American Studies and contributor to this volume, for their good counsel and general encouragement of the whole project. Thanks also to all those from seven different countries who attended the Conference, especially those who gave papers or chaired sessions.

Finally, and most importantly, I wish to thank my postgraduate students, Sylvia Ellis, Sharon Pointer, Fawzia Topan and Steve Walsh for all their efforts before and during the Conference. Particular thanks go to Jenny Walker, who generously put in ludicrously long hours when the going got really tough and was rewarded for her pains by a request to help prepare and index this volume. Janice Cummin and Eleanor Cunningham will know how she felt, having also put in time and effort far beyond the call of duty during the build-up to the Conference, only to find that its successful completion left them with a manuscript to prepare! In this they have been greatly helped by Tricia Brooks, who sorted out word-processing complexities far beyond the understanding of the editors. I am very much indebted to them all for their help, efficiency and patience.

The following organizations and institutions generously contributed to the staging of the 1993 Martin Luther King Jr Memorial Conference. Without their assistance, neither the Conference nor this volume would have been possible: Alcan; The Baring Foundation; The British Academy; The British Association for American Studies; The Fulbright Commission; The Imperial Swallow Hotel, Jesmond; The National Association of Racial Equality Advisors; Nestlé UK; Newcastle upon Tyne City Council; Northern Arts; Procter & Gamble; The Roosevelt Institution, New York; The Roosevelt Study Center, Middleburg; Tyne and Wear Museums; The United States Information Service; The University of Newcastle upon Tyne.

B.W.
Newcastle upon Tyne, 1995

Notes on the Contributors

Tony Badger is Paul Mellon Professor of American History at the University of Cambridge. His publications include *Prosperity Road: The New Deal, Tobacco and North Carolina; North Carolina in the New Deal* and *The New Deal: The Depression Years, 1933–1940*.

Clayborne Carson is a Professor of American History at Stanford University and Director of the Martin Luther King Jr Papers Project. His many publications include *In Struggle: SNCC and the Black Awakening of the 1960s*; *The Eyes on the Prize Civil Rights Reader* (edited with David J. Garrow, Vincent Harding, Darlene Clark Hine and Toby Kleban Levine) and *The Papers of Martin Luther King, Jr., Volume 1: Called to Serve* (edited with Ralph E. Luker and Penny A. Russell).

Robert Cook is a Lecturer in American History at the University of Sheffield. His publications include *Baptism of Fire: The Republican Party in Iowa, 1838–1878* and he is currently writing a general history of the civil rights and black power movements.

Adam Fairclough holds the chair of Modern American History at the University of Leeds. His works on the civil rights movement include *To Redeem the Soul of America: The Southern Christian Leadership Conference and Martin Luther King Jr.* and *Martin Luther King, Jr.* He has just completed a major book on *Race and Democracy: The Struggle for Civil Rights in Louisiana, 1915–1972*. He is currently working on a general history of the civil rights movement, and a study of black teachers in the Movement.

George M. Fredrickson is Edgar E. Robinson Professor of United States History at Stanford University. His numerous publications on race relations include, *The Inner Civil War: Northern Intellectuals and the Crisis of the Union; The Black Image in the White Mind: The Debate on Afro-American Character and Destiny, 1817–1914; White Supremacy: A Comparative Study of American and South African History* and *The Arrogance of Race: Historical Perspectives on Slavery, Racism and Social Inequality*.

Walter A. Jackson is an Assistant Professor of History at North Carolina State University and author of the multiple award-winning *Gunnar Myrdal and America's Conscience: Social Engineering and Racial Liberalism, 1938–1987*.

Richard H. King is Reader in American Studies at the University of Nottingham and a former Chairman of the British Association for American Studies. His publications include, *The Party of Eros, The Southern Renais-*

sance: The Cultural Awakening of the American South, 1938–1955 and *Civil Rights and the Idea of Freedom.*

John Kirk is a Lecturer in American History at the University of Wales, Lampeter. As a graduate student at the University of Newcastle upon Tyne, his essay on 'Dr J.M. Robinson, The Arkansas Negro Democratic Association and Black Politics in Little Rock, Arkansas, 1928–1952' [in *Pulaski County Historical Quarterly*, (1993)], won the F. Hampton Roy History Award.

Emily M. Lewis is a former graduate student at Arizona State University.

Keith D. Miller is an Assistant Professor of English at Arizona State University. His publications include *Voice of Deliverance: The Language of Martin Luther King Jr. and Its Sources* and he is currently conducting preliminary research for a study of black baseball star Jackie Robinson.

Tariq Modood is a former Hallsworth Research Fellow at the University of Manchester and currently working at the Policy Studies Institute in London. His many publications on race and race relations include, *Not Easy Being British: Colour, Culture and Citizenship.*

Mike Sewell is a Staff Tutor in History and International Relations in the Board of Continuing Education at the University of Cambridge. He has published several articles on Anglo-American relations, including, 'The Queen of Our Hearts Today: Queen Victoria's American Image', [in S. Ickringill and S. Mills (eds), *Victorian America*] and 'Political Rhetoric and Policy-Making: James G. Blaine and Britain', [in *Journal of American Studies* (1990)].

Brian Ward is a Lecturer in American History at the University of Newcastle upon Tyne and Director of that institution's Martin Luther King Jr Memorial Conference. His publications include, 'Racial Politics, Culture and the Cole Incident of 1956', [in Melvyn Stokes and Rick Halpern (eds), *Race and Class in the American South since 1890*], and 'A King in Newcastle: Martin Luther King and British Race Relations, 1967–8', [*Georgia Historical Quarterly* (1995)].

John White is a Reader in American History at the University of Hull. His many publications on African-American history and culture include *Black Leadership in America: From Booker T. Washington to Jesse Jackson* and *Billie Holiday: Her Life and Times.* His essay, 'Kansas City, Pendergast, and All That Jazz', [in John White and Brian Holden Reid (eds), *American Studies: Essays in Honour of Marcus Cunliffe*] won the 1992 Arthur Miller American Studies Prize. He is currently working on a biography of E.D. Nixon.

List of Abbreviations

ACMHR	Alabama Christian Movement for Human Rights
ADA	Americans for Democratic Action
AFL	American Federation of Labor
ANC	African National Congress
BBC	British Broadcasting Corporation
BSCP	Brotherhood of Sleeping Car Porters
CARD	Campaign Against Racial Discrimination
CIA	Central Intelligence Agency
CIO	Congress of Industrial Organizations
CND	Campaign for Nuclear Disarmament
CNO	Committee on Negro Organizations
CORE	Congress of Racial Equality
DAR	Daughters of the American Revolution
FBI	Federal Bureau of Investigation
FEPC	Fair Employment Practices Committee
FOR	Fellowship of Reconciliation
FSA	Farm Security Administration
ICC	Inter Civic Council
ILO	International Labour Organization
MFDP	Mississippi Freedom Democratic Party
MIA	Montgomery Improvement Association
MOWM	March on Washington Movement
MRA	Moral ReArmament
NAACP	National Association for the Advancement of Colored People
NAPE	National Alliance of Postal Employees
NCCI	National Committee for Commonwealth Immigrants
NCCL	National Council for Civil Liberties
NICRA	Northern Ireland Civil Rights Association
NPS	National Park Service
NYA	National Youth Administration
OAAU	Organization of Afro-American Unity
PAC	Pan-Africanist Congress
RRB	Race Relations Board
SCEF	Southern Conference Education Fund
SCHW	Southern Conference for Human Welfare
SCLC	Southern Christian Leadership Conference
SCORE	Student Campaign on Racial Equality
SDS	Students for a Democratic Society

SNCC	Student Nonviolent Coordinating Committee
TVA	Tennessee Valley Authority
UAW	United Auto Workers
UDL	United Defense League
UN	United Nations
UNESCO	United Nations Educational, Scientific and Cultural Organisation
USCC	US Civil War Centennial Commission
USO	United Services Organization
WPA	Works Project Administration
WPC	Women's Political Council
YMCA	Young Men's Christian Association
YWCA	Young Women's Christian Association

Introduction

Brian Ward and Tony Badger

On 13 November 1967, Martin Luther King Jr visited the University of Newcastle upon Tyne in England to receive an Honorary Doctorate in Civil Law. Six months later, King was dead. The twenty-five years which separated King's murder and the Memorial Conference from which the papers in this volume are drawn have witnessed a remarkable outpouring of scholarly and popular works dealing with King, the civil rights movement and contemporary race relations in the United States. Historians, political scientists, biographers, sociologists, cultural critics, journalists, novelists, musicians, artists, film-makers and memoirists, have all contributed to this vast and swelling commentary.

During that quarter of a century of representation and analysis, there have been several discernible, if by no means absolute, shifts in the principal concerns of the scholarly literature. Early works tended to concentrate either on King and major protest organizations, like the NAACP, CORE, SCLC and SNCC, or on the diverse white responses to black demands for civil and voting rights at federal and popular levels. In these works the classic phase of civil rights activity was usually fixed geographically in the South and chronologically between the Montgomery bus boycott of 1955–6 and the Selma campaign of 1965. The black power era of the late 1960s and early 1970s was usually reduced to a postscript, characterized by an over-emphasis on disintegration, violence and nihilism. While the implications of the civil rights era and, more particularly, the Voting Rights Act of 1965, received some attention from political scientists, few studies considered the psychological, social and cultural aftermath of the Movement for participants and a new generation of African-Americans.

Since the early 1980s, however, a series of important community-based studies have combined to revise the standard chronology and shift the focus of attention away from national leaders and organizations towards the local figures, organizations and institutions which sustained black protest. A long-hidden history of black struggle, overt and covert, direct and indirect, has been rediscovered. The origins of the Movement have been pushed back into the heart of the Jim Crow era, with the economic, demographic, political and ideological transformations of the New Deal and World War II accorded special importance in the development of mass black activism. While much of this literature has remained largely concerned with the mobilization of southern blacks, there has been a greater appreciation of the relationship between the southern movement and the struggles of blacks elsewhere in the United States and a growing recognition of the importance and complexities of the black power era.

The twelve essays in this volume extend and, in some cases, challenge, many of the agendas established by the civil rights scholarship of the past twenty-five years. Individually, they offer important new insights into the origins, development, representations and international ramifications of the civil rights movement; collectively, they suggest some of the most profitable areas for scholars to probe in the 1990s, offering a wide range of possible new perspectives, methodologies, sources and priorities.

ORIGINS

The first three papers in this collection are concerned with the roots of a mass black civil rights movement in the South. All three employ the detailed study of particular communities and individuals to confirm the inadequacy of the old Montgomery-to-Selma chronology. For Adam Fairclough, John Kirk and John White, it is the careful probing of local affairs, within the context of changing regional, national and international trends and events, which offers the most fruitful insights into the development of mass activism. As Adam Fairclough points out in his essay on 'The Civil Rights Movement in Louisiana, 1939–54', critical changes in the economics and politics of South and nation between 1940 and 1955 meant that by the mid-1950s most of the Deep South was no longer like Mississippi – the classic example of a Jim Crow society. Thus, while paying due deference to the durability and tenacity of black struggle at the local level, the fact is that the modern civil rights movement was crucially shaped, in Louisiana as elsewhere, in partial response to those broader changes.

Fairclough castigates much of the scholarship on the civil rights movement for over-emphasizing the role of Martin Luther King at the expense of local activists and for exaggerating the importance of the black church while neglecting other key centres of black life and protest, such as unions, schools, teachers, businessmen, masonic lodges and other fraternal organizations. The essays by John Kirk on black activism in Arkansas and John White on E. D. Nixon and protest in Montgomery, confirm the value of this heightened sensitivity to the diverse institutional and organizational structure of local black resistance.

While Fairclough, Kirk and White share a desire to push back the origins of mass black protest, separately and collectively their papers warn against the perils of making too many easy generalizations about the nature of white oppression and black resistance before the mid-1950s. Fairclough, for example, argues that the role of the NAACP, long eclipsed by the scholarly focus on newer, allegedly more dynamic, direct action organizations like SCLC and

SNCC, needs to be revaluated. Certainly, in Louisiana in the 1940s and 1950s, the NAACP served as the locomotive of black protest and political activity. By contrast, John Kirk's study of black activism in Arkansas reveals a state in which neither the NAACP, nor labour, nor the black church, played the major role in developing and orchestrating black protest before the 1950s. Rather, as Fairclough also suggested might be the case, teachers, businessmen and masonic lodges appeared at the forefront of the black struggle, while influential local leaders, like the lawyer W. H. Flowers, invariably loomed far larger than national ones.

Moreover, in the avowedly 'progressive' Arkansas of the period between the 1930s and the mid-1950s, politics offered the main arena for collective black action and progress, albeit within the boundaries of Jim Crow. Galvanized by the *Smith* v. *Allwright* decision of 1944, which outlawed the white primary, and encouraged by the success of relatively moderate white politicians like Sid McMath, Arkansas blacks campaigned – with varying degrees of success – to assert their right to the ballot, and organized to exploit the potential of that vote. At the forefront of those efforts was the Committee on Negro Organizations, an early, statewide, example of the sort of 'organization of organizations' which later proved so instrumental in orchestrating local black protests in Baton Rouge, Montgomery and elsewhere in the South. Kirk's study concentrates on the pivotal role of the CNO in Arkansas, paying particular attention to its often fraught relationship with other organizations like the NAACP. Kirk's essay also restores to the historical record W.H. Flowers, architect of the CNO, but a hitherto neglected figure in the history of black protest.

If John Kirk has rescued W.H. Flowers from obscurity, the role of the individual at the heart of John White's piece, E. D. Nixon, has seldom been forgotten: it has merely been much misunderstood. White's study, the first scholarly account of Nixon's career, draws on previously restricted private papers to reassess this forceful character's contribution to black protest in Montgomery – a contribution which culminated, rather than commenced, with his role in the bus boycott of 1955–6. Again in accordance with Adam Fairclough's local study template, White emphasizes how Nixon's links with organized labour, in the form of the Brotherhood of Sleeping Car Porters, and the NAACP, for which he served as president in Montgomery, encouraged his initial activism and later served as the main sources of his influence. Indeed, White explains how Nixon exploited those links, not only to generate funding, but to 'nationalize' the impact of the bus boycott.

White offers ample justification for Nixon's own claims that he was the key figure in black Montgomery protest prior to the boycott and the community's chief tactician at its commencement. Nevertheless, Nixon did not emerge as the leader of the Montgomery Improvement Association and his contribution was ultimately eclipsed by that of Martin Luther King. White

suggests that this was a function both of Nixon's personality – he had little
of King's personal charm or charisma – and the existence of deep cleavages
within the black community in Montgomery which King, as newcomer, holder
of a doctorate and peerless popular orator, was able to transcend. Nixon, in
contrast, held little appeal for the black middle class and found no rapport
with the more progressive clergy who proved so vital in sustaining the boycott.

RESPONSES

The three essays on Origins clearly reveal the existence and diversity of the
protests which predated the civil rights movement of the 1950s and 1960s,
thereby suggesting certain continuities in southern black history. It is important, however, not to lose sight of what was indeed distinctive about the
classic southern civil rights era, 1955–65. There was something quantitat-
ively and qualitatively different about the protests of blacks and their white
allies during this period. Ironically, one group who recognized this fact
immediately were southern whites: liberal and conservative.

Tony Badger's, 'Fatalism Not Gradualism: Race and the Crisis of Southern
Liberalism' considers the apparent vitality, but actual limitations, of southern
racial liberalism during the decade after World War II and seeks to account
for its disintegration in the mid-to-late 1950s, just as the movement for racial
change gathered momentum. Following a detailed discussion of the fate of
white liberals in that most illiberal of southern states, Mississippi, Badger
examines the careers of four liberal southern governors (Sid McMath of
Arkansas, Earl Long of Louisiana, Kerr Scott of North Carolina and Jim
Folsom of Alabama) and explores the motivations of the handful of southern politicians who in 1956 refused to sign the Southern Manifesto, the most
important formal assertion of the region's determination to resist desegregation.
In so doing, he reveals both the internal weaknesses of southern racial liberalism, with its avowedly gradualist agenda, and the external forces which
combined to destroy it in the late 1950s. Ultimately, liberals found themselves unable to sustain their gradualist approach to racial change in the
face of mounting black impatience and activism, increased federal intervention
to affirm and, tentatively, protect black rights and, most importantly, the mobilization of organized massive white resistance to counter those developments.

Yet, according to Badger, the irony of this crisis for southern liberals was
that they never actually spoke up for gradualism at a time when it might
have won the support of the mass of white southerners. It is true that the
South of the mid-to-late 1950s appeared to be no place for moderation or
gradualism on racial matters and liberals responded by variously trying to
ignore the desegregation issue, openly siding with the resistance movement
or, on rare occasions, accepting the Supreme Court's *Brown* decision as the

law of the land – a stance which usually had dire political consequences. Nevertheless, Badger accuses southern liberals of a failure of leadership and commitment to their gradualist beliefs. Southern liberals were afflicted by a fatalism which convinced them that the conservative forces of resistance represented the mass of southern white public opinion and that they had no alternative but to be cautious.

In fact, Badger argues, one of the reasons why conservatives mobilized with such vigour and skill in the massive resistance movement was that they felt it was the liberal agenda on racial change which commanded mass public support. In other words, both conservatives and liberals believed that popular support after *Brown* lay with the other side. The difference was that the conservatives orchestrated a massive campaign of propaganda and legal and extra-legal action to assert white supremacy and halt desegregation. By contrast, liberals, fearing the wrath of their fellow whites, refused to engage in a battle for the mind of the white South. They organized no effective counter campaign urging compliance and thus offered white southerners no viable alternative to resistance, except apathy or resignation.

Like Tony Badger, Walter Jackson is principally concerned with the responses of white Americans to the campaign for black civil rights and with the forces which shaped popular opinion on the issue. More specifically, he investigates the reaction of white intellectuals as represented in the leading national journals of opinion. As Jackson points out, these journals rarely published work by African-American writers and consequently their coverage of the burgeoning Movement often had an 'air of unreality' and occasionally sheer ignorance concerning the black situation. As many black critics later complained, much of this liberal writing was suffused with what James Baldwin called a 'missionary complex' and predicated on the assumption that racial change would be gradual and managed by white elites.

While Jackson accepts that much of this criticism was justified, he does not restrict himself to simple condemnation. Instead, he seeks to explain why white intellectuals had such difficulty comprehending the real character of the civil rights movement in terms of the nature of post-war American liberalism. Just as crucially, Jackson argues that these deeply flawed liberal commentaries had a considerable role in shaping the contours of public debate and governmental thought on racial matters. Consequently, black leaders who recognized the need to forge a national coalition to push for civil rights legislation, most notably Martin Luther King Jr, necessarily did so within the context of a public discourse on race, the character, limits and priorities of which they only partially controlled or endorsed.

The limits of the white liberal agenda on race in America as noted by Badger and Jackson, was dramatically revealed by the unravelling of the civil rights consensus in the decade following the attainment of statutory equality in 1965. Conventionally, this period is portrayed as one of white retreat from the obdurate systemic, social and economic problems which continued to afflict black America and the increased radicalization of black protest in the multifarious forms of black power. Clayborne Carson's essay, 'Rethinking African-American Political Thought in the Post-Revolutionary Era' revises that conceptualization by suggesting both that the southern civil rights movement was more radical than most accounts allow, and that the black power era saw the corruption, rather than the apogee, of that initial radicalism.

Carson argues that the southern civil rights movement initially fused black Christianity, the social gospel and Gandhian tactics to create a radical alternative to the black nationalist, Marxian and liberal traditions which had previously informed much African-American protest. While SNCC, in particular, remained open to certain nationalist ideas − especially those expressed by Malcolm X − and had genuine debts to the Old Left, it had helped to develop a new mass movement committed to nothing less than the radical recasting of American society into a 'beloved community'.

By contrast, Carson charges that the black power era often saw militant rhetoric replace meaningful action and separatism replace coherent efforts to restructure American society. Afrocentrism became the touchstone of black militancy and at its best encouraged a healthy increase in black consciousness and pride. Too often, however, that consciousness remained unharnessed and generated no real political threat to the existing order, particularly at a time when the conservative backlash and brutal repression of black militants were at full tide. In Carson's view, then, the true inheritors of the radical legacy of the civil rights movement were not the black power activists, but those engaged in the ecological, feminist and new age movements, who have retained faith in the value of mass action to realize a better, fairer and more compassionate, pluralistic world.

REPRESENTATIONS

The civil rights movement deployed many tactics in its efforts to secure freedom and equality for African-Americans: boycotts, marches, sit-ins, freedom rides, voter registration drives, lawsuits, educational initiatives and electoral politics all played their part in a diverse and vibrant movement and all have received their share of attention from historians. One of the least examined aspects of the civil rights campaign, however, concerns the politics of the Movement's self-presentation: the very deliberate ways in which the early Movement sought to align itself with the central ideals of American society and manipulate the sacred symbols of American civil religion so as to garner widespread support for its demands. Ultimately, it was the consistent application of social, political and economic pressure from a mass movement, coupled with a blend of legalistic, practical, rhetorical and symbolic appeals to core American values – if not practices – which enabled the civil rights movement to represent itself as a legitimate cause, in pursuit of legitimate ends, by legitimate means.

In rather different ways, the papers by Robert Cook and Keith Miller and Emily Lewis both concern the attempts by the Movement to represent and define itself to the American public by tapping into, in Cook's phrase, the 'commonplace rhetoric and mnemonic baggage' of US nationalism and civil religion. Cook illustrates this project by focusing on the response of the Movement to the Civil War Centennial celebrations which ran from 1961 to 1965. As Cook explains, the Centennial provided the opportunity for various groups in America to articulate and promote very different agendas. For example, the federal government sought to make national unity the central theme of the celebrations, while many southern whites saw them as a chance to reify the myth of the Old South and the Lost Cause. Thus, the Centennial, particularly in its first year, was used by southern politicians to intensify an already passionate commitment to 'the Southern Way of Life' and thereby bolster resistance to desegregation.

The civil rights movement naturally sought to invest the Centennial with a very different meaning, one which served the interests of an ongoing struggle for black rights. Rather than emphasizing the preservation of the Union, civil rights leaders interpreted the emancipation of the slaves as the critical event in the Civil War and urged President Kennedy to make this the focal point of the celebrations. The NAACP, in particular, struggled to influence the public perception of the Centennial. It embarrassed the U.S. Centennial Commission by opposing a segregated celebration at Fort Sumter and constantly urged the government and public alike to recognize that the freedoms for which the Civil War had been fought – in the NAACP's construction of the War's meaning, at least – remained unrealized for blacks.

Somewhere near the heart of the battle for the meaning of the Centennial was a struggle for the symbolic meaning of Abraham Lincoln. As Keith Miller and Emily Lewis point out in their essay on the rhetorical sources of Martin Luther King Jr's 'I Have A Dream' oration and the ritual of the 1963 March on Washington, African-Americans had long sought to harness Lincoln's unique prestige in American public memory to their freedom struggle. Resolutely portraying Lincoln as The Great Emancipator, blacks have always interpreted and represented him primarily as a symbol of racial equality, rather than as the saviour of the Union. Thus, it was no coincidence that some of the most potent appeals for America to respect black civil rights were made in the shadow of Lincoln's memorial in the nation's capital: it was there that the most vivid linkage could be made between national ideals, the unfulfilled promise of Emancipation and the contemporary plight of black Americans.

The essay by Miller and Lewis describes how Marian Anderson's 1939 appearance on the steps of the Lincoln Memorial refined and virtually codified the pattern of mass civil rights demonstrations in Washington. This highly ritualized tradition found its definitive expression on 13 August 1963, during the March on Washington led by Martin Luther King Jr. That day also witnessed the most stunning illustration of another black tradition – a rhetorical tradition, in which champions of black rights since the nineteenth century had routinely deployed so-called 'God Terms', such as freedom and justice, in conjunction with very specific appeals to the American civil creed and religious sensibilities, in order to dramatize the black predicament and denounce racial oppression. Miller and Lewis's close analysis of King's 'I Have a Dream' speech not only reveals its congruency with the style and substance of these earlier black orations but, even more critically, describes how the speech actually 'worked' to move a national audience by invoking a well-established repertoire of revered American ideals, symbols and authorities. As the authors put it, King's speech was brilliant, not because it was original, but because it was so conventional. The ritual and rhetoric of the March On Washington combined to make the civil rights movement quintessentially American.

While Cook and Miller and Lewis are concerned with the ways in which the Movement represented itself to the American people, Richard King shifts the focus of attention to how the Movement has itself been represented in literary accounts. Opening up a rich new territory for interdisciplinary investigation, King argues that fictional(ized) accounts of Movement activities offer a 'simulacrum of the experience of the Movement or at least certain aspects of it' in a way which can significantly enhance historical understanding of that phenomenon. Noting that Martin Luther King's entire social philosophy was predicated on a belief that all human beings have the potential to transcend barriers of race, class, gender and culture in order to communicate with and understand each other, King suggests that literature offers a way into a world of past events which similarly depends upon the existence of mutual recognition, identification and empathy among disparate peoples.

Paying particular attention to Ernest Gaines' *A Gathering of Old Men*, Alice Walker's *Meridian* and Rosellen Brown's *Civil Wars*, King reveals how literature offers special insights into key psychological, emotional and experiential aspects of the Movement and its aftermath, which more orthodox – 'factual' – accounts sometimes note, but rarely capture adequately. King recognizes full well that the fictional depiction of historical incidents and characters can raise important moral, as well as intellectual, problems. Focusing on the controversy surrounding the publication of William Styron's *Confessions of Nat Turner*, King examines the elusive boundary between facts and interpretation and squarely confronts the sensitive question of whether it is legitimate for members of one race – and by extension, of one class, gender, religion or culture – to assume the voice of another race, class, gender, religion or culture and claim to render accurately their experiences.

King's paper indicates that historians would do well to note the predominance in the growing canon of civil rights novels of themes like the quest for individual and collective self-respect, the special role and trials of women within the Movement, the emergence of self-consciously politicized communities, the disintegration of those communities in the face of deep and abiding racial and sexual tensions, the destruction of many personal relationships under those same strains and the awful personal and collective dilemma of how to carry on once the Movement had 'ended', but not truly 'overcome'. Such matters, King suggests, need to be addressed before historians can claim any real understanding of what the Movement actually meant to participants.

COMPARISONS

One of the criticisms most often levelled at scholars of the civil rights movement, and of the African-American experience more generally, is that they have tended to employ the terms race and racism rather uncritically as 'transhistorical' explanations for the events which they describe so ably. In fact, race and racism explain little of the experiences of African-Americans unless those concepts are themselves carefully deconstructed. 'Race', for example, is not a primordial category of social distinction, but a mutable socio-historical construct generated and sustained in particular ways by particular cultures at particular times. Indeed, as Tariq Modood describes in a vigorous critique of the simplistic 'black versus white' paradigm which still controls so much of the scholarship on civil rights and race relations in the West, race as a contemporary sociological category is traversed by many other categories of social, cultural, economic and religious distinction, each with its own claim on the construction of individual and group identities.

Focusing on the British situation, but with frequent reference to the United States, Modood reveals just how brittle and unrewarding the simplistic black–white paradigm is for understanding the dynamics of modern societies. Moreover, he argues that much analysis of British and American race relations is informed by a distortive and reductive Atlantocentrism which has rendered it insensitive to certain critical factors in the creation of minority group identity and undermined its ability to identify the true nature of the oppression and discrimination experienced by specific groups. 'Cultural' racism, for example, is valued less than 'colour' racism in the law, in the media and in race relations studies, yet the discrimination practised against those who endorse 'alien' dietary habits or dress codes is real enough. Religious identity, in particular, is routinely devalued in the Atlantocentric model. Yet Modood maintains that religious beliefs are at the core of many minority groups' sense of selfhood and frequently serve as the occasion of the insults and prejudices most keenly felt by those groups.

The key theoretical point here is that minorities feel oppressed most according to the indices which they value most dearly – not necessarily those which the oppressing group thinks are the most valuable. Indeed, even avowed anti-racists from the dominant culture often miss what is most injurious or insulting to those they wish to help – a trend illustrated by the Rushdie affair, where many of those who would passionately defend British Asians against all manner of colour-based insult, assault and discrimination were totally unable to comprehend the intensity of the Muslim response to a grievous religious slight. In future, historians of the civil rights movement would do well to follow Modood's lead, abandoning their often casual and simplistic use of terms like race, racism and discrimination in favour of more subtle, flexible and, ultimately, useful definitions.

Tariq Modood's essay shares with those by Mike Sewell and George Fredrickson a desire to broaden the focus of civil rights studies and make linkages and comparisons with events beyond the United States. The excellent scholarship on the local and national co-ordinates of civil rights campaigns in the United States should not obscure the fact that there was also an important – if still relatively uninterrogated – international dimension to the Movement. The African-American liberation struggle took place against the backdrop of a global struggle of non-white peoples against colonialism and its aftermath, producing a complex and often ambiguous pattern of influence and counter-influence across national boundaries.

Mike Sewell's essay examines the evolving British responses to the American civil rights movement at both popular and governmental levels. Those responses, Sewell suggests, emerged from and were defined by three overlapping contexts: Britain's own experience of empire and decolonisation; the Cold War; and a global perspective which dictated that the struggle for civil rights and the problems of race relations were rarely seen as exclusively American phenomena, but as a typical condition of the modern world. As Sewell explains, although the British were initially confident that their racial situation was in no way analogous to that of the US, such complacency was eroded by the mounting racial tensions within British society and, especially after Watts and the summer riots of the mid-1960s, was eventually replaced by the belief that the nightmarish American present represented the British future. It was in this context that the British debate over the wisdom of tightening restrictions on immigrants or introducing legislation to protect minority rights took place – although Sewell suggests that the British remained highly sceptical about the efficacy of such legislation in changing racist hearts, minds and practices.

If American events exerted an important influence on the politics and public perception of British race relations in the 1960s, the civil rights and black power movements also had a more direct impact on minority politics and mass protest during that period. As Sewell notes, not only did British immigrant groups variously take their leads from Martin Luther King, Malcolm X and Stokely Carmichael, but other protest groups like the Campaign for Nuclear Disarmament and nationalist groups in Wales, Scotland and, most obviously, in Northern Ireland, borrowed a vocabulary and practical repertoire of protest from the African-American struggle.

Mike Sewell suggests that in Britain, as in America, it was in great measure the use of non-violent direct action tactics that guaranteed widespread white support for the African-American cause between 1955 and 1965. George Fredrickson's essay compares the roots, application and efficacy of those tactics in the southern civil rights movement and the South African defiance campaigns of the 1950s. Fredrickson carefully places the two campaigns within the context of the particular problems and opposition each faced and the prospective support from the dominant culture each could hope to attract. He then considers the similarities between two movements of peoples who defined themselves as black victims of white oppression, revealing an ambiguous and uneven relationship.

The most obvious direct linkage was provided by the figure and social philosophy of Gandhi, whose legacy can clearly be detected in the adoption of non-violent tactics by both the defiance campaigns and the civil rights movement. Nevertheless, because the situations faced by blacks in South Africa and America were actually quite different, Fredrickson argues that they necessarily generated quite separate Gandhian traditions of non-violent direct action. Emphasizing the distinction between those who were committed to non-violence as a practical expedient and those for whom it became a way of life, Fredrickson explains that the defiance campaign and the civil rights campaign had important cultural and structural differences. For example, the African National Congress Youth League members who led the defiance campaigns in the 1950s comprised an intellectual elite with little connection to the churches, schools and colleges attended by the mass of black South Africans. These Youth League members had a highly pragmatic commitment to non-violence and soon rejected it in favour of armed struggle. The southern civil rights movement, by contrast, was led by ministers with a firm faith in the moral rectitude, as well as tactical effectiveness, of non-violence, while the black masses were largely mobilized through the black churches and educational establishments of the American South.

Fredrickson's probing essay exposes many other parallels and divergences between the two campaigns. While the South African defiance campaign was centrally directed, the civil rights movement emerged from local initiatives in southern towns and cities, making it more difficult to supress. Just as importantly, while the South African press was overwhelmingly hostile to black demands and the majority of white South Africans were united to resist them, key elements of the American media supported the goals and methods of the civil rights movement and helped to sponsor substantial white sympathy for its basic goals. By comparing and contrasting these two campaigns of non-violent resistance to white supremacy in this way, Fredrickson not only opens up a genuinely comparative perspective on the American civil rights movement, but significantly advances the theoretical understanding of how social and political movements across the world have worked to overthrow existing racial or ethnic hierarchies. In this, as with so many of the contributions to this volume, George Fredrickson has suggested important new areas for study.

Part I

Origins

1 The Civil Rights Movement in Louisiana, 1939–54

Adam Fairclough

In 1950, in the sweltering heat of a June evening, blacks gathered in a small church in the tiny hamlet of Lebeau, Louisiana, to hear a distinguished guest speaker talk to them about democracy. Alvin Jones held degrees from Columbia University and the University of Pennsylvania; a former schoolteacher, and until recently executive secretary of the New Orleans Urban League, he worked for the Louisiana Progressive Voters League, an off-shoot of the NAACP. A broad-shouldered, distinguished-looking black man in his late forties, Jones reminded the audience that St. Landry Parish, where the tiny hamlet of Lebeau stood, did not have a single black voter. He insisted that now was the time to remedy this situation. The following morning he accompanied five people to the parish court house in Opelousas, which housed the office of the registrar of voters. When they entered the room several policemen assaulted and chased them away. 'I was slugged with the butt of a gun and pounded with a pair of brass knuckles', Jones recounted. 'They left a hole in my head.' Dazed and bloody, he received first aid from a black doctor and then returned to New Orleans. Within eighteen months he was dead.[1]

Although St. Landry Parish lay in the heart of the Acadian triangle, a Catholic area of south Louisiana often regarded as less racially oppressive than the northern, Protestant, half of the state, many blacks regarded it as one of Louisiana's worst. A few months earlier an alleged rapist, Edward Honeycutt, had escaped a lynching party only by diving into the Atchafalaya river. An NAACP lawyer who saw him after his recapture found the surliness of Honeycutt's jailers unnerving: 'I have never in my life experienced a more hostile situation.' Honeycutt's confession had been so obviously beaten out of him that the state supreme court ordered a retrial. (Convicted a second time, Honeycutt went to the electric chair.) A local Catholic priest told black civil rights lawyer A. P. Tureaud that whites in St. Landry Parish were 'immovably opposed' to black voting.[2]

The beating of Alvin Jones, however, gave the NAACP an opportunity that it eagerly seized: here was a dramatic illustration of southern brutality that could advance the cause of black suffrage by goading the federal government into action. Under pressure from the Association, the Attorney General ordered the FBI to conduct a full investigation. But in a pattern that

was becoming wearily familiar to civil rights activists, the 'G-men' drew a
blank. The registrar of voters admitted that he *did* remember some kind of
commotion in his office, but 'he was busy registering voters at the time and
did not notice any of the details of the commotion.' Nothing fazed, blacks
in St. Landry Parish pressed on with their quest for the ballot. Forming a
local branch of the NAACP, they found three men willing to file suit in
federal court against the registrar of voters. A few days after the litigation
began, a deputy sheriff shot and killed one of the plaintiffs. The other two
plaintiffs fled to the comparative safety of Baton Rouge.[3]

White politicians in St. Landry, however, recognized that if the NAACP-
backed suit went to trial, the registrar of voters would probably lose. In
1950, in the first ruling of its kind in Louisiana, federal district judge J.
Skelly Wright had ordered the registrar of Washington Parish to enrol black
applicants; two years later judge Gaston Porterie slapped a similar injunction on the registrar of Bossier Parish, in the northern part of the state.
Black determination and NAACP pressure paid off: in 1953, for the first
time since the wholesale disfranchisement of the black population in 1898–
1904, blacks started to vote in St. Landry Parish. Indeed, black registration
soared. It soon exceeded 80 per cent and composed two-fifths of the total
electorate. Blacks helped to elect a new sheriff, a new mayor, and a new
city council.[4]

To any student of the civil rights movement this is a familiar tale; it
could have happened in any one of hundreds of counties throughout the
length and breadth of the South. Yet, because this particular story unfolded
between 1950 and 1954 – before *Brown* v. *Board of Education*, before the
Montgomery bus boycott, before the civil rights movement 'began' – the
name of Alvin Jones is absent from the list of martyrs that is inscribed on
the Civil Rights Memorial in Montgomery. Nor will Jones's name be encountered in any of the standard histories of the civil rights movement.

When *did* the civil rights movement begin? Precisely when the term 'civil
rights movement' became common currency is unclear. Historians commonly
use it to describe the wave of black protest that swept the South between
1955 and 1965. Those were the years when black southerners, even in the
most oppressive areas of the Deep South, challenged white supremacy head-
on. They developed an insurgency so insistent, so broadly based and so
morally appealing that they overcame every obstacle that white racists threw
at them – legal repression, economic coercion, physical brutality, and murder. The civil rights movement achieved a decisive breakthrough in the long
struggle for racial equality. It tore up the fabric of segregation and transformed the South's political landscape. The words 'civil rights movement'
carry such specific connotations of time, place and character that they immediately conjure up powerful images: images of sit-ins and freedom rides,
of mass meetings and demonstrations; above all, images of Martin Luther

King Jr, on his heroic journey from Montgomery to Memphis.

Yet, in many parts of the South an organized struggle against white supremacy developed much earlier, and had already made giant strides by the time of the Montgomery bus boycott. In a few short years, for example, St. Landry Parish had undergone a dramatic transformation. So had hundreds of other southern counties.

The breakthroughs came earlier and faster in Louisiana than elsewhere in the South. In 1948 black teachers won their eight-year-long campaign for equal pay. In 1949 the City of New Orleans appointed its first black policemen since the 1900s. In 1950 Louisiana State University admitted its first black graduate student; state colleges in Hammond and Lafayette enrolled black undergraduates four years later. In 1954 New Orleans integrated its public libraries. In the same year two African-Americans were elected to the city council of Crowley – Louisiana's first black elected officials for more than fifty years. By 1956 the state's black electorate had grown to 160 000, the highest level of black registration in the South apart from Texas and Florida.

These gains did not simply flow from federal court decisions: they also reflected the courage and determination with which ordinary blacks challenged the status quo. Moreover, many acts of opposition utilized direct action tactics. As far back as 1940, the New Orleans branch of the NAACP had boycotted and picketed a concert by Marian Anderson because seating in the Municipal Auditorium was segregated 'horizontally' rather than 'vertically'. Seven years later the branch picketed four Canal Street department stores that refused to allow black women to try on hats. In 1951 parents and children in Alexandria picketed the Rapides Parish court house after the school board, at the behest of local planters, delayed the start of the school year until cotton picking was completed. In 1953 black children in Lafayette boycotted a new high school because its facilities did not match those of the white high school. The following year, shortly before the *Brown* decision, blacks in New Orleans boycotted McDonogh Day, an annual ceremony in which white and black children honoured the memory of John McDonogh, the nineteenth-century benefactor of public schools in New Orleans and Baltimore. Backed by the city's black teachers, parents refused to let their children take part in the parade when the school board continued to insist that they march at the rear of the procession.[5]

Baton Rouge, the state capital, witnessed the most striking example of direct action. There, in June 1953, blacks boycotted city buses to protest against segregation laws that compelled them to stand over empty seats that had been reserved for whites. An ad hoc organization, the United Defense League, coordinated the boycott, and a young Baptist minister, Theodore J. Jemison, led it. 'We are not going to pay 15 cents and stand up', he declared to a mass meeting. 'This is the onward march of a people who desire to be free. We will not retreat one inch. We have sounded forth the trumpet and we shall not sound retreat. . . . We are going to drive cars until the Council satisfies us.' During the week-long protest, hardly any blacks rode the city buses. 'Operation Free Lift', a car pool made up of about a hundred private vehicles, ferried people to and from work.

The Baton Rouge bus boycott did not gain much national attention; it was too short-lived. Nor did it achieve any great victory: blacks soon accepted a compromise that embodied a more equitable form of segregation. They then made the tactical error of challenging segregation in the state rather than the federal courts, losing the case. Even so, the fact that the boycott happened at all, and that it took place in the heart of the Deep South, was immensely significant. An entire black community had been speedily and effectively mobilized in a protest against segregation.[6]

Such examples of pre-1955 direct action are not, perhaps, all that surprising. Historical epochs do not come in neatly-wrapped chronological parcels; there is always overlapping and fuzziness around the edges. Indeed, when looking for the origins of a social transformation one's search invariably leads further and further back in time; sometimes it is difficult to know when to stop. Seeking the origins of the civil rights movement, historians have burrowed back to the 1940s and even to the 1930s, unearthing roots in the radicalism of the New Deal, the activities of the Communist Party, the militancy of the labour movement, the domestic impact of World War II, the decline of the cotton economy, the urbanization of the black population, and the growth of the NAACP.[7]

Yet, in treating these first stirrings of change, historians have generally accepted the notion that a full-blown movement for civil rights only got under way after 1955. Earlier challenges did not seem to have the force of post-1955 protests. During World War II, for example, black dissatisfaction with segregated buses and streetcars almost reaching boiling point, with black passengers continually disputing the authority of white drivers and conductors. This undercurrent of discontent, however, remained unstructured and ineffective; the countless instances of individual defiance did not add up to collective resistance. When, in 1943, A. Philip Randolph called upon blacks to stage one-day boycotts of segregated trains and buses, blacks in the South took no action.[8]

Historians have also emphasized the profound disjunctures that separated the black activism of the Roosevelt-Truman era from the struggles of 1955–65. The Second World War stoked black militancy and raised black hopes, but then led to cruel disappointments. The Cold War then chilled the political atmosphere, blighting the prospects for social reform. In the late 1940s the spirit of the New Deal expired as southern Congressmen abolished the Fair Employment Practices Committee, established by President Roosevelt in 1941, and killed the civil rights proposals advanced by President Truman.

McCarthyism ushered in the 1950s, destroying left-wing organizations, debilitating the labour movement, silencing radicals, and scaring liberals. Finally, just as the McCarthyite hysteria abated, the upsurge of white opposition to school integration in the mid-1950s – 'Massive Resistance' – decimated the NAACP in the South and kept segregation virtually intact.

According to the most common view, the Montgomery bus boycott did indeed usher in a new historical phase. Black protest increased exponentially and took on a new character – changes that were qualitative as well as quantitative. Inspired by religious faith and democratic idealism, ordinary blacks attacked segregation directly. As Richard King has argued, one should not be so impressed by its antecedents as to lose sight of what was fresh and unique about the civil rights movement of 1955–65. August Meier and Elliott Rudwick, looking at previous instances of non-violent direct action, concluded that changing black reactions to a changing social context, not the evolution of an established tradition, explained the dramatic growth of black protest between 1955 and 1965. In short, the *struggle* for civil rights became the civil rights *movement*.[9]

That last word encapsulated the defining qualities of the civil rights movement of 1955–65. Participants simply called it 'The Movement', a term that connoted not only organization but also mass participation; not simply activism but also non-violent direct action; not merely reform but also the moral regeneration of society. 'The Movement' also implied momentum: the kind of motive power that is generated when numbers fuse with courage and faith – hence that quality of 'unstoppability', that unshakeable belief in its own inevitable triumph, expressed so memorably in 'freedom songs' like 'We Shall Overcome' and 'Ain't Gonna Let Nobody Turn Me Around'.

It might seem anachronistic, therefore, to speak of a 'civil rights movement' between 1939 and 1954. Nevertheless, the central assertion of this paper is that the 'Montgomery-to-Selma' account of the civil rights movement, which focuses almost exclusively on the period 1955 to 1965, needs to be extended and revised. As Gerald Horne has argued, this narrative has become a historical myth. It is a myth not in the sense of being untrue, but in the sense of providing a simplified version of history that is readily comprehensible, morally edifying and politically acceptable. 'The traditional myth', writes Horne, 'is centred on Martin Luther King, Jr, with Rosa Parks and the Student Non-Violent Coordinating Committee playing pivotal and supporting roles. All of a sudden, in the mid-1950s – during a period, we are told, for some reason otherwise somnolent – Negroes, led by Dr. King and assisted by brilliant attorneys . . . started marching and getting their rights.' This is a caricature, of course, but we can recognize various elaborations of that myth in many, if not most, histories of the civil rights movement.[10]

This myth might suffice for a high-school textbook, but it should be abandoned by serious historians. As a framework for understanding the dynamics of racial change in the modern South, the 'Montgomery-to-Selma' narrative is woefully inadequate. It places far too great a burden of historical explanation on the shoulders of Dr King. It exaggerates the importance of the black church, failing to appreciate the complexity of the social networks that sustained black protest. It is biased towards the generation of activists that came of age in 1960, neglecting the generation of 1940. It wrenches the civil rights movement from its political context, failing to examine how the Cold War shaped the landscape of the late 1940s and 1950s. Above all, it telescopes the history of the civil rights struggle. Put simply, it omits the first half of the story – the fifteen years or so when, thanks to a melding of labour unionism, wartime militancy, and NAACP activism, the legitimacy of white supremacy had been so weakened, and the black community so strengthened, that open rebellion by blacks finally became possible. We need to extend the narrative of the civil rights movement so that it begins around 1940 – or even earlier – not in 1955.[11]

A longer perspective enables us to penetrate the miasma of McCarthyism to recognize the importance of the Old Left in the civil rights struggle. On the face of it, McCarthyism destroyed the Old Left so decisively that left-wing organizations bequeathed no tradition of protest and no legacy of tangible change. Between the early 1930s and the late 1940s, however, the Communist Party and its satellite organizations encouraged black militancy in many ways. The International Labor Defense, for example, made the Scottsboro case an international cause célèbre that led to pivotal Supreme Court rulings. The Southern Negro Youth Congress stimulated black interest in the ballot with its 1940 'Right-to-Vote' campaign. And the Communist-influenced labour unions kept the issue of racial discrimination to the forefront of the labour movement and pulled working-class African Americans into the NAACP. The Montgomery-to-Selma narrative, however, sanitizes the movement's history by removing any suggestion that Communists played any significant or positive role.

It would be wrong to see too many connections between the Old Left and the civil rights struggle of 1955–65. One of the most striking aspects of Robin Kelley's study of Communists in Alabama during the Great Depression is how completely the party's influence had faded by the 1950s. Even in its death throes, however, the Old Left merits study. Anti-communism, in its many guises, reshaped black protest during the 1950s. Its influence could be seen in the image and message projected by Martin Luther King Jr, as well as in the political circumspection of the NAACP. Indeed, a better understanding of the sheer force of anti-communism might soften the sometimes harsh judgements that have been rendered on the anti-communism of the NAACP. During the McCarthy years survival was the name of the game: the NAACP survived. If left-wing activism ground to a halt after 1950, the

NAACP provided the civil rights struggle with a strong ballast of continuity between the 1940s and the 1960s.

Here is another advantage of a longer perspective: by examining specific black communities over time the remarkable depth and duration of black protest becomes evident. As historians redirect their gaze from the top leadership of the civil rights movement to the grass roots activists, and away from the few famous confrontations toward the many unheralded struggles, we can see how the work of SNCC, CORE and SCLC in the 1960s depended upon the efforts of 'local people' (to use the title of John Dittmer's study of Mississippi) who had been organizing and struggling for many years. And we can recognize that the civil rights movement began to take shape in the 1930s and 1940s, a period that saw, to quote Jeff Norrell's model case study of Tuskegee, Alabama, 'not just a few tantalizing moments of protest but a widespread . . . struggle to overthrow segregation and institutionalized racism'.[12]

The example of Louisiana suggests that one can find, if one only looks, a long and continuous history of black organization and protest in many cities, towns and counties. For many local activists the struggle for civil rights was not merely a year-by-year affair but often a decade-by-decade one. And for many who joined the NAACP it was a lifetime commitment. One could cite the example of Rev. John Henry Scott, president of the NAACP in Lake Providence, East Carroll Parish, from 1938 to 1968. Or of William Bailey, the first black voter in Washington Parish, who headed the NAACP in Bogalusa from 1950 to 1972. Or, most strikingly, of lawyer Alexander Pierre Tureaud, who joined the NAACP in the 1920s and handled all of its important litigation in Louisiana from 1940 to the late 1960s.

The NAACP supplied, in most cases, the core element of continuity in local black activism. Yet, historians have until quite recently both neglected and underestimated that organization. In most histories of the civil rights movement it receives short shrift, virtually disappearing from sight after *Brown* v. *Board of Education* save for an occasional comment disparaging its effectiveness. (The present writer, in an earlier work, made this very mistake.)

The reasons for this neglect are not hard to fathom. The NAACP lacked a charismatic leader – Roy Wilkins was an uninspiring figure. It also lacked a cadre of action-oriented field-workers of the kind that gave SNCC and CORE their hard-hitting edge and appeal to young people. The NAACP was slow-moving, overly bureaucratic, and dominated by middle-aged and elderly men. The response of the New Orleans branch to the outbreak of the student sit-in movement epitomized these weaknesses. Instead of organizing a sit-in, the branch appointed a committee to examine the legal ramifications of having a sit-in. The Young Turks who had revitalized the branch in 1940 were the 1960s Old Guard. Meanwhile, as the NAACP dawdled, members of CORE simply went down to Canal Street and sat-in at a Woolworth lunch counter.

Police arrested them. Their dramatic initiative suddenly shifted the civil rights struggle into a higher gear.[13]

Assessments of the NAACP's effectiveness circa 1960, however, must take into account the segregationist counter-attack known as Massive Resistance. In 1956 ultra-segregationists across the South unleashed a campaign to smash the NAACP. This onslaught almost succeeded. Persecuted by the state authorities, the NAACP in Louisiana was decimated. Members resigned en masse and all but two of its 50 branches disbanded. It took ten years to recover from the blow. The creation of SCLC, and the emergence of Martin Luther King Jr as the pre-eminent southern black leader, were due in part – perhaps in large part – to the repression of the NAACP. It was no accident that SCLC's birthplace and heartland was Alabama, where a state court injunction forced the NAACP to cease its operations entirely.

Hence the generation of 1960 encountered the NAACP in an enfeebled state. Moreover, they usually knew little of the history of the civil rights struggle in particular local communities and made little effort to find out. What happened in 1956, let alone 1946, was ancient history. Historians, however, should not be so present-minded. Too often they have accorded significance to older NAACP stalwarts only to the extent that they paved the way for SNCC, CORE or SCLC. As Julian Bond once put it, the Amzie Moores and the E. D. Nixons were part of the civil rights movement's 'pre-history'. But such activists were actually much more than that: they belonged to the same phase of history, to the civil rights movement itself. Southern whites tried to destroy the NAACP not because the organization was ineffective, but because its combination of courtroom action, political pressure and popular mobilization was proving all *too* effective. It would be a great irony if Massive Resistance achieved a posthumous triumph by erasing the NAACP's golden age from the history books.[14]

It is important to determine precisely when and how the NAACP became the driving force of the early civil rights movement. In the 1930s Charles Houston and Thurgood Marshall initiated a campaign of litigation against inequalities in public education, a campaign that ultimately led to the triumph of *Brown* v. *Board of Education*. Yet, before the 1940s the NAACP lacked the popular support to constitute anything approaching a 'movement'. Indeed, writing in 1940, black political scientist Ralph J. Bunche described the NAACP as an elitist organization whose unimaginative pursuit of narrow, legalistic goals had rendered it irrelevant to the vast majority of blacks. The Association's national leaders, he complained, showed a 'pitiful knowledge of mass technique'. And its local leadership, he continued, rested with an 'exclusive, often class and color snobbish, self-appointed Negro upper class group'. Although his criticisms were tendentious and overstated, they did not stray far from the truth insofar as they described the NAACP in 1939, when Bunche carried out his research.[15]

Yet, by the time Bunche's analysis found its way into Gunnar Myrdal's *An American Dilemma*, published in 1944, it was already out of date. The NAACP's national membership had increased tenfold and new southern branches were sprouting like mushrooms. In Louisiana, branches in Baton Rouge, Shreveport, Lake Charles, and Monroe boasted at least a thousand members each. The New Orleans branch, which in 1938 had barely three hundred members, now claimed 6000. Nationwide, membership had increased from 50 000 in 1940 to about half a million in 1946. The NAACP had been transformed into a mass membership organization with roots in cities, towns and counties throughout the South.[16]

The transformation of the NAACP involved more than numbers. The Association also became more militant, more effective, and more closely attuned to the interests and aspirations of ordinary, working-class African-Americans. As Ray Gavins has written in respect of North Carolina, at the local branch level the NAACP was 'less bureaucratic and more people-oriented'.[17]

The Association's spectacular growth during the 1940s is usually attributed the Second World War, and rightly so. What is not so often recognized, however, is that the NAACP's expansion began *before* the war, and that it was closely related to a shift in its branch leadership from the black upper class to the black working class. To understand the reasons for that shift, we need to look at the labour militancy of the late 1930s and the unionization of black workers.

The metamorphosis of the New Orleans branch typified this development. In 1939, the executive committee of the New Orleans NAACP read like a *Who's Who* of the black bourgeoisie. It included nine top executives of the leading black insurance companies, two members of the most prestigious undertaking business, and the city's most eminent black surgeon, Dr Rivers Fredericks. Fredericks, former chief surgeon to a rebel army in Honduras, chief surgeon of Flint-Goodridge hospital in New Orleans, and principal stockholder of the Louisiana Industrial Life Insurance Company, left assets worth $1.5 million when he died in 1954.[18]

This interlocking directorate of doctors, insurance men, and funeral directors had served the NAACP well; nurturing the New Orleans branch during its difficult infancy, they provided vital financial support and organizational competence. Yet a social and class gulf separated them from the black lower classes, inhibiting the NAACP's ability to attract popular support. Above all, they were hostile to the CIO, which had entered New Orleans in 1936 to organize longshoremen, warehousemen, truck drivers and factory workers. In 1940, when black insurance agents struck for union recognition, the leadership of the NAACP refused to back the strikers, causing a bitter division between the executive committee and the younger rank-and-file members who had already mounted an unsuccessful bid to gain control of the branch.

The insurgents called themselves 'The Group'. Formed in 1939, The Group numbered about two dozen people; it included truck drivers, insurance agents, letter-carriers, and postal clerks. None of them were remotely upper-class, and with the exception of a couple of teachers and a lawyer, A. P. Tureaud, none could be classified as professionals.

The core of The Group comprised a handful of Post Office workers. Indeed, postal workers, not ministers, were the principal source of leadership for the NAACP in many towns and cities. Although the job of postal worker might seem relatively humble, in the 1930s and 1940s it ranked highly in the black social structure. Postal workers were federal employees and enjoyed job security, decent pay and flexible hours. The Post Office attracted blacks of talent and education, and by the 1930s black postal workers had become a force to be reckoned with. In 1913 black mailmen formed the National Alliance of Postal Employees (NAPE) and set about challenging discrimination within the service. In 1937 NAPE members in New Orleans started their own newletter, *The Postcript*, edited by John E. Rouseau, Jr. When President Roosevelt created the FEPC, NAPE succeeded in lifting a ban on the hiring of black clerks which had been in effect since the 1920s. Other members of The Group were also strong union men.

When The Group narrowly lost the branch election in 1939, they decided to launch their own newspaper, each member chipping in $100 of his own money. The *Sentinel* was left-of-centre, pro-labour and pro-NAACP. Unlike the other black newspapers, it remained independent of the white political factions. Defeated a second time in the NAACP branch elections, The Group sought an issue that would both boost the *Sentinel*'s circulation and prod the NAACP into more militant action. They contacted Thurgood Marshall and laid plans for a suit in federal court to equalize the salaries of black teachers in New Orleans. In 1941, on its third attempt, The Group captured control of the branch.

Drawing upon the experience of mass organization they had gained in the labour movement, members of The Group boosted the branch's membership and infused it with new energy. They hired black lawyers; they filed voting and education suits in federal court; they built a statewide NAACP organization; they cemented an alliance with the Louisiana Colored Teachers Association. Key members of The Group provided stable leadership for the NAACP, both in New Orleans and in Louisiana, for the next quarter of a century.[19]

During the early 1940s the ferment of war inspired the NAACP with a sense that all things were possible. And when the war ended, returning veterans tried to make democracy a reality. In 1946 blacks gathered at court houses across the state to apply to register to vote, proudly-uniformed veterans leading the way. In another sign of the NAACP's new boldness, officers of the New Orleans branch drove hundreds of miles to Minden, Louisiana, to investigate a lynching – before the war it would have left this job to white investigators. It was a tribute to the NAACP's growing effectiveness that

Louisiana's first post-war lynching was also its last. The NAACP had become an organization to be reckoned with.

And it *did* challenge white supremacy head-on. The example of St. Landry Parish shows the importance of not drawing too sharp or dogmatic a distinction between the legalistic methods preferred by the NAACP and the direct action techniques later wielded by SNCC, CORE and SCLC. Nor should that distinction be equated with conservatism and militancy.

As Mark Tushnet and Genna Rae McNeil have reminded us, the NAACP viewed litigation not only as a legal strategy but also as an organizing technique. Lawsuits acted as a catalyst for the organization of black protest at the local level: blacks had to come forward as plaintiffs; 'citizens committees' had to raise money. Moreover, black lawyers were still a comparative rarity in southern courtrooms during the 1940s: the sight of Thurgood Marshall and others openly challenging discrimination – often quizzing white officials in the witness box – was utterly novel. When Marshall argued an equalization suit in Jefferson Parish in 1942, 'the courtroom was so filled with Negroes that the court reversed the order of segregation and put the white people in the rear.' At the second trial of Edward Honeycutt in 1950, the appearance of NAACP lawyers caused a sensation. 'To the astonishment of all observers,' reported the *Louisiana Weekly*, 'some 1,000 Negro spectators flocked to the court house, jamming the Negro balcony and overflowing into the corridors and upon the grounds.' It was no coincidence that Alvin Jones travelled to St. Landry a few days after this trial ended in order to stir up interest in voting.[20]

As SNCC discovered when it began working in Mississippi in 1961, the white authorities drew no distinction between direct action and 'conventional' activities like litigation and voter registration. They treated both equally harshly. Voter registration *was* direct action in that it directly challenged white supremacy and evoked severe repression. So was litigation, as many a black plaintiff found out to his or her cost. The conditions that prevailed in Mississippi in the early 1960s confronted the NAACP throughout most of the South during the 1940s and early 1950s. Then, to organize an NAACP branch, to file a petition asking for equal schools, to apply to register to vote, to protest against lynching and police brutality – even, in some areas, to sell a black newspaper – exposed blacks to danger. Ella Baker, the NAACP's director of branches for much of the 1940s, recalled that: 'At that time the NAACP was the . . . cutting edge of social change. I remember when NAACP membership in the South was the basis for getting beaten up or even killed.' In 1944, for example, the leaders of a newly-formed NAACP branch in New Iberia, Louisiana, were expelled from the town by the sheriff. The branch president, J. Leo Hardy, was badly roughed up; his injuries hastened his death a year later. Still, the branch survived, and by 1956 blacks in New Iberia were voting in large numbers.[21]

The relationship between the pre-Montgomery and post-Montgomery phases of the civil rights struggle is a complex one. But an awareness of discontinuities, and an appreciation for the distinctive qualities of the Montgomery-to-Selma years, does not lessen the argument for treating the two periods as inextricably linked. Instead of viewing 1940 to 1955 as a mere prelude to something much bigger, we should see it as the first act of a two-act drama.

To state the matter baldly, in 1940 the whole South was not unlike Mississippi; by 1955 that was no longer the case. In 1940, lynching was still an ever-present threat; by 1955 it had become such a rarity that each incident evoked national condemnation and international opprobrium. In 1940 southern whites were still implacably opposed to black voting; by 1955 the areas of hard-core white resistance were increasingly isolated. I am not arguing, of course, that the voter registration and direct action campaigns of the 1960s were a mere mopping-up operation. I am simply asserting that the registration of one and a quarter million black voters between 1944 and 1956 represented an achievement of equal magnitude and significance.

As King was the first to acknowledge, his leadership was created by, and responded to, the aspirations and activism of ordinary people. By the same token, ordinary people became stronger and more courageous when they found a leader such as King. The Montgomery bus boycott and the emergence of King were critically important in intensifying black protest. But they also represented a further stage in a struggle that went back ten, fifteen, twenty years. And these earlier years were just as critical; they should not be lightly passed over. At stake is more than the remembrance of civil rights martyrs like J. Leo Hardy and Alvin Jones; more than the apportioning of credit to this or that organization. At stake is our understanding of what shaped and propelled the most important social movement of twentieth-century America.

NOTES

1. *Louisiana Weekly,* 10 June 1950. Lebeau was named after a nineteenth-century Catholic priest who ministered to blacks. Another Catholic priest had encouraged black interest in voting and helped to facilitate Jones's visit.
2. U. Simpson Tate, 'Report on Interview with Edward Honeycutt', 13 April 1950, in Oakley Johnson Papers, Schomburg Library; A. P. Tureaud to Gustave Auzenne, 5 May 1950, box 56, folder 15, A. P. Tureaud Papers, Amistad Research Center, Tulane University.
3. Auzenne to Tureaud, 8 June 1950, box 56, folder 16, Tureaud Papers; '[Deleted]–Subjects: Alvin Jones et al.–Victims', 16 June 1950, FBI file 44–3207–6; *Louisiana Weekly,* 27 October, 3, 25 November 1951; Thurgood Marshall to James I. McInerny, 23 November 1951, FBI file 44–3207–24; Doris M. White,

'The Louisiana Civil Rights Movement's Pre-*Brown* Period, 1936–1954', MA, University of Southwestern Louisiana, 1976, p. 69.

4. J. K. Haynes, Vanue LaCour and Murphy Bell, interviewed by Patricia Rickels, c. 1978, transcript, University of Southwestern Louisiana; *Louisiana Weekly*, 11 October 1952; Mary Alice Fontenot and Vincent Riehl, *The Cat and St. Landry: A Biography of Sheriff D. J. 'Cat' Doucet of St. Landry Parish, Louisiana* (Baton Rouge, 1972), pp. 87, 100; Southern Regional Council, 'Negro Voter Registration in the South', 7 June 1957.

5. Joseph L. Logsdon, 'An Oral History of A. P. Tureaud, Sr.', transcript, in possession of Joseph Logsdon; *Louisiana Weekly*, 29 November, 20 December 1947; 15 September 1951; Daniel E. Byrd to Thurgood Marshall, 5 March 1953, box 1, folder 11; Byrd, 'Activity Report', March 1953, box 4, folder 1, Daniel E. Byrd Papers, Amistad Research Center; August Meier and Elliott Rudwick, 'The Origins of Nonviolent Direct Action in Afro-American Protest: A Note on Historical Discontinuities', chap. in *Along the Color Line: Explorations in the Black Experience* (Urbana, 1976), pp. 360–1; Kim Lacy Rogers, 'Humanity and Desire: Civil Rights Leaders and the Desegregation of New Orleans, 1954–1966,' PhD, University of Minnesota, 1982, pp. 96–9.

6. *New York Times*, 16, 21 June 1953; *Baton Rouge Morning-Advocate*, 16–22 June 1953; *Pittsburgh Courier*, 4 July 1953; Harold D. Buell, 'The Politics of Frustration: An Analysis of Negro Leadership in East Baton Rouge Parish, 1953–1966,' MA, Louisiana State University, 1967, pp. 116–27; Aldon D. Morris, *The Origins of the Civil Rights Movement: Black Communities Organizing for Change* (New York, 1984), pp. 17–25; Meier and Rudwick, 'Origins of Nonviolent Direct Action', pp. 365–6.

7. See, for example, Robin D. G. Kelley, *Hammer and Hoe: Alabama Communists during the Great Depression* (Chapel Hill, 1990); Gerald Horne, *Communist Front? The Civil Rights Congress, 1946–1956* (Rutherford, NJ, 1988); Robert Korstad and Nelson Lichtenstein, 'Opportunities Lost and Found: Labor, Radicals, and the Early Civil Rights Movement', *Journal of American History* 75 (December 1988); Harvard Sitkoff, *A New Deal for Blacks: The Emergence of Civil Rights as a National Issue: The Depression Decade* (New York, 1978); Raymond Gavins, 'The NAACP in North Carolina in the Age of Segregation', in Armstead L. Robinson and Patricia L. Sullivan (eds), *New Directions in Civil Rights Studies* (Charlottesville, 1991); Neil A. Wynn, *The Afro-American and the Second World War* (New York, 1976); Doug McAdam, *Political Process and the Development of Black Insurgency* (Chicago, 1982); Morris, *Origins of the Civil Rights Movement*.

8. A. Philip Randolph, 'March on Washington Movement Presents Program for the Negro', in Rayford W. Logan (ed.), *What the Negro Wants* (Chapel Hill, 1944), p. 151; Meier and Rudwick, 'Origins of Nonviolent Direct Action', pp. 334–49. For tensions on buses and streetcars see Howard W. Odum, *Race and Rumors of Race* (Chapel Hill, 1943); Robin D. G. Kelley, 'We Are Not What We Seem: Black Working-Class Opposition in the Jim Crow Era', *Journal of American History*, 80 (June 1993), pp. 75–112.

9. Richard H. King, *Civil Rights and the Idea of Freedom* (New York, 1992), p. 4; Meier and Rudwick, 'Origins of Nonviolent Direct Action', passim.

10. Gerald Horne, '"Myth" and the Making of *Malcolm X*', *American Historical Review* 98 (April 1993), p. 440.

11. John Dittmer, *Local People: The Struggle for Civil Rights in Mississippi* (Urbana and Chicago, 1994), stresses the long-term, grass-roots and independent character of the civil rights struggle in Mississippi. He also forcefully makes the point

that the civil rights movement received very little support from black ministers
– even in the 1960s.

12. Robert J. Norrell, *Reaping the Whirlwind: The Civil Rights Movement in Tuskegee*
(New York, 1985), p. x.

13. Adam Fairclough, *Race and Democracy: The Civil Rights Struggle in Louisiana,
1915–1972* (Athens, 1995), pp. 273–6. Although women participated in the civil
rights movement in Louisiana at every level, especially at the level of local
grass-roots activism, the movement there seems to have been more male-dominated than it was in, for example, Mississippi. Among black elected officials
today, the underrepresentation of women is more marked in Louisiana, and significantly so, than in any other southern state; see *Black Elected Officials: A
National Roster 1993* (Washington, DC 1994), p. xxiii.

14. Julian Bond, lecture, University of Virginia, 1990.

15. Ralph J. Bunche, 'The Programs, Ideologies, Tactics, and Achievements of Negro
Betterment and Interracial Organizations', 1940, pp. 142–55, Carnegie-Myrdal
Papers (microfilm), Alderman Library, University of Virginia.

16. Figures on the NAACP's growth, both nationally and in Louisiana, can be found
in NAACP, *Annual Report, 1947*, copy in Alderman Library, University of Virginia; New Orleans branch, 'Annual Report, 1942–43', box 12, folder 25; South-
western Regional Advisory Board, minutes, 12–14 March, box 12, folder 12,
both in Tureaud Papers.

17. Gavins, 'The NAACP in North Carolina during the Age of Segregation', p. 106.

18. Composition of the executive committee of the New Orleans branch is detailed
in James Lewis to Walter White, 11 November 1939, part 1, series G, box 83,
NAACP Papers, Library of Congress.

19. The history of The Group can be traced in the A. P. Tureaud Papers; in the
New Orleans branch files of the NAACP at the Library of Congress; and in
Logsdon, 'Oral History of A. P. Tureaud, Sr.', transcript of tape 8. An interview with John E. Rousseau, Jr (31 March 1992), one of the original editors of
The Sentinel, was also extremely valuable. Four members of The Group played
especially noteworthy roles in the NAACP. Rousseau acted as the NAACP's
chief link to the black press. Civil rights lawyer A. P. Tureaud handled every
NAACP suit in the field of education, and many more besides, from 1940 to
the late 1960s. Daniel Byrd, a leader of the 1940 insurance agents' strike, became a field secretary for the NAACP Legal Defense Fund, working mainly on
school desegregation until his retirement in 1976. Arthur J. Chapital became
president and mainstay of the New Orleans NAACP until his death in 1969.

20. Mark Tushnet, *The NAACP's Legal Campaign against Segregated Education,
1928–1950* (Chapel Hill, 1987); Genna Rae McNeil, *Groundwork: Charles
Hamilton Houston and the Struggle for Civil Rights* (Philadelphia, 1983); Logsdon,
'Oral History of A. P. Tureaud, Sr.', transcript of tape 11; *Louisiana Weekly*,
3 June 1950.

21. Baker quoted in Gerda Lerner, (ed.), *Black Women in White America: A Documentary History* (New York, 1973), p. 346; Adam Fairclough, *Race and Democracy*,
pp. 84–98.

2 'He Founded a Movement': W. H. Flowers, the Committee on Negro Organizations and the Origins of Black Activism in Arkansas, 1940–57
John Kirk

In recent years civil rights historians have begun to move beyond the exploration of national events, figures and organizations, which much of the initial body of literature addressed, towards a probing of local developments, assessing their impact upon the dramatic social upheavals taking place between the mid-1950s and mid-1960s in American society. Works like Robert J. Norrell's study on the civil rights struggle in Tuskegee, Alabama, and William Chafe's on Greensboro, North Carolina, have helped set a new agenda of issues for other scholars to follow up on. In particular, the growing number of community studies have highlighted the inadequacy of the existing chronology of the civil rights movement. Tracing the origins of black protest back into the 1930s and 1940s, they have stressed that an understanding of developments in those decades is fundamental to fully comprehending changes which occurred in later years.[1]

Building upon work already done in uncovering local movements elsewhere, this paper focuses on the rich and vibrant history of black protest in Arkansas. More specifically, it seeks to highlight the role of W. H. Flowers and the Committee on Negro Organizations (CNO) in the continuing struggle for black rights. At a time when the National Association for the Advancement of Colored People (NAACP) was reluctant to offer help, the CNO emerged as the premier focus for encouraging organized direct action protest in the state. This paper traces the development of the organization, its changing strategies and agendas, and locates its local campaigns in the context of the New Deal and Second World War. Also, the paper explores the complex relationship between Flowers, the CNO and other centres of power, protest and influence in the state, as efforts were made to assemble a united black front in an 'organization of organizations'.[2] Above all, it seeks to consider the ways in which Flowers and the CNO established precedents and served as catalysts for civil rights activities which captured national attention only in later years. Both in the way they laid the groundwork for later direct action protests and challenged black perceptions of themselves and their capacity to resist Jim Crow at the time, Flowers and the CNO played a vital role in the story of black protest in Arkansas.

On 10 March 1940, at the Buchanan Baptist Church in Stamps, Arkansas, six young professional men sat on a raised platform in front of a gathered assembly of around two hundred blacks. These men formed the core of the CNO. W. H. Flowers, a young lawyer and driving force behind the initiative, stood to speak. He charged that there was a 'blackout of democracy' in Arkansas. There was, he claimed, no adequate organization to serve the needs of its Negro citizens; to publicize and stand up against the daily racial injustices which they were forced to encounter. Realizing the magnitude of the task in filling such a void, Flowers expressed the belief that the young leadership of the CNO possessed 'enough brain power and courage to revolutionize the thinking of the people of Arkansas'.[3]

William Harold Flowers had been born in Stamps in 1911, son of a businessman and schoolteacher. His family belonged to a professional elite which formed the upper echelons of black society there; Maya Angelou, who grew up in the same town, referred to Flowers' grandmother as the 'aristocrat of Black Stamps'.[4] Inspiration to pursue a legal career came early. Trips as a child with his father to watch jury trials at the courthouse had given him his 'first peep into the judicial system'. Later, at the age of 16, he was given an insight into another side of southern justice. On a visit to Little Rock, he witnessed the burning of a lynched black man, on the main black downtown business throughfare, on a funeral pyre built with pews plundered from a nearby black church. It was at this sight, he would recall in later years, that he was 'truly converted to be a lawyer'.[5]

Graduating from Robert H. Terrall law school in Washington, DC, Flowers had returned to Arkansas, setting up a practice at Pine Bluff in 1938. Young, eager and idealistic, with his first-hand experiences of southern injustices towards blacks, from the outset he wished to use his legal talents to further the cause of the race there. Originally, he wanted to work through the NAACP. In October of 1938, Flowers wrote to Walter White, President of the NAACP, emphasizing the fact that Arkansas badly needed organization and leadership, and that it was a fertile field for NAACP activity. Flowers stated that he had returned to his home state 'to practice law and render a distinct service to my people.' He wished to have the job of organizing Arkansas blacks anew, but needed financial backing for his endeavours. As a novice lawyer, just starting out in practice, he could barely afford to give away time whilst building up his new business.[6]

No offers of help from the central offices of the NAACP were forthcoming. Instead, further communications came trying to appease Flowers' frustrations. A letter from Charles Houston, one of the NAACP's leading attorneys, empathized with the situation in Arkansas and recognized the fact that Flowers could not take time out of his office without due recompense. However, he also explained that the NAACP worked through local volunteers, which prevented branches from turning into financial rackets. He admitted that this meant protests were sporadic and relied upon the efforts of a few dedicated individuals, but this was the way the NAACP chose to work. Thurgood Marshall, another aspiring NAACP attorney, writing soon after, conceded the fact that not much progress had been made concerning the organization of Arkansas and advised that the matter be left in abeyance until the next NAACP national conference.[7]

The ambivalent attitude of the NAACP had grown out of previous dealings with the state. The first local branch had been established in 1918 at Little Rock.[8] One of the most celebrated cases of the NAACP's early history, the defence of twelve prisoners sentenced to death for their alleged role in the Elaine Race Riot, followed the year after. A lengthy and expensive five years of litigation finally brought a reprieve for the 12 convicted men.[9] Arkansas's abysmal lynching record meant that there were many more forays for the NAACP into the state. Yet beyond the efforts of a few dedicated black female secretaries, most notably Mrs Carrie Sheppherdson, who won the Madam C. J. Walker Gold Medal in 1925 for her outstanding fundraising drive, there was very little interest in NAACP activities.[10] As Mrs H. L. Porter summed up in 1933, 'the lawyers, Doctors, preachers and businessmen . . . are just a bunch of egotistic discussers and not much on actual doings', adding that they were 'a very slow bunch in turning loose a little money'.[11]

Largely, the lack of interest in the NAACP was due to the fact that many local organizations seemed to offer a better forum for racial advancement. The Grand Mosaic Templars of America provide an outstanding case in point. Established in 1882 by John Bush and Chester Keats, two members of Little Rock's black middle class, the organization acted as a fraternity-cum-insurance agency: at the height of their success, in 1924, they boasted a membership of 108 000 people in 24 states and combined assets of $280 000. The Templar building, a four storey and particularly ornate downtown edifice, offered a central meeting place for many of the black professional, civic, political religious and fraternal associations in the city. There, the NAACP occupied one room amongst many other groups dedicated to advancing the cause of black citizens.[12]

One of the rare applications for NAACP help came from Dr J. M. Robinson, head of the Arkansas Negro Democratic Association, in 1928, for what turned out to be an unsuccessful challenge to the all-white Democratic Party primary elections.[13] From the outset the NAACP were reluctant to help. They thought that too much money was being asked to fund the lawsuit, besides which, similar cases were also being argued in both Virginia and Texas at the time. But, in a memo to Arthur Spingarn at head office 'another reason to feel that we should not give much, if anything, towards this case' was given. 'Despite all the money we have spent in the Arkansas cases . . . we have never been able to get any considerable support from the state. For example, the Little Rock branch sent to the National Office during 1928 only $48, and this year only $44.25'. A concluding recommendation suggested that 'we send say fifty or one hundred dollars as a contribution towards this case so that in the event that it turns out to be the one on which we get the definitive decision, we will at least have given something'.[14]

The 1930s increased the need for NAACP assistance. The Depression hit home hard amongst the black middle classes, heralding the end of many successful enterprises like the Mosaic Templars. By the end of the decade, not only was there a lack of finances to sustain local organizations, but also a new agenda of concerns had moved beyond their capacity to handle. Although the majority of blacks had been hit harder by economic upheaval than the black elite, the potential for change which had been glimpsed in the New Deal brought new optimism and raised hopes. Albeit still limited by segregation and discrimination, the New Deal had built more black facilities like schools and hospitals than ever before; it had provided jobs, training and a greater access to education; it had shown the potential of the federal government to make a difference in their daily lives. Blacks had begun to move off the land and into urban areas where they were less vulnerable to white attacks; lynchings slowly but steadily began to decline. The war accelerated all these trends and gave further heart to those who thought that a better way of life was coming within their grasp.[15]

Looking to build upon the promise of change which the New Deal had brought, an enlivened constituency of support for a more aggressive pursual of black rights developed through the war years. Yet in spite of a potential base for mass support there was a distinct lack of direction and leadership in the state for such a movement. An entrenched conservative elite still wielded considerable influence and still dominated organizational activities. Compounding these problems was the continuing lack of NAACP interest in the state which might have given outside help in tackling the local stagnancy of black protest. By 1940 only six local branches existed in Arkansas, with a membership of not more than 600 people.[16] It was the problem of bridging an activist agenda with a conservative leadership, in the absence of outside help, that Flowers and the CNO sought to address. Half a generation younger than the older established leadership, this group of professionals recognized the need to harness the support of the masses to bring benefits for the whole of the black population.

By the time that the NAACP had rebuffed all requests for help, Flowers had decided he could wait no longer for them to act. At the meeting on 10 March in Stamps an independent CNO platform had been adopted. *The CNO*

Spectator, a bimonthly fly-sheet, keeping citizens informed of the groups activities, heralded this platform as the 'most forward looking ever . . . touching every field of social activity'. The programme stated that the CNO's purpose was to provide a 'single organization sufficient to serve the social, civic, political and economic needs of the people'. It stood for the rights of Negroes to have a say in the government which they supported, to fight 'un-American activities . . . enslaving the Negro people' and to devise a 'system of protest' to remove them. It outlined its particular areas of concern: education, politics, health, housing, jobs, equal opportunities in the armed forces and wartime industries, provision of truly 'equal' facilities for Negroes and a fair allocation of farm benefits to help remove the 'existing evils' in the landlord–tenant relationship. Within each broad area the CNO had specific aims. For example, in education there were demands for equalizing school facilities, teachers' salaries, and graduate opportunities, along with calls to appoint Negroes to policy-making boards at state and local levels.[17]

The cornerstone of the CNO's whole programme was to secure widespread, organized political participation. Only through raised political awareness and activity could blacks gain the leverage with the white power structure to have their demands enforced. In Arkansas, unlike many other southern states, blacks were not denied the franchise at general elections: through the payment of a $1 poll tax they were eligible to cast their vote. However, since Arkansas was ruled by the Democratic Party (V. O. Key referred to it in 1949 as 'the purest one party state in the South'[18]), it was the vote in their primary elections which determined who held office. The general election was provided only for the ratification of a (usually unopposed) Democratic nominee. Blacks were prevented from voting in these primary elections on the grounds that the Democratic Party was a private organization which could draw up its own racially exclusive membership rules.[19]

Attempts at securing black political participation had been in progress since Reconstruction. Scipio Jones had fought a long battle against 'lily white' factions in the Republican Party to maintain a black political voice there.[20] In 1928, Dr J. M. Robinson had filed a lawsuit against local Democrats in order that blacks could gain a say in that party.[21] However, all previous attempts had been by middle-class leaders who wished to win representation in politics so that the educated few, like themselves, could exercise a voice in the parties on behalf of their race. Moreover, this political voice had always been seen as a way of articulating grievances but never actually issuing a wholesale challenge to existing inequalities. Flowers, even though a staunch Republican, was attempting to go beyond party politics. He proposed the creation of an independent mass black political organization, representative of the whole of the black population, as a way of tackling the common problems which they all faced.

The first step towards political participation was payment of the poll tax.

Once blacks began to purchase poll tax receipts and turn up on election day to vote, showing there was an interest and awareness of voting rights amongst the Negro population, then it would be easier to challenge white Democrats and push for equal rights. To attain the goal of a mass political mobilization, organization would be needed. This reached the very essence of the CNO's sense of mission: its central platform was 'to seek the endorsement of Negro church, civic, fraternal and social organizations'.[22] Only by bringing about unity and direction of purpose, and exerting the sheer strength of numbers in a state-wide representative body, could the task of raising a political consciousness be effectively carried out. This would mean creating a coalition in an 'organization of organizations', pooling individual and group bases of influence throughout the state. Thus, the whole programme hinged upon the CNO's ability to gain a wide base of recognition and support throughout the black community.

Although the 'independent' programme of the CNO was essentially the same as that put forward by the NAACP at the time, it set itself apart in one very important aspect: it was entirely community oriented. As the NAACP concentrated on winning court rulings which would have a national impact, the CNO focused on the immediate needs of those living in Arkansas. Consequently, the programme was attuned specifically to local activities and needs. No one knew these better than W. H. Flowers and perhaps no one was quite so well equipped to tackle them. Flowers' father had been not only a businessman, but also a leading Mason. His mother was a schoolteacher. He was a lawyer. All had strong links to the church. Theirs was a well-respected and well-known black Arkansas family. With a working, first-hand knowledge of how power was structured in the black community in Arkansas, and direct links to its various strands, Flowers knew just which channels to work through and where success for his endeavours would come from.

After the Stamps meeting, Flowers set off on a speaking tour of the state to raise the profile of the CNO and muster support from grassroots organizations in the various communities. To do this meant tapping into, harassing and redeploying the already existing centres of influence, which resided in different institutions, organizations and individuals in different places. On 7 April 1940, under the sponsorship of the Hope Interdenominational Ministerial Alliance, in southern Arkansas, around three hundred blacks turned out to hear the CNO programme explained. The message was reported as 'enthusiastically received'. At Potsdelle, in eastern Arkansas, on 14 April approximately six hundred people listened to a meeting held under the auspices of the local branch of the NAACP. On 16 April the Negro Business Club of Morrillton sponsored a mass meeting in central Arkansas of over two hundred citizens. On 5 May the Lewisville Negro Taxpayers Association in southern Arkansas acted as hosts. There, more than two hundred and fifty persons pledged their support to the programme. Although not under the direct guidance of the CNO, similar meetings were held throughout the state.[23]

These meetings culminated in the 'First Conference on Negro Organization', on 27 September 1940, held at Lakeview Junior High school, a recently completed Farm Security Administration (FSA) project. Located in the Delta, the conference exposed the CNO to graphic demonstrations of the kinds of inequalities against which it was fighting. Difficulties were encountered from the outset. Chairman of the local schoolboard Lester Wolfe ordered FSA officials to prevent the meeting from taking place, claiming he had been 'misled' about its true purpose. In spite of black local leaders from the NAACP calling for the conference to be cancelled, because of the possibilities of angering whites, Flowers stood his ground, proclaiming that the meeting would take place 'even if we have to use the banks of the lake which borders this *United States Government* project'.[24]

Local white officials eventually relented and the meeting went ahead. At his opening address, Flowers told the crowd that they had met to 'devise a program of action' to combat discrimination against Negroes 'merely because of the color of their skin'. He spoke of organizing Arkansas's half-million Negroes through a programme of definite aims and objectives, with a leadership pledged to carry them out. 'For six months we have obtained the endorsement of twenty-one organizations with a numerical strength of approximately ten thousand Negro citizens', he said. Further, he outlined the achievements of the CNO to date. Thirty-five investigations had been carried out over colour discrimination in public works employment. It had brought about the removal of a ban in Jefferson County, preventing blacks from participating in opportunities provided by the National Youth Administration (NYA). It had also been responsible for the appointment of a Negro census enumerator in St. Francis County. Sixteen mass meetings had been carried out successfully, with a total attendance of over four thousand people.[25]

After a successful three-day conference, speaking dates continued. On 1 January 1941, Flowers spoke to the White County Chapter of the Lincoln Emancipation League, urging them to build an organization which would be 'truly representative of the people'. Moving on to the Salem Baptist Church he warned that 'A voteless people is a hopeless people'. Explictly drawing upon the fight against racism in Europe, and America's possible entry into the Second World War, he declared that 'the success of our effort to make democracy a way of life for the peoples of the world must begin at home, not after a while, but now'. He blamed the existing leadership of professionals, preachers and businessmen for 'the inaction on the part of citizens voting at elections in Arkansas', particularly lambasting 'the pussyfooting educators on the public pay roll, who are only submissive to those responsible for their jobs'.[26]

Speeches continued throughout the year in a state-wide effort to mobilize support. Poll-tax drives began in September 1941 to meet the 1 October deadline for voter qualification. Under the direction of the CNO, Dr Roscoe C. Lewis, a physician from Hope, promoted poll-tax purchases in southern Arkansas, whilst W. L. Jarrett, an undertaker from Morrillton, supervised in the North. Attesting to the ever-expanding base of CNO support, more and more organizations began to assist in the campaign. Amongst them were the Warren, Phillips County and Potsdelle branches of the NAACP; the Morrillton Business Club; the Conway Negro Business League; the El Dorado and St. Francis Negro Civic Leagues; the Lewisville Negro Taxpayers Association; the Camden, Menifee, Crossett, Dermott and Fort Smith indigenous CNO organizations; the Tau Phi Chapter, Omega Psi Phi fraternity; the Order of the Eastern Star and the Free and Accepted Masons of Arkansas; the Beth-lehem District Association of the Missionary Baptist Church; the Phillips, Lee, Monroe and Desha District Baptist Associations; the Middle Western District Baptist Association and the Texarkana and Brinkley Negro Chambers of Commerce.[27]

'Drive To Increase Race Votes Is Successful' headlined the *State Press*, Arkansas's leading black newspaper. A record turnout at the polls was ex-pected.[28] Emboldened by this expectation, the CNO petitioned Governor Homer Adkins to assist Negro graduate students who were denied an education in Arkansas, which did not provide such facilities for blacks. 'We direct your attention to the growing unrest on the part of the Negro race', Flowers wrote to the Governor: 'They no longer are willing to remain on their knees beg-ging for the rights, privileges and immunities of American citizenship'.[29] Adkins passed the issue to the State Department of Education, who suggest-ed using the latest increase in funds at Pine Bluff AM&N, Arkansas's only publicly funded Negro college, to pay for out-of-state scholarships. With the implementation of this plan left to college trustees, no action was taken. Dissatisfied with this, Flowers called together influential Negro educators from throughout the state for a conference with State Commissioner of Ed-ucation Ralph B. Jones. A few weeks later, the first of fourteen $100 awards that year was given to Flowers' brother, Cleon A. Flowers, to help with his studies at Meharry Medical College in Tennessee.[30]

After two years of persistent effort, the CNO could claim a number of concrete achievements. In the same year that the *Arkansas State Press* printed Flowers' photograph with the caption 'He Founded a Movement', one of the most important of these, and one of the biggest steps forward for black rights in the state to date, was being taken.[31] In March 1942 Susie Morris, a black Little Rock schoolteacher, initiated a court suit for the right to be paid the same salary as white teachers in the district. It proved to be the first successful attempt by blacks in Arkansas to win equal rights through the courts.[32] Flowers had particularly entreated the teachers, as one of the oldest and strongest of the professional associations in Arkansas, to take a stronger involvement in the active pursuit of black rights, chastising them for being more concerned with 'dress than redress'.[33]

The success of the teachers' salary suit acted as the catalyst for further initiatives which would have a profound effect on the unfolding struggle for civil rights in Arkansas. Thurgood Marshall had been in town for the case and his presence had raised the profile of the NAACP there. With such a renowned national figure visiting Little Rock, a new interest was awakened in the organization and, according to reports from the local branch secretary, membership dues had taken a dramatic upswing. 'He sure did shoot them some straight dope as to their part and membership to be played in the NAACP cause' declared Mrs H. L. Porter. 'Then and there at that meeting we collected $68.50 in membership'.[34] In response to this rising local interest (and more money coming in), the national NAACP headquarters began, in turn, to take more of an interest in the state. By 1945 a State Conference of Branches had been put into effect. Soon afterwards W. H. Flowers took charge of its statewide recruitment drives.[35]

The year before the State Conference came into existence, the *Smith* v. *Allwright* decision of 1944 outlawed the all-white Democratic Party primaries which had previously prevented blacks from exercising a meaningful vote at elections. Although white Arkansas Democrats tried to preserve racial exclusion by instituting a complex system of 'double primaries', in which local and state primaries remained segregated, whilst those for federal office did not, the expense, plus the time-consuming, cumbersome and bureaucratic procedures involved, soon led to its collapse.[36]

Because of the work of Flowers and the CNO, when blacks could finally reap the benefits of the vote in the late 1940s, they started to do so in significant numbers: from 1.5 per cent of voting age blacks registered in 1940, the number had expanded to 17.3 per cent by 1947.[37] Through poll-tax drives, voter education and a general raising of political awareness, the CNO had already paved the way for blacks to have an immediate impact at elections.

The CNO gradually became a victim of its own successes. Along with the NAACP moving into the state, the political empowerment of the black community gave rise to a new set of local organizations dedicated to mobilizing the vote and using it as a tool with which to carve direct concessions from the white community. For example, in Little Rock, Charles Bussey's Veterans Good Government Association and Jeff Hawkins's East End Civic League used a black block vote to pressure white politicians into improving street-lighting, roads and pavements in their communities. They also managed to win bond money from the city for the construction of a new black park. These groups, riding on the rising tide of black activism which had been set in motion by Flowers across the state, began to focus on translating a raised political consciousness into action and, ultimately, concrete gains on a day-to-day basis in their own communities.[38]

Flowers continued as a pioneer in his own right. In 1947 the Wilkerson case provided the crowning glory of his legal career. In the case, two black men stood accused of killing two white men. Routinely this had brought an automatic death sentence. However, in this instance, Flowers managed to get their sentences commuted to jail terms. At the same trial Flowers demanded, and received, some black jurists to sit in on the case, the first time this had happened in Jefferson County since Reconstruction. These achievements were even more remarkable given the fact that Flowers was one of the few black lawyers in the state at the time who represented his clients alone, without the counsel of a white lawyer, flaunting established court 'etiquette'. Wiley Branton, a leading NAACP lawyer also from Arkansas, recalled that the case had 'a major impact on the view of black people . . . that maybe there is justice after all'.[39]

In 1948 Flowers personally handled the admission of Silas Hunt to the law school at the University of Arkansas, Fayetteville. Not only was this the first time a black student had attended classes with white students in Arkansas, it was the first time such a situation had existed anywhere in the South since Reconstruction.[40] The following year, Flowers brought the first school case to trial in Arkansas, when he petitioned the De Witt schoolboard to equalize its facilities for black and white students. The judgment handed down, as the case was ruled in favour of the plaintiffs, stated that facilities should be equalized 'within a reasonable amount of time'.[41] The wording of the judgment foreshadowed the same ambiguity of the 'with all deliberate speed' clause of the *Brown II* implemention order of 1955. The case also drew the battlelines for the many courtroom battles over school desegregation which would continue in the decades ahead.

Along with this career of personal achievement, Flowers continued his struggle with the forces of black conservatism within the state. When the NAACP instituted a State Conference of Branches in 1945, they had put Rev. Marcus Taylor at Little Rock in charge of operations whilst allowing Flowers to pursue a role as organizer of new branches. Quite early the mutual antipathy which existed between the two became clear. With no establishment of communications between Little Rock and Pine Bluff, Rev. Taylor began to accuse Flowers of financial misdemeanours, suggesting that he was keeping half of the funds collected from new NAACP branches for himself.[42] Although funds were generally slow in making their way to national headquarters, an investigation into Flowers' activities gave no reason to relieve him of his duties.[43]

In fact, it seemed that activists were beginning to gain an upper hand in the state. In 1948 Flowers was elected as President of the Arkansas State Conference of Branches after building up the Pine Bluff NAACP branch to

4382 members, by far the largest in the state. 'I will admit that I may have underrated Pine Bluff and its leadership', wrote Lucille Black, national Membership Secretary.[44] Donald Jones, NAACP Regional Secretary, attended the Arkansas State Conference meeting in 1948 and reported that spirits were 'high and militant'. He continued: 'Largely responsible for the fine NAACP consciousness in Pine Bluff and the growing consciousness in the state is Attorney Flowers, whose success in the Wilkerson case and tremendous energy have made him the state's acknowledged leader.'[45]

Later the same year in Little Rock, Daisy Bates, who ran the *State Press* there with her husband, L. C. Bates, filed an application to form a 'Pulaski County Chapter of the NAACP'.[46] The move came out of a direct disillusionment with the local Little Rock branch which was still in the grip of Rev. Marcus Taylor. The Bateses were good friends with Flowers and came from the same activist ilk as he did. Flowers had written in the *State Press* under the assumed name of Francis Sampson and considered the Bates's home his place of residence whilst in Little Rock. The *State Press* provided an effective forum for the dissemination of an activist agenda; reports on the CNO had appeared from the founding of the newspaper in 1941.[47] In response to the application for a new NAACP branch, head office tried to reconcile the differences between the two existing factions by pointing out that a branch in Little Rock was already operating and suggested that members wishing to help join up there.[48]

In 1949, the issue of finances reared its head again. The Arkansas State Conference of Branches defaulted on its contribution towards the Southwest Regional Conference fund. As a response, Regional Secretary Donald Jones recommended that Flowers be given the choice of either resigning from office or facing dismissal.[49] The Pine Bluff Branch then issued a proclamation deploring the 'unrest, discord and disunity now existent in NAACP activities in Arkansas'. Furthermore, it recommended that the Arkansas State Conference of Branches withdraw from the NAACP, to concentrate upon pressing local matters that needed attention. It also suggested that monies already collected be used to fund local battles instead of going to out-of-state concerns.[50] Only after strong letters from leading figures in the NAACP, pleading for the Pine Bluff branch to reconsider its actions, did local activists repent. Disillusioned, Flowers resigned from office.[51]

Flowers was replaced by Dr J. A. White of Warren, Arkansas. But activists resentments still continued to be voiced. Lulu B. White, of the Texas State Conference of Branches, reported that 'no place in the country is there so much strife and division amongst Negroes as it is in Arkansas'. Commenting on attitudes there, she wrote: 'They say that the work of the NAACP is in charge of a few favorites in the state, who are Lackies, what ever that is, for New York, and New York is not worth a D— to them'.[52]

In 1951, Dr White fell ill and resigned his position. W. L. Jarrett, who had been one of the principal workers in the CNO poll-tax campaigns of the 1940s, became temporary President of the State Conference of Branches.[53] In 1952, Daisy Bates became head of the NAACP in Arkansas. Gloster B. Current, Director of Branches for the NAACP, voiced concerns over Mrs Bates's election. He questioned her ability to work with the existing leadership and reported that she 'tends to go off the deep end at times'. 'I am not certain that she was the proper person to be elected,' he confided to U. Simpson Tate, head of the Southwest Regional Council, '[but] I permitted it because there was no one else to be elected who offered any promise of doing anything to further the work of the NAACP in Arkansas.'[54]

Mrs Bates's election to head of State Branches was the culmination of a long struggle. Finally, an activist was head of the NAACP who also had a base in the state capital at Little Rock. Mrs Bates was thus now in a better position to take on conservative elements within the organization and amongst black leadership in the state by introducing a more militant agenda. The very year of Mrs Bates's election the first negotiations with white Schoolboard members commenced, over the desegregation of schools in Little Rock. After a breakdown in talks, Mrs Bates was ready for the local branch to file a lawsuit; national office advised her to wait for the outcome of other suits pending in the courts at the time.[55] One of these eventually led to the famous *Brown v. Board of Education* ruling in 1954, which outlawed separate but equal schools and ordered desegregation.

Although the Little Rock schoolboard had been one of the first to move towards compliance with the *Brown* decision, it soon began to backtrack on its initial plans. The starting date for integration was moved back. Then provisos were added, like the building of new segregated black and white schools in different parts of town before Central High, in the middle, could be desegregated. By February of 1956 the schoolboard's claims to be acting in 'good faith' had worn thin. Daisy Bates, along with an aspiring young black lawyer from the Pine Bluff group of activists, Wiley Branton, formulated a lawsuit. After a year of wrangling through the courts a ruling was eventually handed down ordering the schoolboard to go ahead with plans to integrate Central High, at the beginning of the fall term, 3 September 1957.

On the evening of 2 September, the night before term was about to begin, Arkansas Governor Orval Faubus surrounded Central High School with National Guardsmen. The next morning as lone black student Elizabeth Eckford tried to enter the school the armed guard turned her away and a gathered white mob began to harass her. Pictures of the scene were relayed all over the world via television and newspaper photographs. Events raised not only a national, but also an international outcry. Only after negotiations broke down between Governor Faubus and President Eisenhower did the latter, still reluctantly, federalize the National Guard and send in the troops of the Airborne 101st unit to uphold the forces of law and order. Finally, under a federal, armed escort, nine black students entered Central High School on 23 September 1957.[56]

Yet as the cameras moved away from Little Rock after the events of 1957, and on to the next dramatic story to capture national attention in the battle for civil rights, the local struggle continued. At the end of the year, Governor Faubus closed all the city's schools. Two years of bitter infighting ensued before they were reopened on an integrated basis in 1959. Even then, much still remained to be done. Segregation continued to exist at lunch counters, movie theatres, golf courses, parks, swimming pools and a whole range of other public and private facilities. Blacks still faced discrimination when applying for jobs or obtaining housing, amongst other forms of prejudice which bolstered the Jim Crow system. The school crisis had been the culmination of one particular phase of the ongoing fight for black rights, but it had also marked the beginnings of another phase, which would bring with it new demands for more wide-ranging changes to take place and a new set of tactics to achieve its goals. Heading into the 1960s, another younger generation of activists were ready to take their place in the continuing story of black protest in Arkansas.

NOTES

1. William H. Chafe, *Civilities and Civil Rights: Greensboro, North Carolina, and the Black Struggle for Freedom* (New York, 1980); Robert J. Norrell, *Reaping the Whirlwind: The Civil Rights Movement in Tuskegee* (New York, 1985). Other work of note includes: David R. Colburn, *Radical Change and Community Crisis: St. Augustine, Florida, 1877–1980* (New York, 1985); Neil R. McMillen, *Dark Journey: Black Mississippians in the Age of Jim Crow* (Urbana, 1989); John Dittmer, 'The Politics of the Mississippi Movement, 1954–1964' in Charles Eagles (ed.) *The Civil Rights Movement in America* (Jackson, 1986). Two unpublished studies, Robert G. Corley, 'The Quest for Racial Harmony: Race Relations in Birmingham, Alabama, 1947–1963', PhD, University of Virginia, 1979, and Marcellus Barksdale, 'The Indigenous Civil Rights Movement and Cultural Change in North Carolina: Weldon, Chapel Hill and Monroe, 1946–1965', PhD, Duke University, 1977, are worthy of note, amongst many others too numerous to mention here.
2. The terminology is borrowed from Aldon D. Morris's *The Origins of the Civil Rights Movement: Black Communities Organizing for Change* (New York, 1984). Morris provides excellent analysis of what he terms local 'movement centers' which 'mobilize, organize and co-ordinate collective action'. He continues

> They are dynamic forms of social organization within which activists prepare communities for collective action and actually initiate struggles against the power-holders to bring about social change. These struggles often pursue limited goals perceived as attainable and positive steps toward realizing ultimate goals.

Analysts and participants often measure the success or failure of a movement by the attainment of its announced limited goals. Use of that criterion [however] ignores the overall benefits such efforts may have for the infrastrucure of a movement. (p. 100)

As this paper indicates, the CNO provides an ideal-type of a local movement centre, right down to the 'organization of organizations' model which, as Morris explains, they typically encompass. However, there is one important difference to note. Whereas the groupings which Morris looks at – the UDL (Baton Rouge, Louisiana, 1953), MIA (Alabama, 1955), ICC (Tallahassee, Tennesee, 1956) and ACMHR (Birmingham, 1956) – are all located in a more traditional time-period, the CNO emerged at a significantly earlier stage in the struggle for civil rights. This not only leans toward a confirmation of the benefits of studying earlier developments in local communities organizing for change, but also suggests that the energy, capability and potential support for such direct-action protest organizations existed, and were exploited, long before they captured national attention and met with greater success at a later stage in the movement.

3. Press Release, (n.d.), W. H. Flowers Papers, Pine Bluff, Arkansas. The W. H. Flowers Papers (WHFP) are unprocessed and uncollected at his law offices in Pine Bluff, as he left them at the time of his death in September 1990. Research was conducted with the kind permission of Ms Stephenie Flowers, W. H. Flowers' daughter and custodian of the papers, without whose understanding and co-operation this paper could not have been written.
4. Maya Angelou, *I Know Why the Caged Bird Sings* (New York, 1970) p. 47.
5. *Arkansas Gazette*, Sunday, 31 July 1988.
6. W. H. Flowers to Walter White, 31 October 1938, WHFP.
7. Charles Houston to W. H. Flowers, 22 November 1938; Thurgood Marshall to W. H. Flowers, 14 April 1939, WHFP.
8. Application for Charter and Official Authorization, Papers of the NAACP: Part 12: Selected Branch Files, 1913–1939. Series A: The South. Microfilm Reel 4: Group I, Series G, Branch Files: Group I, Box G-12. Little Rock, Arkansas Branch. University Publications of America, Bethesda, Maryland. University of Arkansas at Little Rock, Special Collections (UALRSC). Frames 0785–0787.
9. August Meier and John H. Bracey Jr, 'The NAACP as a Reform Movement 1909–1965: To Reach the Conscience of America', *The Journal of Southern History*, Vol. LIX, No. 1, February 1993, 13. For a detailed account see Richard C. Cortner, *A Mob Intent on Death: The NAACP and the Arkansas Riot Cases* (Middletown, Connecticutt, 1988).
10. W. A. Springfield to William Pickens, 5 January 1925. NAACP Microfilm, UALRSC.
11. Mrs. H. L. Porter to Roy Wilkins, 2 November 1934, ibid.
12. A. E. Bush and P. L. Dorman, *History of the Mosaic Templars of America* (Little Rock Central Printing Company, 1924).
13. John Kirk, 'Dr J. M. Robinson, the Arkansas Negro Democratic Association and Black Politics in Little Rock, Arkansas, 1928–1952', *Pulaski County Historical Review*, Vol. 41, No. 1, Spring 1993, 2–16 and Vol. 41, No. 2, Summer 1993, 39–47.
14. Memo to Arthur Spingarn, 7 November 1929. Miscellaneous Correspondence, 1917–25, 1928–32, NAACP, Little Rock. Microfilm, University of Arkansas at Fayetteville, Special Collections.
15. Harvard Sitkoff, *A New Deal For Blacks: The Emergence of Civil Rights as a*

National Issue (New York, 1978) provides an excellent overview of the plight of blacks in the Depression decade. For local developments see *Survey of Negroes in Little Rock and North Little Rock* compiled by the Writers Program of the WPA in the State of Arkansas, Sponsored by the Urban League of Greater Little Rock, Arkansas, 1941. The best collection of primary materials on the effects of the New Deal in Arkansas are the Floyd Sharp Scrapbooks 1933–43, at the Arkansas History Commission, Little Rock, Arkansas. Floyd Sharp was co-ordinator of the WPA in the state.

16. William Pickens to W. H. Flowers, 10 May 1940. NAACP Papers, Library of Congress. Group II, Series C, Branch Files 1940–1955: Container 10, 'Pine Bluff, Ark., 1940–1947'.

17. *The CNO Spectator*, 1 July 1940, WHFP.

18. V. O. Key, *Southern Politics in State and Nation* (New York, 1949), p. 183.

19. J. Kirk, 'Dr J. M. Robinson', Vol. 41, No. 1, Spring 1993, 6–13.

20. Tom W. Dillard, 'Scipio Jones', *Arkansas Historical Quarterly*, Vol. 31, Autumn 1972, and 'To the Back of the Elephant: Racial Conflict in the Arkansas Republican Party', *Arkansas Historical Quarterly*, Vol. 33, Spring 1974.

21. J. Kirk, 'Dr J. M. Robinson', Vol. 41, No. 1, Spring 1993, 6–7.

22. *The CNO Spectator*, 1 July 1940, WHFP.

23. Ibid.

24. Press Release, 12 October 1940, WHFP. Accounts seem to have appeared in various black newspapers about the meeting, perhaps most notably the *Pittsburgh Courier*, Penn. (See Flowers to William H. Nunn, Editor, 5 October 1940, WHFP.)

25. 'Partial Text of Keynote Address of W. Harold Flowers, delivered Friday Evening, 27 September 1940 at the opening of the "First Conference on Negro Organization" held at Lakeview, Arkansas', dated 27 September 1940, WHFP.

26. Press Release, 1 January 1941, WHFP.

27. Press Release, 4 September 1941, WHFP; *State Press*, Friday, 19 September 1941.

28. *State Press*, Friday, 19 September 1941.

29. Press Release, 11 September 1941, WHFP.

30. Ibid.; *State Press*, 15 May 1942.

31. *State Press*, 6 March 1942.

32. T. E. Patterson, *History of the Arkansas State Teachers Association* (Washington, D.C., 1981), pp. 89–91.

33. *The CNO Spectator*, 15 July 1940.

34. Mrs H. L. Porter to William Pickens. NAACP Papers, Group II, Series C, Branch Files 1940–1955: Container 9, 'Little Rock, Arkansas, 1940–1947'.

35. W. H. Flowers to Ella Baker, Director of Branches, NAACP, 18 August 1945. NAACP Papers, Group II, Series C, Branch Files 1940–1955: Container 11, 'Arkansas State Conference, April 1945–December 1948'.

36. J. Kirk, 'Dr J. M. Robinson', Vol. 41, No. 1, 8–13; C. Calvin Smith, 'The Politics of Evasion: Arkansas Reaction to *Smith* v. *Allwright*, 1944', *Journal of Negro History*, Vol. 67, Spring 1982, 40–51.

37. Steven Lawson, *Running For Freedom: Civil Rights and Black Politics in America* (New York, 1991), p. 85.

38. J. Kirk, 'Dr J. M. Robinson', Vol. 41., No. 2, Summer 1993, 39–40.

39. *Arkansas Gazette*, Sunday, 31 July 1988. Interview with John Hofheimer.

40. Guerdon D. Nichols, 'Breaking The Color Barrier at the University of Arkansas', *Arkansas Historical Quarterly*, Vol. 27, Spring 1968.

41. *State Press*, 15 July 1949.

42. Rev. W. Marcus Taylor to Ella Baker, 4 December 1945. NAACP Papers, Library of Congress. Group II, Series C, Branch Files, 1940–1955: Container 9, 'Little Rock, Arkansas, 1940–1947'.
43. Memorandum, Gloster B. Current to Thurgood Marshall, (n.d.) NAACP Papers, Library of Congress. Group II, Series C: Branch Files 1940–1955, Container 11, 'Arkansas State Conference, April 1945 – December 1948'.
44. Lucille Black to W. H. Flowers, 15 January 1948. NAACP Papers, Library of Congress. Group II, Series C: Branch Files 1940–1955, Container 10, 'Pine Bluff, Ark., 1948–1955'.
45. Memorandum, Donald Jones to Gloster B. Current, (n.d.) NAACP Papers, Library of Congress. Group II, Series C: Branch Files 1940–1955: Container 11, 'Arkansas State Conference, April 1945 – December 1948'.
46. Mrs L. C. Bates to Miss Mary W. Ovington. NAACP Papers, Library of Congress. Group II, Series C, Branch Files 1940–1955: Container 10, 'Little Rock, Ark., 1948–1955'.
47. Irene Wassell, 'L. C. Bates: Editor of the *Arkansas State Press*', Masters Thesis, University of Arkansas at Little Rock, 1983, pp. 36–7, UALRSC.
48. Gloster B. Current to Mrs L. C. Bates, 19 January 1949. NAACP Papers, Library of Congress. Group II, Series C, Branch Files 1940–1955: Container 10 'Little Rock, Ark., 1948–1955'.
49. Donald Jones to Gloster B. Current, 24 February 1949. NAACP Papers, Library of Congress. Group II, Series C, Branch Files 1940–1955: Container 11, 'Arkansas State Conference 1949–1950'.
50. 'Resolution', 3 September 1949. NAACP Papers, Library of Congress. Group II, Series C, Branch Files 1940–1955: Container 10, 'Pine Bluff, Ark, 1948–1955'.
51. Walter White to Pine Bluff NAACP, 25 February 1949; Roy Wilkins to Arkansas Branches of the NAACP, 10 May 1949. NAACP Papers, Library of Congress. Group II, Series C, Branch Files 1940–1955: Container 10, 'Pine Bluff, Ark, 1948–1955'.
52. Lulu B. White to Gloster B. Current, 1 November 1950. NAACP Papers, Library of Congress. Group II, Series C, Branch Files 1940–1955: Container 11, 'Arkansas State Conference 1949–1950'.
53. 'Memorandum to the Staff, Branches and Regional Offices from Gloster B. Current, 7 August 1951. NAACP Papers, Library of Congress. Group II, Series C, Branch Files 1940–1955: Container 11, 'Arkansas State Conference 1951–1952'.
54. Gloster B. Current to U. Simpson Tate, 20 August 1952. NAACP Papers, Library of Congress. Group II, Series C, Branch Files 1940–1955: Container 11, 'Arkansas State Conference 1951–1952'.
55. Georg Iggers, 'An Arkansas Professor: The NAACP and the Grassroots', in Wilson and Jane Cassells Record, *Little Rock, U. S. A.: Materials for Analysis* (San Francisco: Chandler, 1960), pp. 283–91.
56. Daisy Bates, *The Long Shadow of Little Rock* (Fayetteville, 1987).

3 Nixon *Was* the One: Edgar Daniel Nixon, the MIA and the Montgomery Bus Boycott
John White

In 1948, the distinguished French socialist Daniel Guerin travelled across the United States, and in his later published account of American race relations commented on an encounter in Montgomery, Alabama, with

> a vigorous colored union militant who was the leading spirit in his city both of the local union of Sleeping Car Porters and the local branch of the NAACP. What a difference from other branches of the Association, which are controlled by dentists, pastors and undertakers. [This man] has both feet on the ground. He is linked to the masses, he speaks their language. He has organized the work of race defence with the precision and method of a trade unionist. Men like E. D. Nixon ... incarnate the alliance which has at last been consummated between the race and labor.[1]

Guerin's 'colored union militant' himself once remarked, 'The labor movement gave black people the opportunity to do things that the civil rights movement gave [them] the right to do.'[2]

Edgar Daniel Nixon had been a notable figure in Montgomery twenty years before the creation of the Montgomery Improvement Association (MIA) and the subsequent bus boycott. By 1955 his long-standing connections with organized labour, friendships with such prominent liberal white Montgomerians as Joe Azbell, Aubrey Williams, Clifford and Virginia Durr, and in the African-American community with Mrs Rosa Parks, Jo Ann Gibson Robinson, and the lawyer, Fred Gray, had placed Nixon in a unique and commanding position.[3] Not least, it was E. D. Nixon who early recognized the charismatic qualities of a recently-arrived young African-American preacher who was to achieve national and international fame when he assumed (with Nixon's endorsement) leadership of the MIA. Unhappily, Nixon, well before his death in 1987, believed (with some justification) that his own contributions to the boycott, the MIA and racial progress in Montgomery had been eclipsed in both popular and scholarly accounts by Martin Luther King's towering reputation. In June, 1957, Nixon resigned as Treasurer of the MIA, informing Dr King: 'Since I have only been treasurer in name and not in reality, it will not be hard to find someone to do what I have been doing, even a schoolboy.' Although Nixon's belief that the MIA was mis-handling its funds was the occasion of his resignation, his accompanying statement – 'I resent being treated as a newcomer to the MIA. It is my dream, hope and hard work since 1932 and I do not expect to be treated as a child' – suggests divisions within the MIA and Montgomery's black community which also deserve consideration.[4]

E. D. Nixon was born in Montgomery on 12 July 1899, the fifth of eight children. His father was a tenant farmer and an untrained Primitive Baptist preacher. Nixon's mother, a maid and cook, died when he was eight and he was brought up by his paternal aunt, Winnie Bates, a laundress. By his own accounts, Nixon had little more than a third-grade education, and left home in 1911. In 1923, after working briefly in a meat-packing plant, a store in Birmingham, and on a streetcar line, Nixon was a baggage-room porter in Montgomery, and in 1925 became a Pullman porter, taking regular runs from Montgomery to Florida. Although they were regarded as among the elite of the African-American working class, Nixon deeply resented the treatment of Pullman porters – by white passengers and the Pullman Company.[5] But his experiences on the railroad literally (and metaphysically) widened Nixon's horizons. As he declared on many occasions: 'I was over 20 years old before I knew the whole world wasn't like Montgomery'.[6] Already convinced of the necessity of a union for porters, Nixon's Road to Damascus came in 1929 when he heard A. Philip Randolph speak in St Louis and immediately joined the Brotherhood of Sleeping Car Porters. In 1937, twelve years after the first meeting of the BSCP in New York, the Pullman Company recognized the union and signed a labour contract that improved the working conditions of black porters.

This recognition undoubtedly increased Nixon's standing and influence in Montgomery's African-American community – where he had already organized the Montgomery Welfare League to assist blacks who needed relief during the Depression – and in 1938 he was elected as president of the new union's Montgomery local, an office he held for 25 years. During the 1930s, Nixon was involved with Myles Horton's Highlander Folk School in Tennessee in an attempt to secure union organization of cucumber pickers in Alabama. The young labour militant had also been attracted to the NAACP – which formed a Montgomery chapter in 1918 – because of its record in securing black rights through legislation, litigation and lobbying. Defeated in his bid for branch president in 1944, he was elected in 1945, re-elected the following year, and served as president from 1946 to 1950, when he was replaced by Robert L. Mathews – the man he had defeated in 1945. In 1947 Nixon became president of the Alabama Conference of NAACP chapters, after defeating the incumbent, Emory O. Jackson, a Birmingham newspaper editor. But with national and local NAACP officials hostile to Nixon's lack of formal education and his allegedly dictatorial tendencies, he was not re-elected to the state post in 1949.

A summary of Nixon's other activities in the 1940s and 1950s would include his involvement in Randolph's March on Washington Movement, the securing of a water fountain and toilet facilities for blacks (provided by Sears Roebuck) in Montgomery's train station, and the construction during World War II of a United Services Organizations Club for black military personnel stationed near Montgomery. This last achievement was gained with the help of Eleanor Roosevelt. Earlier, when the First Lady had been a passenger on Nixon's train, he had requested (and received) an audience, which marked the beginning of their life-long friendship.

In 1940, Nixon organized the Montgomery Voter's League – to register black voters – and on 13 June 1944, led 750 African-Americans to the board of registrars, demanding to be allowed to qualify to vote. Less than 50 blacks were registered. Nixon himself had paid the $36.00 poll tax in Montgomery and tried to register to vote for ten years – and then had to file one lawsuit and threaten another – before being registered in 1945. From May to October, 1944, Nixon took leave from his porter's job and travelled through Alabama to organize black voters – the number of black voters in the state increased from 25 000 in 1940 to 600 000 by 1948. In 1948 Nixon described himself as being 'very busy in this fight for the right to vote for Negroes', and stated, 'I wish I could sell the people on this one idea of full citizenship . . . but these crackers here have did [*sic*] a good job of keeping the Negro afraid and also keeping him unlearned.'[7]

As president of the Montgomery NAACP, Nixon handled many cases involving police brutality, the rape of black women, murder and lynchings. In one instance, he managed to persuade Alabama Governor Chauncey Sparks to commute the death sentences of three African-American men found guilty of raping a white woman to terms of life imprisonment. A man of undoubted personal courage, Nixon was openly contemptuous of southern white liberals who confined their ostensible concern for African-Americans to armchair discussion. When Amanda Baker, a Negro schoolgirl was raped and murdered near Montgomery, Nixon went to see Governor Sparks, and later recounted:

> I was walking to the Capitol [and] passed a church where the Southern Conference for Human Welfare was having a meeting, talking about the terrible things going on. I went in . . . and was sitting in the back, when the chairman, [an] elderly white woman, seen me and said, 'I see we got a new face here this morning, and I'm going to let the gentleman come up and identify himself.' So I walked up and said, 'Good morning – I'm E. D. Nixon, president of the NAACP, and I'm on my way up to Governor Sparks to ask for a reward for the arrest and conviction of the guilty party who committed the crime against Amanda Baker, and all I want to ask is if there is one man or woman here, white or black, that has the courage to go with me, because if you do, I'd be glad to have you.' I

stood there a few minutes, and not a word did I get out of them. Finally, I said, 'Madam chairman, I'm sorry I've taken up your time, and I see now that nobody here really believes in what you are talking about'.[8]

In March 1947, the Montgomery chapter celebrated the twenty-fifth anniversary of the founding of the NAACP with a rally at Holt Street Baptist Church. The programme carried a short entry on Nixon, its president, in which he was described as 'well versed on the problems confronting Negroes in Montgomery', and as having 'spent long hours working toward the time when the two races will have a better understanding as regards each other. He is respected by all who know him and many members of our race rely upon his judgement'.[9] In 1952, Nixon won election to the presidency of the Montgomery chapter of the Progressive Democratic Association, the organization of Alabama's African-American Democrats. During the 1950s, Nixon pressured the city and county commissioners into hiring black policemen, creating a food stamp programme for poor blacks and whites, and after the 1954 *Brown* decision, attempted (unsuccessfully) to integrate the William Harrison High School in Montgomery. The minutes of a special Executive Committee meeting of the Montgomery chapter of the NAACP for 17 May 1955, celebrating the first anniversary of the Supreme Court's *Brown* decision recorded that: 'Mr E. D. Nixon said that we had not done very much about implementing the May 17 Supreme Court decision . . . The NAACP and other organizations should join in letting it be known in Washington that segregation in public schools must be abolished.'[10]

When Davis Lee, African-American publisher of the Newark, New Jersey *Telegraph*, who opposed school desegregation – on the grounds that it would result in the loss of many Negro teaching posts – was scheduled to speak in Montgomery in July 1953, Nixon as leader of the Montgomery Progressive Democrats and the BSCP, joined the Women's Political Council, Bethel Baptist Church and Association of Women's Clubs in placing 'An Open Letter to the People of Montgomery' in the *Advertiser*, protesting the visit. As a consequence of the 'Open Letter' and pickets outside the City Auditorium when Lee appeared, he addressed a sparse gathering. An estimated 75 spectators, of whom only 25 were Negroes, attended.[11]

In May 1954, Nixon filed as candidate in the Montgomery Democratic primary for membership of the county Democratic Executive Committee, the first black to seek public office in the state since Reconstruction, and lost by only 97 votes (with some white support). He was also chosen by Montgomery's blacks as the *Alabama Journal's* 'Man of the Year' – the prize included a free haircut and shoe shine, dry cleaning vouchers, theatre tickets, two turkey dinners, a shirt and tie, a large family photograph, presentation during the half-time period at the Tuskegee State game, and a certificate from the management of the *Journal*. The accompanying profile stated that

Nixon was 'very unassuming, yet militant . . . aggressive, yet not a radical'.[12]

Nixon again made headlines in the local press when in 1955 he tried to purchase a ticket to the Democratic party Jefferson-Jackson Day dinner in Birmingham, Alabama. Refused admission on the grounds of race, Nixon (now characterized by the *Montgomery Advertiser* as 'the NAACP Mau Mau chief') protested against his exclusion and in response, the principal scheduled speaker, Governor G. Mennen Williams of Michigan, cancelled his appearance.[13] (Always sensitive to policies of racial exclusion/segregation, Nixon in the 1950s went three years without a telephone in Montgomery rather than accept one on a four-party 'all colored' line).

Three weeks before Rosa Parks's historic refusal to give up her seat to a white passenger, New York Congressman Adam Clayton Powell, at Nixon's request, visited Alabama State College in Montgomery to speak to the city's chapter of the Progressive Democratic Association. The flamboyant Powell, who stayed overnight with Nixon in Montgomery, caused a double sensation. Governor James E. Folsom sent the state limousine to Montgomery airport to meet Powell and to convey him to the governor's mansion for a drink – a gesture which severely tarnished Folsom's political image in the state. In private, Folsom declared: 'Adam Clayton Powell is one son of a bitch I wish I'd never seen'. In his address to the Progressive Democrats, Powell asserted that the economic pressures of the racist White Citizens' Council 'can be counter met with our own [black] economic pressure'. Given that Powell had organized a bus boycott by African-Americans in New York City in 1941 and that blacks in nearby Selma had recently staged a boycott of white-owned businesses following the firing of black petitioners seeking school integration, the African-American leadership in Montgomery – and almost certainly E. D. Nixon – doubtless drew the appropriate conclusions.[14]

The WPC in Montgomery, organized in 1949 to urge African-American women to register to vote, had lodged several complaints with the City Commission about the mistreatment and humiliation of black female passengers on the city's busline, but had achieved little amelioration of conditions. Several incidents (all involving African-American women) had aroused the black community – the most notable being the arrest on 2 March 1955 of a teenager, Claudette Colvin, who had refused to vacate her seat when ordered to do so by the bus driver, Robert W. Cleere. After Colvin pleaded not guilty to violating Alabama's segregation law (and to assault and disorderly conduct), E. D. Nixon (who initially consulted Clifford Durr and Fred Gray on using the Colvin incident as a test case) decided – to the anger of some members of the WPC – that Colvin, an unmarried pregnant teenager, was hardly the ideal choice for lengthy, expensive and uncertain litigation.[15]

The arrest of Rosa Parks, a known activist and a respectable member of the black community, on 1 December 1955, however, provided Nixon – and Jo Ann Robinson, the most active member of the WPC – with an ideal opportunity to mount a protest against continuing discrimination on the city's buses. Rosa Parks, who became chapter secretary of the NAACP in 1943 and was later an adviser to its youth auxiliary, recalled that when she first met E. D. Nixon (in 1943), he had urged her to become a registered voter: 'Mr Nixon explained to me very fully the qualifications of being a voter, and the necessity of getting registered.'[16]

After Nixon lost the presidency of the NAACP, Mrs Parks worked for him at his union office, and it was Nixon who introduced her to Mrs Virginia Durr.[17] It was Mrs Durr (for whom she worked on a part-time basis as a seamstress) who arranged for Rosa Parks to attend Highlander Folk School in the summer of 1955. On her return to Montgomery, and to the great satisfaction of Nixon, Mrs Parks presented a report to the NAACP on her attendance at a workshop on desegregation.[18]

It was also E. D. Nixon (with Clifford and Virginia Durr in attendance) who paid Rosa Parks's bail bond, and gained her permission to use her arrest as a test case of the segregation laws. Again it was Nixon (and the WPC) who decided that the protest would take the form of a one-day boycott by Montgomery's blacks of the Montgomery City Lines. As he liked to relate, on the day following Mrs Parks's arrest, Nixon began to call the city's black civic leaders and ministers (beginning with Ralph Abernathy) informing them of the decision, and soliciting their support. According to Nixon, when he called Dr King, he was told, 'Brother Nixon, let me think about it a while and call me back.' When Nixon called again, King said that he would support the protest and elicited from Nixon the riposte, 'I'm glad you agreed because I have already set the meeting up to meet at your church.'[19]

Because of his railroad commitments, Nixon could not be present at the Dexter Avenue Baptist Church meeting, but before leaving town for his Chicago run, called *Montgomery Advertiser* reporter Joe Azbell and alerted him to the proposed boycott and the pamphlets printed and about to be circulated by Jo Ann Robinson and the WPC, advising blacks: 'Please stay off all buses [on] Monday.' As Nixon anticipated, the *Advertiser*, in its Sunday edition, carried the headline 'Negro Groups Ready Boycott of City Lines'. Following the successful one-day boycott, a meeting was held at Mt. Zion AME Baptist Church at which it was decided that a permanent organization, the MIA headed by Dr King, would continue and coordinate the protest already launched by the actions of the WPC. The initial demands of the MIA – reflecting earlier proposals by Nixon's Progressive Democratic Association – were for more courtesy from bus drivers, the hiring of black drivers on predominantly black routes, and the seating of blacks towards the front and of whites from the front towards the back (without a section being assigned for each race). The decision was to be put to a mass meeting at Holt Street Baptist Church, later that day. Sensing that some black ministers favoured a return to the buses, while others, aware of the press photographers present, were reluctant to speak and favoured mimeographing and distributing the MIA's recommendations secretly at the planned meeting, Nixon angrily upbraided them and later recalled:

> I got up and said 'Let me tell you gentlemen one thing. You ministers have lived off of these washwomen for the last 100 years and never done anything for them. Now you have a chance to pay them back for some of the things they've done for you. If this program isn't accepted and brought out into the open tonight (and there will be over 1000 people at that church), I'll take the microphone and tell the people that the reason we don't have a program is because you are all too cowardly to stand on your feet and be counted . . . We ought to be men enough to stand on our feet and be counted or admit to ourselves that we are a bunch of scared boys'.[20]

This outburst – whether calculated or spontaneous – had the desired effect. As Martin Luther King observed: 'With this forthright statement the air was cleared. Nobody would again suggest that we try to conceal our identity or avoid the issue head on. Nixon's courageous affirmation had given new heart to those who were about to be crippled by fear.'[21]

Again, it would seem that although Nixon informed the local chapter of the NAACP of the decision to extend the boycott, he decided that a new organization should lead the protest, since

> the man who was president of the NAACP at that time said 'Bro Nixon, I'll have to wait until I talk to New York to find out what they think about it.' I said, man we ain't got time for that. He believed in doing everything by the book. And the book stated that you were suppose[d] to notify New York before you take a step like that.[22]

Nixon can also claim some credit for the MIA's decision, in February 1956, to file a civil case in federal court testing the legality of Alabama's segregation ordinance, rather than awaiting the outcome of its appeal against Mrs Parks's conviction. Attorney Fred Gray (who cites Nixon as being instrumental in finding five black lawyers who sponsored his original application to law school) accordingly filed suit on behalf of five black women – Aurelia S. Browder (40), Susie McDonald (77), Jeanetta Reese (64), Claudette Colvin (16), and Mary Louise Smith (19) – all of whom had experienced discrimination on municipal transportation during the preceding year.[23] In *Browder* v. *Gayle*, a Federal district court ruled that bus segregation violated the Fourteenth Amendment, and the Supreme Court upheld the ruling in November 1956, bringing the Montgomery boycott to its ultimate and 'legal' conclusion. Although Dr King later asserted that the decision to file suit in federal court was a response to the intransigence of the Montgomery City Commission and the bombing of his own and Nixon's homes, Nixon relates that in January 1956, and after conferring with Clifford Durr, he proposed such a measure to King and Abernathy. He reminded them of the Viola White episode, a similar case to Rosa Parks's in the mid-1940s, and pointed out that ten years later, it was still pending in the courts. In Nixon's retelling:

> I came in from my run on the second Sunday in January 1956 and I called Reverend King and Reverend Abernathy, and I told them, I got news for you boys. I said I can call you 'boys' because I got a son that's older than either of you. I said, you all think we goin' to the Supreme Court in Mrs Parks's case. The city fathers knows we feels that the only outlet we got is that case, and they goin' to freeze us out. I told them what we would have to do.[25]

Nixon's repeated accounts of his role in the events immediately preceding and following Rosa Parks's arrest and the formation of the MIA are in some respects contradictory, and have been variously interpreted.[26] His activities *during* the 381-day boycott, as Treasurer and fund-raiser for the MIA – which have never received adequate scholarly recognition – were undoubtedly crucial to its success.

The first collection for MIA funds was taken at Holt Street Baptist Church and approximately $500 was raised. Nixon, as Treasurer, left the meeting with the money, and pointedly asked the local police in attendance to escort him home for protection. They complied and drove him in a patrol car, in what was to be the only gesture of cooperation between the MIA and the Montgomery Police Department.[27] Nixon also proposed that the MIA should use its capital surplus, together with a loan from the federal government, to establish a Negro bank, which would also contain office space for African-American professional men. Such an enterprise, Nixon argued, would provide much-needed capital for the development of the Negro section of the city, but his suggestion was never taken up.[28]

From the inception of the boycott, Nixon was acutely aware that the MIA needed substantial funds to mount its operations. On one occasion, when he phoned a labour leader in Los Angeles and explained the MIA's financial needs, 'the man replied that he had no authority as a union president to commit his group for any sum of $100.00 or over, without getting authorization from the membership. He did promise, though, to send along a check for $99.99 every week for ten weeks'.[29]

In March, 1956, Nixon was the guest speaker at a BSCP-sponsored Meeting of the National Committee for Rural Schools, in New York City. His topic was the Montgomery Bus Boycott, and he began his address by announcing:

> I am from the heart of Dixie, but sometimes I wonder whether Dixie has a heart . . . I would like to say that . . . Rosa Parks's case was not the sole

foundation for this mass protest ... the papers named it a boycott. But over a period of years, we have had different things happen on the buses and in the streets [and] police brutality ... we have called on the city's commissioners and the bus company with reference to these situations ... but we found that we were not able to get anywhere.[30]

Nixon then recounted his role in calling Montgomery ministers after Rosa Parks's arrest, and the *Montgomery Advertiser's* notice of the proposed boycott. 'They gave us a two-page column down the front page ... we could not have bought this as an advertizement for $500.00. Aside from giving us two pages in the paper, they gave us radio and television, and thousands of people who would have never known about what we was trying to do was able to read about it in the paper and hear about it on radio and television.'

Nixon also stated the 'many objectives' of the MIA as of March 1956. 'Our prime interest right now is to adjust the seating arrangements on the bus, and we're trying to do that within the existing law. We knew that we'd eventually have to go to court and we is hoping to renew the Rosa Parks case. But ... we have filed a case [*Browder* v. *Gayle*] in federal court in the name of five people who was a party to that.' Nixon then explained the organisation and operation of the MIA's transportation committee and its car pool, with 47 pick-up stations and 300 cars – which now provided 'a better job ... than the Montgomery bus line has done in 20 years'. After describing to a northern audience the etiquette of Jim Crow on southern buses, and his own activities in providing car transportation, Nixon claimed, 'I think I'm more involved in this thing than most peoples, and ... I have contributed 25 years of my life to this thing, and I believe if I'd died two, three years ago, without living to see this thing, I'd say to the Lord, "Jesus, you've already discriminated against me once." I wouldn't have missed it for nothing'.

He also stressed that if and when the MIA achieved its immediate objective, it would remain in existence to fight police brutality and other forms of racial discrimination. He ended by retelling a favourite joke about a small boy going down the street with a basket, selling puppies. Asked their price by a lady, the boy replied '25 cents'. The lady was tempted, but decided not to buy a puppy. The next day, she saw the boy again, and asked him if he had any more puppies. The boy said he had, and the lady was about to ask him for one when he said that a puppy cost 50 cents. Lady: 'Why are they 50 cents today and only a quarter yesterday?' Boy: 'Their eyes are open.' Nixon: 'I'd like to leave this with you people here tonight – that the Negroes' eyes are open in Montgomery and they aren't being sold for 25 cents anymore.'[31]

Nixon also addressed the National Committee on the following day when he was introduced by A. Philip Randolph as 'the foundation of this spirit being expressed in this protest against the Jim Crow bus'. On Nixon's behalf,

Randolph appealed to delegates to support the boycott. 'Brother Nixon tells me that it costs $3,500 a week to keep the automobile pool rolling that carries the people to and fro, from work, from day to day . . . the porters in Chicago sent him a hundred dollars. The porters in Jacksonville sent him $25, and I believe that the porters here have the same sort of devotion that they have all over the country.' Nixon began his second address by bringing greetings to the delegates from Montgomery, Alabama, 'The cradle of the Confederacy that has stood still for a long, long time, prior to December 1st, but is now being rocked by 50 000 Negroes in Montgomery.'

After paying a warm tribute to his hero and mentor, Randolph, Nixon again recounted the events surrounding Rosa Parks's arrest, and stressed the importance of the mass meetings in Montgomery in maintaining the impetus of the boycott and the donations which the MIA was receiving from across the country. In an aside, he observed that the Montgomery city fathers had 'tried to say that Reverend King came from up North, so we had to let them know if Atlanta, Georgia, was "up North," then we were guilty'.

He ended on both a rhetorical and an entrepreneurial note. 'The Negroes in Montgomery is tired of being kicked around . . . of being Jim-Crowed on the Montgomery City Line or any other form of transportation . . . They have made up their mind that they're going to fight it until the court says they don't have to do it.' But the need was for funds – to pay for court costs, oil and gasoline and all the expenses incurred by the car pool. 'I still believe in prayer,' Nixon concluded, 'had I not believed in it, I wouldn't have come here. So one thing, you can pray for us, and the next thing . . . you can put your hand in your pocket and make a contribution. Whether it's large or small, the MIA will be eternally grateful.'[32]

In April 1956, a press release by the International Union of United Automobile, Aircraft and Agricultural Implement Workers of America announced that 'an attentive, and at times demonstrative, audience of more than 1500 UAW members' had attended a Civil Rights Rally, sponsored by UAW Region 1 (Detroit's East Side) to hear E. D. Nixon, treasurer of the MIA 'tell how his home was bombed by terrorists after he had led a "No Ride" protest of Negroes against racial segregation and inhuman treatment on the Montgomery buses'. Nixon had informed the audience: 'They couldn't find the man who bombed my house, so, they arrested me.' Among those present at the Detroit rally were UAW Secretary Treasurer Emil Mazey and Vice-Presidents Norman Matthews and Pat Greenhouse. Acting Chairman George Merrelli opened the rally with a review of current civil rights injustices and the need for organized labour to support the Montgomery struggle both morally and financially. Mazey presented Nixon with a cheque for $500 from the International UAW, and the financial secretary of Chrysler Local 7 'presented a check for $50 from his Local plus a membership collection of $483.71'. The press release also noted that: 'Local 212 President Pat Caruso gave

Nixon a check for $500 from the Local and a cash donation of $110 from third shift members.' Local 208 reported that it had raised $379 in cash 'and were pledging an additional $100 per month for the duration of the bus stoppage'. Local 410 indicated that it was pledging $100 a month, while a pledge of $500 was received from Local 351. In addition, 'a total of $326.25 was donated by those attending the rally, as they left the hall'.

Nixon, the release observed, had 'roused the audience to a great shout when he asserted that "I don't believe the people of Montgomery will ever accept Jim Crow travel again"'. After expressing his gratitude to the ministers for the 'job they have done in Montgomery', Nixon – 'the fighting Negro leader' – had declared: 'We've got to win not only for the people of Montgomery but for the people everywhere who believe in freedom and justice.'[33]

The following month, Nixon made a great impression when he appeared at a NAACP/BSCP/AFL–CIO civil rights rally in Madison Square Garden, together with Eleanor Roosevelt, A. Philip Randolph, Tallulah Bankhead, Martin Luther King and Adam Clayton Powell Jr. As the last scheduled speaker, Nixon brought the audience of 16 000 people to its feet when he stood up and announced:

> I'm E. D. Nixon from Montgomery, Alabama, a city that is known as the Cradle of the Confederacy and the city that stood still for more than ninety-three years until Rosa Parks was arrested and thrown in jail like a common criminal, and 50,000 Negroes rose up and caught hold of the cradle and began to rock it until the Jim Crow rocker began to reel and the segregated slats began to fall. I'm from that city.[34]

Roy Wilkins remembered that 'People began to shout and yell and thump one another on the back, and the Garden resonated with enough joy and hope to keep all of us going for months afterward.'[35]

From the outset of the bus boycott, Nixon's activities were extensively covered in the BSCP newspaper, *The Black Worker*. In its December 1955 issue, the paper announced: 'Bro. Nixon Steps Up the Fight For Civil Rights', and recounted how following Rosa Parks's arrest, Nixon, together with Fred Gray had posted $100 bond to have her released from custody. The resulting bus boycott was now almost 100 per cent successful and 'our hats are doffed to you once again, Brother Nixon'.[36] Three months later, A. Philip Randolph prefaced a *Black Worker* profile of Nixon with the comment that he was a leading member of the BSCP and 'particularly, and unquestionably . . . a leader of the citizens of Montgomery'.[37] In February 1956 the paper carried the headline 'Nixon Helps Lead Bus Boycott' and in the accompanying article observed that:

> This notable exhibition of courage, determination, unity and intelligence

by the boycott of jim crow buses in Montgomery ought to serve as a source of inspiration and hope to the Negroes not only in Dixie, but throughout the country ... We salute the Rev. L. M. [sic] King, Jr., and E. D. Nixon, president of the Montgomery Division of the Brotherhood of Sleeping Car Porters, whose homes were bombed, upon their integrity, courage and devotion in this great and significant struggle for human dignity for black citizens.

A separate feature carried a full account of the bombing of Nixon's home in Montgomery, and noted that it followed the earlier bombing of 'the home of a Negro minister, Rev. L. M. [sic] King, Jr., who like Nixon is also a leader in the boycott of the Montgomery buses'. But the paper's focus was definitely on Nixon who, readers were reminded, 'has for more than a score of years given an enlightened and aggressive type of leadership in Montgomery', and, 'Brother Nixon seems not disturbed or deterred by the bombing but on the contrary, with his wife, he is more determined to play his part with other Negroes in Montgomery in all efforts to eliminate racial inequities and other undemocratic practices.'

Nixon was reported as having said that black Montgomerians 'are madder than ever' and that 'whoever is responsible for these bombings isn't going to end the boycott that way. We are all in this to the end'. The *Black Worker* concluded that Nixon was a credit to the BSCP, and deserving of its support. 'Brother Nixon is one of the Brotherhood's most aggressive, courageous and forward looking leaders. A man of great ability, forthrightness and integrity, he is well prepared to lend leadership in this historic period when the walls of racial segregation are beginning to crumble.'[38]

Nixon's response to the bombing (and its aftermath) was also revealed in a personal 'note' to A. P. Randolph:

Well the bom [sic] missed my house about 12 ft. No police protection here as the whole city force mayor and all are members of the white Citizens Council. They have made every effort to intimidate me but I dont scare easy. I get about 50 threatening [sic] calls every 24 hours, (smile) but they wont come out in the open, a bunch of cowards. I was not home but they tell me in 20 minutes after the bom went off there was 2,000 people and shortly after there was 5,000 including most of the porters.[39]

In reply, Randolph applauded 'the reaction which resulted in thousands of your admirers gathering around the home to give you protection. This shows that the people believe in your sound and courageous leadership.'[40]

Aubrey Williams, publisher of the *Southern Farmer*, and himself a supporter of the Montgomery boycott, wrote to Randolph in May, 1956 – while the boycott was still in progress – concerning Nixon 'your great admirer and I am proud to say, I think my good friend'. Nixon, Williams asserted 'is and has been the real leader of the bus protest', and had devoted his time to it 'in an amount which must have been very hard on his earnings'. Reporting as 'one on the scene who can and does testify to his indispensibility,' Williams believed that: 'this magnificent show of strength, character and power would never have happened but for his leadership. It is the fruit of a lifetime of courage and single-purposed pursuit of an ideal.'[41] Responding to this encomium, Randolph expressed himself 'in complete accord with your thinking that this great spirit of Negroes in Montgomery in the boycott of the jim-crow buses is the outgrowth and expression of a long, courageous and unselfish struggle on the part of Brother Nixon for freedom and manhood rights for Negroes in Montgomery'. And, Randolph informed Williams: 'Knowing of his [Nixon's] dedication to this cause of civil rights, I have sought to involve him in various meetings and conferences here in the North, in order that his position in the struggle may be better known.'[42]

Two months later, Randolph wrote to Nixon 'to congratulate you and the Montgomery Improvement Association upon the great fight being made to abolish jim crow transportation on buses in Montgomery'.[43]

In April 1956 the Chicago Division of the BSCP hosted 'A Salute to A. Philip Randolph' in the Grand Ballroom at the Midland Hotel. E. D. Nixon was the keynote speaker before the 600 guests and as the *Black Worker* duly reported, 'The address presented by Brother E. D. Nixon gave the people present a ringside view of the important undertaking being carried on successfully by the Negroes in Alabama. Brother Nixon detailed the origin and purpose of the Montgomery Improvement Association, of which he is treasurer and which is the group behind the bus boycott in Montgomery. Brother Nixon's address was most inspiring.'[44]

Nixon's contributions to the bus boycott were also reported in *The Militant*, the newspaper of the Workers Party of America. In 1956, reporter William Bundy characterized Nixon as 'an old time civil rights and union fighter in Montgomery', and cited an anonymous Montgomery source as saying: ' . . . if it hadn't been for E. D. Nixon this movement wouldn't be where it is today'. The article also quoted Nixon to good effect: 'Some of us tried to get something done about the buses long before this protest. We tried to talk to the city officials, but they wouldn't even listen. When Mrs Parks got arrested that was the last straw.' Nixon also informed Bundy that: 'We could have settled this thing long ago if the white leaders had just sat down and talked to us, but after that first day it was too late. We had to go on. Our people just insisted. They voted to go on with the protest until we got something definite, and we organized the association [MIA] right there on the spot.'[45]

The Militant also reviewed Daniel Guerin's *Negroes on the March*, with its mention of Nixon, and noted that his 'current role as one of the most prominent boycott organizers and treasurer of the Montgomery Improvement Association, bears out the author's foresight of seven years before'.[46] In a later article on 'The Civil Rights Fight and the White Worker', Nixon was described as a 'symbolic figure' who 'epitomized the necessity of an alliance between the labor movement and the Negro freedom fighters'.[47]

On the occasion of the tenth anniversary of the Montgomery bus boycott, Nixon was guest of honour at a dinner sponsored by the socialist Militant Labor Forum in New York City. Noting that Nixon had not been invited to the anniversary celebrations in Montgomery, Farrell Dobbs, National Secretary of the Socialist Workers Party, observed to the assembled guests that: 'We of the Militant Labor Forum felt that he should be included, that he before all others should be recognized as the pioneer, the founding father, the initiator, the spark plug and principal man of the hour in the battle.' In his address, Nixon – described in the *Militant's* report of the proceedings as 'an authentic spokesman who emerges from the ranks of a working class movement' – observed that the MIA 'was not started just because someone came to town or someone felt it was the proper thing to do at this time. It was started because there had been a struggle of the people for long years'. In a lightly-veiled reference to his disagreements with the middle-class leadership of the MIA, Nixon had asserted that:

> in every organization there are people who get carried away by big words. There are sometimes people who get carried away by how the words are said. But ... there are two things that are important in dealing with organizations. One of them is not how much you say but how much you do. The other thing is not just to say things but to tell the truth about the things you deal with. And that's what I have tried to contribute to the Montgomery Improvement Association and to any other organization I have dealt with.[48]

On the twentieth anniversary of the boycott, in a letter to Mrs Johnny Carr, president of the MIA, Nixon rejected an overture from that organization 'after twenty years' and asserted:

> ... it was I that bonded Mrs Parks out of jail, it was I who called the people together to organize the MIA, it was I who wrote the 3 recommendations, it was I who selected Rev. King to be the spokesman, and during the early part of the MIA, it was I who made contact with organized labor, and politicians across the country, and during this period that I served as Treasurer of the MIA, and I cut checks for $415,000.00 ... I personally raised $97,000.00 myself, and I had $68,000.00 that came to my house in letters from across the country, and I begged 5 automobiles, and no one brought back an automobile except me, and when they arrested the 90 odd of us, and Fred Gray was out of town, everybody was all excited and didn't know what to do ... and I personally called Attorney Thurgood Marshall, who advised us the next step to take. In view of

these things, and other contributions that I made to help serve the community through the MIA, and to find for 20 years that I have been completely left out of the picture of the MIA ... I feel as a Christian and a dedicated worker who are [*sic*] really sincere, I'm forced to decline your invitation.[49]

E. D. Nixon had always claimed that he was a 'founding father' of the MIA, and a major contributor to the Montgomery bus boycott. In certain crucial respects this was true: Nixon was the one who (with Martin Luther King) brought a grass-roots protest to national attention. As the late Alex Haley observed, Nixon, through his affiliation with organized labour and left-wing protest groups, helped to nationalize the Montgomery movement, while these same connections 'gave him the foresight and the organizational skills to impress and mobilize Montgomery's black community'.[50] That he was not impressed by and did not appeal to the college-educated, middle-class and largely clerical leadership of the MIA is revealed in Mrs Johnny Carr's comment: 'Mr. Nixon was a hardworking man, a fine leader and everything, but he [didn't] have that thing that could weld people together in a movement like ours ... I have heard Mr. Nixon say that "When I walk into an MIA meeting, don't nobody clap or say anything, but when Dr. King walks in, everybody stands up and claps." Now he [Nixon] had been working down through the years and all, but it was just one of those things.'[51]

Although he was conspicuously absent from the civil rights protests which followed after the Montgomery boycott, Nixon continued to work for the city's working-class community. Ironically, in his last years E. D. Nixon began to receive belated recognition – including celebratory newspaper articles by Joe Azbell and an honorary doctorate from Alabama State University – by the city's white and black establishments as 'A Forgotten Hero'.[52]

In 1986, Nixon's home on Clinton Street, Montgomery, was registered as 'a significant landmark' by the Alabama Historical Commission, with the endorsement of Governor George Wallace. A historical marker in front of the now dilapidated house (still lived in by Nixon's widow, Arlet), accurately records that:

Edgar D. Nixon, Sr., posted bail for segregation law violator Rosa Parks. In her defense, Nixon gathered the support of Montgomery blacks in implementing the successful 1955–56 Montgomery Bus Boycott. His commitment and active involvement as a grassroots organizer, civic leader and founder of the Montgomery NAACP chapter has paralleled local movement for the advancement of blacks ... As chief strategist of the Montgomery Bus Boycott, Nixon spearheaded a local protest which launched a massive movement of social reform and earned him local recognition as "The Father of the Civil Rights Movement".

60   *John White*

NOTES

1. Daniel Guerin, *Negroes on the March: A Frenchman's Report on the American Negro Struggle* (New York, 1956), p. 179.
2. Jack Santino, *Miles of Smiles, Years of Struggle: Stories of Black Pullman Porters* (Urbana, 1989), p. 55.
3. There is no scholarly biography of Nixon, but see the short and privately printed *Freedom is Never Free: A Biographical Portrait of Edgar Daniel Nixon, Sr.*, by Lewis V. Baldwin and Aprille V. Woodson (United Parcel Service, 1992). Informative depictions of Nixon by fellow Montgomerians are to be found in: Rosa Parks (with Jim Haskins), *Rosa Parks: My Story* (New York, 1992); David J. Garrow (ed.), *The Montgomery Bus Boycott and the Women Who Started It: The Memoir of Jo Ann Gibson Robinson* (Knoxville, 1987); Uriah J. Fields, *The Montgomery Story: The Unhappy Effects of the Montgomery Bus Boycott* (New York, 1959); and Hollinger F. Barnard (ed.), *Outside the Magic Circle: The Autobiography of Virginia Foster Durr* (Tuscaloosa, 1985, 1990). In his account of the boycott, Martin Luther King pays a generous tribute to Nixon. See: Martin Luther King, Jr., *Stride Toward Freedom: The Montgomery Story* (New York, 1958). Nixon receives only a passing mention in Coretta Scott King's *My Life With Martin Luther King, Jr.* (London, 1970): 'Mr Nixon was a fiery Alabamian. He was a Pullman porter who had been active in A. Philip Randolph's Brotherhood of Sleeping Car Porters, and in civil rights activities.' p. 126.
4. Nixon to Martin Luther King Jr, 3 June 1957 (MLK Papers, Special Collections, Mugar Memorial Library, Boston University).
5. These and subsequent biographical details are drawn from materials in the E. D. Nixon Collection, Special Collections, Alabama State University, Montgomery, Ala. Hereafter EDN Collection. For Nixon's published reflections of his experiences as a Pullman porter, see Studs Terkel, *Hard Times: An Oral History of the Great Depression* (New York, 1970), pp. 117–22, and Santino, *Miles of Smiles*, pp. 53–5.
6. Eliot Wigginton (ed.), *Refuse to Stand Silently By: An Oral History of Grass Roots Social Activism in America, 1921–1962* (New York, 1992), p. 23.
7. Quoted in Paula F. Pfeffer, *A Philip Randolph: Pioneer of the Civil Rights Movement* (Baton Rouge, 1990), p. 173.
8. Earl and Miriam Selby, *Odyssey: Journey through Black America* (New York, 1971), pp. 51–2.
9. EDN Collection.
10. NAACP Minutes, Montgomery Branch, 1954–55, Schomburg Center, New York City.
11. *Montgomery Advertiser*, 6 July 1953.
12. *Alabama Journal*, 22 November 1954. Front page.
13. *Montgomery Advertiser/Alabama Journal*, 2 October 1955, 2B.
14. George E. Sims, *The Little Man's Big Friend: James E. Folsom in Alabama Politics, 1946–1958* (Tuscaloosa, 1985), p. 176. Powell's visit to Montgomery was reported in the *Advertiser*, 6 November 1955. See Also: Wil Hayward, *King of the Cats: The Life and Times of Adam Clayton Powell, Jr.* (Boston and New York, 1993), pp. 204–6. On the Selma boycott see J. Mills Thornton III, 'Selma's Smitherman Affair of 1955', *Alabama Review*, Vol. XLIV, No. 2 (April, 1991), 112–31. For the background and course of the Montgomery boycott, see Mills Thornton's important article 'Challenge and Response in the Montgomery Bus Boycott of 1955–1956', *Alabama Review*, Vol. XXXIII, (July, 1980), 163–235, and his more recent summary in 'Municipal Politics and the Course of the

Movement', in Armstead L. Robinson and Patricia Sullivan (eds), *New Directions in Civil Rights Studies* (Charlottesville, 1991), pp. 44–7.

15. The Colvin episode is discussed in John A. Salmond, *The Conscience of a Lawyer: Clifford J. Durr and American Civil Liberties, 1899–1975* (Tuscaloosa, 1990), pp. 172–3, David J. Garrow, *Bearing the Cross: Martin Luther King, Jr. and the SCLC* (New York, 1986), pp. 15–16 and in Taylor Branch, *Parting the Waters: America in the King Years, 1954–63* (New York, 1988), pp. 120–3. See also, Garrow, *The Montgomery Bus Boycott and the Women Who Started it*, pp. 37–9; 41–3, and Steven M. Millner, 'The Montgomery Bus Boycott: A Case Study in the Emergence and Career of a Social Movement', in David J. Garrow, ed., *The Walking City: The Montgomery Bus Boycott, 1955–1956* (New York, 1989), pp. 339–40.

16. Rosa Parks: Videotape, 'Edgar D. Nixon: A Forgotten Hero', ASU Special Collections.

17. Parks, *My Story*, p. 95.

18. NAACP Minutes, Montgomery Branch: Schomburg Centre. For Rosa Parks's experiences at Highlander, see John M. Glen, Highlander: No Ordinary School' (Lexington, 1988), pp. 136–7, and Cynthia Stokes Brown (ed.), *Ready from Within: Septima Clark and the Civil Rights Movement* (Navarro, California, 1986), pp. 17–18.

19. Howell Raines, *My Soul is Rested: Movement Days in the Deep South Remembered* (New York, 1979), p. 45. Abernathy's recollections of Nixon's phone call and his role in the boycott are recounted in: R. D. Abernathy, 'The Natural History of a Social Movement: The Montgomery Improvement Association', originally written as an MA thesis in the Department of Sociology, Atlanta University, 1958, and reprinted in Garrow, *The Walking City*. In 1958, Abernathy characterized Nixon as: 'an aggressive and fearless fighter for the rights of Negro people in Montgomery for many years ... a pullman porter ... [who] does not have a formal education, but ... a very courageous man', and 'a tall, raw-boned man of blunt directness [with] both tenacity and stamina ... long before the bus crisis, he was meeting threats and turning them back in language sometimes as picturesque as a Missouri mule skinner', pp. 111, 143. In *And the Walls Came Tumbling Down: An Autobiography* (New York, 1989), Abernathy writes that Nixon 'had a powerful voice that he used to great advantage, sweating prodigiously as he waved his arms or pounded the table', but adds that when Nixon was mentioned as a possible leader of the MIA, Martin Luther King 'objected to the fact that Nixon was uneducated and used poor grammar' p. 143.

20. E. D. Nixon interviewed by Judy Barton, 25 January 1972. Martin Luther King Center Oral History Project. Transcript, 10.

21. King, *Stride Toward Freedom*, p. 57.

22. Aldon D. Morris, *The Origins of the Civil Rights Movement: Black Communities Organizing for Change* (New York, 1984), p. 54. Morris asserts: 'Here is a concrete example of how a bureaucratized organization was inappropriate in the early mobilization stage of a mass protest. The group proceeded to form "an organization of organizations," and Abernathy named it the Montgomery Improvement Association'. ibid. See also Roy Wilkins (with Tom Mathews), *Standing Fast: The Autobiography of Roy Wilkins* (New York, 1982). Wilkins states: 'E. D. Nixon, an old friend of mine, had served several times as head of the NAACP in Montgomery, and ... had also been an organizer for the BSCP. He was straight as a ramrod, tough as a mule, and braver than a squad of marines. When he took up the [Rosa Parks] case, the white establishment of Montgomery didn't have a chance'. p. 226.

23. Burt M. Rieff, 'Browder v. Gayle: The Legal Vehicle for the Montgomery Bus Boycott', *Alabama Review*, XLI, No. 3 (July 1988), 193–208, 197. Fred D. Gray, Interview with John White, Tuskegee, Alabama, 23 September 1992.

24. Thomas J. Gilliam, 'The Montgomery Bus Boycott of 1955–56', in Garrow, *The Walking City*, pp. 261–62.

25. Milton Viorst, *Fire in the Streets: America in the 1960s* (New York, 1981), pp. 46–7.

26. Lawrence D. Reddick, King's colleague in the MIA and subsequently his first biographer, quotes approvingly Daniel Guerin's estimate of Nixon's importance in Montgomery as being 'doubtless true at that time, 1948'. But Reddick believes that Nixon later regretted not allowing himself to be nominated for the presidency of the MIA. 'Accordingly, on occasion he so strongly projected his part in the creation and development of the MIA that many a passing reporter came away with the impression that Nixon really was the man'. L. D. Reddick, *Crusader Without Violence: A Biography of Martin Luther King, Jr.* (New York, 1959), p. 125. See also, Branch, *Parting the Waters*, p. 132.

27. Gilliam, 'Montgomery Bus Boycott', p. 221.

28. *Ibid.*, 231.

29. *Ibid.*, 230.

30. Joseph F. Wilson, *Tearing Down the Color Line: A Documentary History of the Brotherhood of Sleeping Car Porters* (New York, 1989), pp. 240–6 *passim*.

31. *Ibid.*

32. *Ibid.*, pp. 252–8 *passim*. Nixon, commenting on the role of music and speeches at MIA meetings, explained: 'If you are going to lead a group of people you are going to have to put something into the program that those people like. A whole lot of people came to MIA meetings for no other reason than just to hear the music, some came to hear the folks who spoke'. Morris, *Origins of the Civil Rights Movement*, p. 47.

33. *News From the UAW*, 20 April 1956.

34. Raines, *My Soul is Rested*, p. 37.

35. Wilkins, *Standing Fast*, pp. 236–7.

36. *Black Worker*, December 1955, 1.

37. Ibid, 15 March 1956, 2/8.

38. Ibid, February 1956, 1, 3, 6.

39. E. D. Nixon to A. P. Randolph, 5 February 1956, BSCP Papers, Library of Congress. At the suggestion of *Liberation* magazine, the civil rights strategist Bayard Rustin visited Montgomery in February 1956, and duly reported: 'This afternoon I talked with E.D. Nixon, whose home was bombed on February 1. For years he has been a fearless fighter for Negro rights. He suspects that his home will be bombed again but says: "They can bomb us out and they can kill us, but we are not going to give in"'. *Down the Line: The Collected Writings of Bayard Rustin* (Chicago, 1971), p. 55.

40. A. P. Randolph to E. D. Nixon, 29 February 1956, BSCP Papers, Library of Congress.

41. Aubrey Williams to A. P. Randolph, 3 May 1956, BSCP Papers, Library of Congress. On Williams's friendship with Nixon, see John Salmond, *A Southern Rebel: The Life and Times of Aubrey Willis Williams, 1890–1965* (Chapel Hill, 1963), pp. 252–3, and Richard A. Reiman, 'Aubrey Williams: A Southern New Dealer in the Civil Rights Movement', Alabama Review, Vol. XLIII, No. 3 (July 1980), 180–205.

42. A. P. Randolph to Aubrey Williams, 8 May 1956, Library of Congress BSCP Papers.

43. A. P. Randolph to E. D. Nixon, 26 July 1956, Library of Congress BSCP Papers.
44. *Black Worker*, 27, No. 4, April 1956, 1/3.
45. *The Militant*, 19 March 1956, p. 2. See also Bundy, 'E. D. Nixon – Trade Unionist, Negro Leader', *Militant*, Vol. XX, 26 March 1956, 3.
46. *The Militant*, 14 May 1956.
47. *The Militant*, 13 May 1957, 2.
48. *The Militant*, 20 December 1965, 8.
49. E. D. Nixon to Mrs J. Carr, 9 October 1976, EDN Collection.
50. Alex Haley, Foreword to *Freedom is Never Free*, p. xi. For a persuasive statement to the effect that the protest leaders who orchestrated the bus boycott were replaced by 'accommodationist' African-American leaders within 18 months of its resolution, see Ralph H. Hines and James E. Pierce, 'Negro Leadership After the Social Crisis: An Analysis of Leadership Changes in Montgomery, Alabama', Phylon, 26, 2nd Quarter (1965), 162–72.
51. Millner, 'Emergence and Career of a Social Movement', p. 530.
52. See: *Dr. E. D. Nixon: Father of the Modern Civil Rights Movement – "A Forgotten Hero"* (n.d.) (EDN Collection). Profiles of Nixon which stress his pivotal role in the MIA and the Montgomery bus boycott include: Donald Cox, 'Edgar Daniel Nixon: Kingmaker', *Black World*, Vol. 20, No. 4 (February 1971), 87–98; Vernon Jarrett, 'A Forgotten Hero: He Rallied Blacks to Famed Boycott', *Chicago Tribune*, 1 December 1975, reprinted in *The Forgotten Heroes of the Montgomery Bus Boycott* (n.d.) (Alabama Department of Archives and History); Richard Blake Dent, 'The Father His Children Forgot', *American History Illustrated*, Vol. XX, No. 8 (December 1985), 10–17; Joe Azbell, 'E. D. Nixon of Montgomery: The Man Who Made M. L. King', *Montgomery Independent*, 30 January 1975, and 'Random Notes From a Reporter's Week', Montgomery Independent, 17 April 1980.

Part II

Responses

4 Fatalism, Not Gradualism: The Crisis of Southern Liberalism, 1945–65
Tony Badger

I

Mississippi in the 1950s may have been a 'closed society', seemingly cut off from the intellectual and racial forces of change affecting the rest of the nation. Yet the New Deal and World War II had unleashed changes in the state that gave hope to a new generation of white liberals in the Magnolia State.

In World War II a quarter of million Mississippians, black and white, served in the armed services. One of the whites was Frank Smith. As he recalled, 'More men came home from World War II with a sense of purpose than from any other American venture'. Smith himself had grown up in Sidon in Leflore County in the heart of the Delta. His memories of the 1930s made him a New Deal liberal.

> The several farm programs of the first eight Roosevelt years brought a stable and relatively prosperous farm economy to Leflore County ... The days of the WPA, NYA and distribution of surplus food commodities were the first that Sidon ever knew without sharp pockets of poverty and even just plain hunger in some corners of the community.

At the end of the 1930s Smith had gone to read history at the University of Mississippi where he started life-long friendships with Jim Silver and Bell Wiley. During the war he wrote from France to his future wife, 'The racial haters at homes [sic] are fascists at heart, whether they know it or not. The tragic fact is that they do not know it.'[1]

On his return from the War, Smith joined a fledgling 'liberal' newspaper, the Greenwood *Morning Star*, a paper that in its brief existence gave a start to John Herbers, who later covered so much of the civil rights movement for the *New York Times*. One of the events Smith covered was a speech to the local service club by Circuit Judge John Stennis, who made an impassioned speech in support of the United Nations. Stennis argued that UNESCO might be the most important of the UN agencies to contribute to lasting peace and that, for the UN to work, the American people had to be prepared to give up some national sovereignty to the international agency.[2]

When Stennis later that year announced he would run for the Senate to succeed Theodore 'The Man' Bilbo, Smith went to work for him as publicity director. Stennis campaigned without mentioning the race issue and pledged 'to plow a straight furrow down to the end of my row'. He won. At the same time Frank Smith was elected to the State Senate. There, in January 1948, he joined 30 or 40 veterans, some still GI students at the University of Mississippi. 'I knew either directly or indirectly' recalled Smith, 'that most of them were idealists who hoped to have a part in making a better day. We had no illusions about completely remaking Mississippi, but we did believe we could contribute to its improvement'.

That legislature, the youngest in Mississippi's history, enacted a model workmen's compensation law. The legislature between 1945 and 1950 enacted the most progressive welfare legislation, especially for children, in the state's history. Because of war-induced prosperity, Mississippi had for the first time been able to afford to take part in the categorical assistance schemes of the Social Security Act, programmes which required states to match federal spending. There were more women in the 1952 state legislature than ever before or since.[3]

Meanwhile, in the heart of the Delta, Frank Smith got elected to Congress in 1950 by campaigning against the old guard political leaders. His economic philosophy was simply to extend the benefits the New Deal had brought to the state: 'federal programs were necessary to get more money into the hands of the people'. Mississippi did not have the tax base to produce the revenue for economic development: the money for roads, rural electrification, and even schools, had to come from the federal government. Economic development was crucial since it was Smith's belief that 'large-scale economic progress was the only avenue likely to lead to solution of the race problem in Mississippi'.[4]

The man who had helped set up the newspaper Smith had worked on was Hodding Carter, the editor of the Greenville *Delta-Democrat Times*. During the War, Carter served in Cairo as editor of the Middle East editions of *Stars and Stripes* and *Yank*. He saw the bitterness that British colonial rule inspired in the local population. 'Men with white skins are in the minority in this world,' he noted in 1945, 'and an even smaller minority are white-skinned men who look upon darker skins with contempt.' In Carter's first novel, *Winds of Fear*, a young newspaperman returning from the war fights the Thing [fear, hatred and prejudice] and concludes 'If you stood against the Thing, people would eventually listen'. In real life Carter exhorted his readers to 'shoot the works in a fight for tolerance' and won the 1946 Pulitzer Prize. He later argued in the Cold War, 'Whenever anyone adds fuel to the flames of intolerance, he is in fact helping to bring Communism a step nearer'.[5]

Before 1954 Carter personally believed, like Smith, that the maintenance of segregation, with the provision of genuinely equal facilities, was the best way forward for gradual racial change in the South. But when the *Brown* decision was handed down, he editorialized that 'the Court could not have made a different decision in the light of democratic and Christian principles and against the background of today'.[6]

Just after the *Brown* decision was handed down, *New York Times* editor Turner Catledge returned to his home town of Philadelphia in Neshoba County and talked to the students in the white high school. He was bombarded with questions about the decision, in particular from one young pretty blonde, Florence Mars. These intelligent, open-minded students left Catledge optimistic that his home state would adapt to the *Brown* decision responsibly.[7]

In Holmes County, the editor and owner of the *Lexington Advertiser* was an attractive socialite, Hazel Brannon Smith, who named her house Tara, in the style of *Gone with the Wind*. In 1948 she enthusiastically supported the white supremacy Dixiecrat revolt and supported Joe McCarthy with some zeal. Her reforming editorial campaigns were directed at gambling and bootlegging and the blind eye to them turned by local law enforcement officers. But as a passionate evangelical who disliked violence, she also launched a series of editorial attacks on local law enforcement officers who had attacked blacks. She excoriated the sheriff who shot a black man in the back when the man was simply following the sheriff's order to leave the scene of an incident. She condemned the sacking of a black schoolteacher and her husband after the teacher had been shot in the arm by a white driver. The teacher had complained to the driver when he damaged her yard by turning his car in it. The white assailant was not arrested. Brannon Smith refused to support the segregationists between 1954 and 1961. While she did not openly espouse the cause of civil rights before 1961, that summer she praised the freedom rides and the sit-ins. In 1964 she welcomed Freedom Summer volunteers and Martin Luther King to her home, endorsed the Civil Rights Act and backed Lyndon Johnson for the Presidency.[8]

In the tiny community of Petal, just outside Hattiesburg, P. D. East had started out like Hazel Brannon Smith as an utterly conventional local newspaper editor. East was no economic or racial liberal. At the age of 16, he 'learned that the South had lost the Civil War. It's unbelievable but that is a fact. I was surprised at the news, but not especially alarmed'. He was a something of a misfit. He was always getting into fights. He also found it hard keeping his job on the Southern Railroad and suffered a nervous breakdown. He took the opportunity to take up a small weekly newspaper in Petal after promises from local businessmen of volume advertising. He followed the formula of success of other weeklies 'Love America, Motherhood, and Hate Sin'. He aimed to please everybody.[9]

Like Smith, East favoured segregation but he had an iconoclastic streak that found it difficult to stomach the idiocies perpetrated by the defenders of white supremacy. He innocently ran into trouble for praising Abraham Lincoln and making jokes about the liquor question: $1 million worth of whiskey was sold each year in his county but it still voted dry. Not that his readers always understood his sarcasm – when he suggested that Mississippi replace the Magnolia as symbol of the state with the crawfish which always moved backwards to the mud from which it came, two men who were to be charter members of the local Citizens Council praised him for 'telling them niggers where their place is, by God'. He was praised for his spoof on the 'Professional Southerners Club, addressed by the Honorable Jefferson D. Dixiecrat' by a local merchant who agreed 'its about time the black bastards learned to keep their place'. But even the most obtuse segregationist could understand the spoof citizen's council advert:

> Yes YOU too, can be *SUPERIOR* Join the Glorious Citizens Clan Next Thursday Night. Worried about being socially acceptable? Learning to play the piano by ear? Using the right toothpaste? Join the Citizens Clan and be safe from social worries. BE SUPER SUPERIOR. Compare these 10 Freedoms with other old fashioned offers. Freedom to Interpret the Constitution of the United States to your own advantage. Freedom to yell 'Nigger' as much as you please without your conscience bothering you. Freedom to be superior without Brain, character or principles. Not to join could mean you're a Nigger lover. The Clan needs YOU but most of all, YOU may need the Clan.[10]

East found congenial spirits in William Faulkner and Will Campbell. The novelist had long bemoaned the tragic fate of Mississippi and the South, cursed as they were by the race question. Campbell, a self-taught Baptist preacher, was Director of Religious Life at the University of Mississippi where he turned the YMCA into a centre of free-ranging discussion of social and racial issues.[11]

Together in July 1956 they produced and printed *The Southern Reposure*, a revised and edited version of *The Nigble Papers* that had been mimeographed by students at Ole Miss. The banner headline read 'Eastland Elected by NAACP as Outstanding Man of the Year'. The alleged publisher, Nathan Bedford Cooclose, aimed to keep the Scotch-Irish segregated from the rest of the white community:

> The average Scotch-Irish is a repulsive and obnoxious creature who is apt, if the notion strikes him, to pull a highland fling on the main street of any one of our towns in Mississippi. In addition, they have come to expect to be served oatmeal in our finest restaurants simply because they have the required fifteen cents ... They breed like turtles. In addition to

poor breeding, they are vulgar to an unbearable point. How many times have you heard one exclaim, 'Hootman', or 'Begorrah!' How disgusting! . . . Do you want your daughter to marry a windbag, highland flinging, kilt wearing creature . . . If God had wanted the Scotch-Irish to mix with the rest of the white race he would not have put them on an island off the coast of Europe.

Readers were invited to join the *Anti-Scotch Irish Council* whose aims included keeping 'the Scotch-Irish in their place' and keeping 'The R Rolling Children Out of Our Fine Southern Schools'.[12]

But dissenters like the Smiths, Carter, East and Campbell were not the force of the future in the South. Most liberals in Mississippi became at best, in the words of Hodding Carter, 'closet moderates'. The white supremacy leaders in Mississippi created a climate of conformity in Mississippi by a combination of propaganda, economic pressure and terrorist violence, orchestrated by the Citizens Councils and encouraged by the State Government, aimed at both blacks and white dissenters. Mississippi became the 'closed society' so memorably described by James Silver, or in the words of Jessica Mitford 'a concentration camp of the mind'.[13]

Frank Smith sadly noted in 1964:

The Negro has been an underlying issue in Mississippi politics since 1845, and he has been the dominant issue throughout the lifetime of the present-day Mississippians. In the past few years, he has become the only issue, with top prizes going to those who shout against him the loudest and demonstrate the most convincing hatred for his friends in national politics.

Smith had clung on to his seat until redistricting compelled his defeat in 1962, but he did so only by avoiding the race issue wherever possible, and mouthing segregationist platitudes on occasion. He assiduously attended to constituency needs and worked tirelessly for economic development measures. But that could not save his political career in the end. His support of the Kennedys, despite the federal benefits it brought his district, was the kiss of death. After his defeat in 1962 he went into exile. Appointed a director of the TVA, Smith moved to Knoxville.[14]

In 1955 Washington journalist Tris Coffin went to Mississippi:

I saw and met a charming people living on the edge of a precipice. They drank frosted mint juleps and held the conversation rigidly on small matters that no one really cared about. I sensed they were frightened by the immense forces that lived on both sides of them, the poor white bigots with their capacity for savage cruelty and the Negroes, a sticky force gradually hardening.

I talked in private with the Governor and business leaders and they all told me segregation was through but there would be violence and terror. None of them seemed to have thought through any system for preventing terror. And although I may be wrong, I sensed that there might be reason to have terror as a weapon, not for the Negro but for labour organizers.[15]

In February 1956 Virginia Durr reported from neighbouring Alabama, 'My grandfather who fought with General Forrest [in the Civil War] used to say that there were only two things he hated: A man that scared easy and a woman that raped easy. Mississippi seems full of both'.[16]

In March that year, leading Jackson businessman Boyd Campbell talked to southern utility leaders. He warned them that 'the greatest deterrent to our economic growth in the South for the foreseeable future was a relationship between the races that was deteriorating rapidly'. The voices of moderation had been driven out by extremists on both sides. 'This continual preoccupation with segregation vs integration is becoming almost psychotic.' He hoped that 'a group of really distinguished leaders – native-born, mature, conservative and respected might explore some move toward getting together in a group, however small, to search for the possibilities for encouraging a more objective and wholesome attitude toward our problems in the years ahead'. Instead, that month, former moderate John Stennis helped draft the Southern Manifesto, a blast of defiance at the Supreme Court which promised to resist the *Brown* decision by all lawful means.[17]

Faulkner was alarmed by the prospect of white mob violence to prevent Autherine Lucy enrolling at the University of Alabama. In a *Sunday Times* interview in March 1956 he reiterated his opposition to compulsory integration and implored the NAACP to 'Go Slow Now, Stop Now for a time, a moment . . .' In the event of a clash between Mississippi and the federal government over race, Faulkner announced, 'As long as there is a middle ground, all right, I'll be on it. But if it comes to fighting, I'd fight for Mississippi against the U.S. even if it meant going out into the street and shooting Negroes.' The interview encapsulated his belief in gradualism, his fatalism about white racism and his opposition to outside intervention.[18]

Later that summer, after the publication of the *Southern Reposure*, East met Faulkner to discuss forming a group of moderates. Faulkner had little taste for political organization and collaboration with others. East reported, 'It was decided, finally, that it was impossible. Faulkner felt that we'd spend all our time fending off attacks rather than in getting anything worthwhile accomplished.'[19]

East struggled on largely alone. His *Petal Paper* was increasingly difficult to sustain. Its advertising revenue dried up. East himself was ostracized. Only the financial support of northern friends sustained him. No one bought the paper in Hattiesburg. Eventually he physically and emotionally collapsed.[20]

Hazel Brannon Smith's newspaper faced a similar collapse in circulation. She had to confront an advertising boycott, cross-burnings on her lawn, and the establishment of a rival paper backed by the Citizens Council. At the height of her unpopularity, Smith sold more newspapers outside the state, than inside her home county.[21]

Will Campbell had plans to challenge segregation at the University by getting a young black minister to apply to the School of Continuing Education. Playing table tennis against the minister at the campus YMCA, Campbell was spotted by university police and reported to the Dean. The Dean was unpersuaded by Campbell's defence that table tennis was a quintessentially segregated game, with separate but equal bats, a tightly-drawn net dividing the two men, and a white ball. Shortly afterwards, Campbell found excreta coated in sugar floating in the punch at a YMCA student reception. He finally responded to his brother's entreaties and the university's hostility and left the state.[22]

Hodding Carter stayed and continued to edit the Greenville paper. But when his son took over, he remembered that each night he taped the bonnet of his car so that he could see next morning if it had been tampered with and a bomb placed in the vehicle.[23]

Turner Catledge was horrified to learn that it was his home town of Philadelphia, Neshoba County, where the three civil rights workers were taken from custody and murdered in 1964. Florence Mars, the young blonde who had been so bubbling and inquisitive in 1954, attempted to cooperate with FBI and Justice Department efforts to flush out the involvement of the Klan and the connivance of local law officers in the murders. Her stockyard was boycotted and she was eventually forced to sell. She was arrested for drunk driving and removed from her position of Sunday school teacher.[24]

Yet racial change did come to Mississippi and it came very quickly. But the changes owed little to the work of Mississippi white liberals, rather change was imposed from outside and was accepted when whites in the state finally saw that resistance was impossible or counter-productive. The efforts of the white liberals were largely irrelevant.

In retrospect, the turning point was the riot at Ole Miss in 1962 which prompted President Kennedy to send in troops to ensure that James Meredith was admitted to the University. The first impact of this was to strengthen the position of segregationist leaders like Governor Ross Barnett, to heighten the paranoia which affected the white population, and to drive the forces of moderation even further underground as the fate of those local clergy, driven out by their congregations when they attempted to rally support for calm, indicated. But the riot and the federal response demonstrated for the first time to many Mississippians, even if they did not want to admit it immediately, that the federal government and the courts would eventually triumph. As one Yazoo editor plaintively acknowledged, 'I didnt know until after the

Meredith case. That is what gets me. I didnt know we were whistling in the wind. *I didnt know.*' Looking back, one businessman summed up the stark reality of Mississippi's position, 'It's like looking down the barrel of a cannon, you can't fight back with a peashooter.'[25]

In 1964 Jackson business leaders decided to comply with the new Civil Rights Act and not to fight the September desegregation of the city's schools. In Neshoba County, where the three civil rights workers were murdered, the schools were desegregated peacefully less than two years later. The 1965 Voting Rights Act achieved almost overnight what voter registration workers had laboured for in vain: the mass registration of black voters. Registration of voting-age black Mississippians rose from 6 per cent to almost 60 per cent in two years. By 1967 the white terrorism which had scarred the state with the bombing of homes and churches and the murder of civil rights activists had been more or less stamped out.[26]

What had secured dramatic racial change in the state was not the patient efforts of liberals to secure gradual change from within, but the coercive impact of legislation and judicial decisions imposed from outside. The key figures in persuading white Mississippians to accept that change was unavoidable were business leaders and conservative political leaders who belatedly recognized that economic development and the violent defence of white supremacy were incompatible. The white liberals did have a part to play. As the 'closet moderates' came out of the closet, they constituted, as William McCord observed, 'a reserve force to exert the final push forward after the federal courts and Negroes had done their work.'[27]

Mississippi was obviously an extreme example: the troops of reaction were stronger, the forces of moderation more beleaguered. But these cameos of Mississippi liberals, their fate and the eventual process of racial change in the state do suggest with broad brush-strokes the nature of the crisis of southern liberalism in the post-war years. They illustrate the post-war optimism in a new order and the faith in New Deal-style economic liberalism as the answer for the region's problems; the faith that economic progress would ultimately solve the racial problem; the idiosyncratic road to racial moderation of individual liberals and the limitations of their racial liberalism. The liberals favoured gradual racial change, preferably within the system of segregation, and feared that federal intervention would be counter-productive. The resistance the liberals faced testified to the determination of the advocates of traditional race relations to mount a crusade to stir up segregationist sentiment and to stamp out dissent from racial orthodoxy. Those liberals who did stand out faced violence, ostracism and economic intimidation. Most ran for cover, paralysed by their conviction that white public opinion was irresistibly arrayed against them. When substantial racial change eventually came in the 1960s the efforts of the Mississippi liberals were largely irrelevant.

II

'World War II', argued Morton Sosna, 'probably had a greater impact on the South than the Civil War'. Wartime prosperity and federal military spending created the new urban jobs to absorb the surplus rural population, created an internal market for consumer durables, and created local markets for the products of a diversified mechanized agriculture. The war was the catalyst for self-sustaining economic growth in the region. These changes promised to break the stranglehold on the region of the hitherto all-powerful rural and small-town elites. Throughout the South new-style younger politicians were elected who appealed to a broad-based coalition of blacks, veterans, organized labour, women and lower-income whites. The liberals emerged at all levels: in the United States Senate, Lister Hill and John Sparkman of Alabama, Claude Pepper of Florida, Estes Kefauver of Tennessee; in the House not only Frank Smith in Mississippi but Albert Gore in Tennessee, Charles Deane in North Carolina and Carl Elliott in Alabama; in the state houses, governors like Sid McMath in Arkansas, Kerr Scott in North Carolina, Jim Folsom in Alabama, and Earl Long in Louisiana; in the cities reform mayors like DeLesseps Morrison in New Orleans.[28]

The key to liberal success had to be the extension of political participation in the South. The low levels of pre-war political participation ensured conservative hegemony. The groups in southern society which might have pushed for liberal welfare and spending programmes designed to benefit the disadvantaged – the blacks and lower-income whites themselves – were effectively disfranchized. The New Deal and the war, however, raised black expectations and led to black voter-registration drives. In the 1930s Thurgood Marshall and Charles Houston had tirelessly travelled the South urging blacks to form NAACP branches and to supplement legal action with voter registration. In the 1940s NAACP field secretary Madison Jones reported from the South that the war had 'caused the Negro to change almost instantly from a fundamentally defensive attitude to one of offense'. After the 1944 Supreme Court decision outlawing the white primary, black voters' leagues sprang up all over the South. Blacks who had served in the armed forces outside the South returned home determined to exercise their right to vote. The percentage of the black voting-age population registered to vote quadrupled in the 1940s.[29]

The role of the war in raising black expectations has long been asserted. Yet, as the case of Frank Smith indicated, the war also had an effect on southern whites who served overseas. Throughout the region returning soldiers joined GI revolts which aimed to overthrow the traditional local power structures. A recurring theme in these revolts was that honest elections and a freely exercised vote would end the power of the old-time bosses. Young liberal candidates like Sid McMath in Arkansas and DeLesseps Morrison in

New Orleans capitalized on their distinguished war records. Some advocated increasingly internationalist views. While in Mississippi John Stennis advocated a more powerful role for the United Nations, in North Carolina the youngest and most liberal candidate for governor in 1948, R. Mayne Albright, was chairman of the North Carolina branch of the World Federalists.[30]

Like blacks and returning GIs, organized labour had a vested interest in seeing a new southern politics. If the CIO was to make the decisive breakthrough in union organization in the region, which it hoped to achieve through Operation Dixie in 1945–6, the unions desperately needed the election of sympathetic politicians: local sheriffs who would not harass union organizers, state legislators and governors who would repeal right-to-work and anti-closed shop laws. The unions endorsed, and provided funds for, candidates like Kerr Scott in North Carolina and Jim Folsom in Alabama.[31]

Southern women also played a significant, and as yet largely unacknowledged, role in the liberal politics of the 1940s. The assumption has been that during World War II and the Cold War women, whose leaders had wielded unprecedented political and policy influence in the New Deal, returned to 'greater concerns emanating from daily living'. Southern women exhibited a 'widespread disinterest . . . in public affairs and feminist issues'. It has increasingly been recognized that such a view is seriously flawed for the black community. The activities of the WPC in initiating and sustaining the Montgomery bus boycott is just one example that gives the lie to notions of black passivity. But this interpretation is also an inadequate picture of the activities of white women. Everywhere in the South reinvigorated branches of the League of Women Voters campaigned for liberal candidates. In Georgia, Helen Douglas Mankin was elected to Congress in a special election in 1946 with the overwhelming support of Atlanta's newly enfranchised black voters. Women were prominent as state campaign managers for Henry Wallace's Progressive Party. Liberal politicians, in turn, responded to the women's activism. Estes Kefauver in 1948 was the first candidate in Tennessee to appoint women campaign managers in every county. Kerr Scott and Jim Folsom as governors appointed the first women to state and appeal court judgeships in North Carolina and Alabama. As for Earl Long, he characteristically explained, 'I'm for the women, I've appointed more women than all other Louisiana governors put together.'[32]

There is not an inevitable link between female political activism and economic and racial liberalism. It is not enough simply to celebrate a litany of heroic individuals like Hazel Brannon Smith. The women in the Mississippi legislature were just as segregationist as their male colleagues. Women voted for segregationist candidates and joined the Citizens Council. Two of the most rabid segregationist groups were the Mothers' League of Central High and the Women for Constitutional Government in Mississippi.[33]

Race relations, however, involved two areas where traditional notions of domesticity gave a certain legitimacy to a public role for women: the church and education. Southern cultural norms gave middle-class white teachers and church women a measure of protection from community assault. Women did use the church to promote racial change. From Atlanta, Dorothy Tilly organized the Fellowship of the Concerned which enlisted over 4000 women to be the 'shock absorbers' of racial change by organizing local workshops to prepare the way for desegregation. Throughout the region, middle-class women and the YWCA were responsible for interracial groups that gave many white students their first contact with their black contemporaries. Frances Pauley in Georgia transferred her leadership of the League of Women Voters to the fight to save public education. Pat Derrian and other women played a similar role in the Mississippi campaign to keep the public schools open.[34]

Just as there is a history of southern women after 1945 to be written, so there is still to be written a history of the relationship of southern white churches and race relations. The way in which the more fundamentalist churches, particularly Baptist churches, bolstered the segregationist cause has been amply documented. While segregationist pastors vocally supported the cause of Massive Resistance, other ministers who might have dissented from racial conformity were reluctant to offend their congregations' white supremacy sensibilities. But there were clergymen who took a more courageous line. Mark Newman's massive work on southern Baptists and race relations shows that even the Baptists were not a monolithic bloc in favour of the racial status quo. Groups like the Fellowship for Southern Churchmen organized interracial workshops and communion services and aimed to '[p]ractice shock therapy by taking the initiative in the violation of traditional taboos which stood in the way of complete justice and equality'. The Catholic Committee of the South organized workshops for priests on race and labour relations. We need to know more about the activities of southern Methodists and the activities of the American Friends Services Committee and, especially, to know more about the work of YMCAs on southern campuses. Will Campbell's work at Ole Miss was duplicated round the region and exposed a new generation of white students to interracialism.[35]

The southern liberal politicians who emerged after 1945 fashioned an appeal to their lower-income white and black constituents that combined a traditional popular style and new economic benefits. They mounted colourful personal campaigns and excoriated opponents as tools of the big interests but they also offered the voters the welfare and educational services that the conservatives had long denied them. They advocated a New Deal modernization strategy for the South: a strategy that depended on economic growth sustained by mass purchasing power. The relative prosperity of the 1940s enabled their states to participate fully in New Deal programmes that required states to match federal money, programmes that southern states had been too poor to take real advantage of in the 1930s. They enthusiastically supported measures of federal government assistance – ultimately only federal aid could solve the region's problems. This strategy starkly contrasted with the conservative modernization strategy which rested on the attraction of low-wage industries to the region by promising low taxation and a non-unionized labour force. To the southern liberals, the federal government was the answer to their problems; to southern conservatives, the federal government was the problem.[36]

The southern liberal politicians stressed economic issues because they believed that an emphasis on common economic problems would unite their coalition of lower-income white and black supporters on class lines and divert their attention away from the divisive issue of race. But it was not only for practical political reasons that they stressed economic ones. They genuinely believed, as Frank Smith had exemplified, that, at its core, the South's racial problem was an economic one and that economic growth would largely eradicate it. This emphasis on the primacy of economic issues accompanied a faith that black needs could be best met gradually, within the system of segregation and without the assistance of outsiders. These tenets of gradualism and paternalism were firmly within the tradition of southern white liberalism so ably documented by Morton Sosna and John Kneebone. They were the views eloquently expressed by the region's celebrated liberal newspaper editors like Ralph McGill of the *Atlanta Constitution*, Harry Ashmore of the *Arkansas Gazette*, and Jonathan Daniels of the *Raleigh News and Observer*. Anthony Lake Newberry in the most comprehensive analysis of the racial views of 'middle-of-the-road' southerners has identified two characteristic strands: a persistent paternalism and an emphasis on the dangers of precipitate action. These opinions, which professed optimism but advocated caution, had a compelling influence over many northern Democratic politicians and liberal intellectuals in the 1950s who, listening to those they considered southern moderates, advocated restraint in implementing civil rights policy.[37]

There were, however, a small number of more radical white southerners who believed that the conundrum of race and economics had to be resolved the other way round: the precondition of a sound prosperity in the South, of creating mass purchasing power, was the solving of the region's racial problem. Southerners like Will Alexander, Clark Foreman, Aubrey Williams, and Clifford Durr, who had served in New Deal agencies in Washington in the 1930s, knew from their contacts with national black leaders that southern blacks would not be satisfied with continued segregation. Other whites, influenced both by the Social Gospel and by Marx, had worked in the South in local community organizing alongside blacks in the 1930s in the Communist Party, in the student movement, amongst tenant farmers, and in labour unions. During the war, they argued that the full resources of the nation, and the South in particular, could not be used effectively against Hitler unless the debilitating effect of racism was eradicated. Unlike the liberals, these radicals, many of whom worked in the 1940s for the SCHW, were convinced that segregation had to be eliminated before genuine progress could be made in the South.[38]

III

But as in Mississippi the liberals and moderates were not able to promote gradual and peaceful racial change from within the region. After the *Brown* decision of 1954 southern politics were dominated by conservatives who most vehemently protested their loyalty and announced their intention to defy the Supreme Court. Liberal politicians were no match for the forces of Massive Resistance. What went wrong?

It is tempting to say that the liberal opportunity of the 1940s was a mirage: that the overwhelming forces of popular racism doomed the cause of racial moderation from the start. The war stimulated white violence and racial tension as much as it raised black expectations. Organized labour's attempts to unionize the region were almost a complete failure. Women's political activism and church-inspired interracial work went behind closed doors in the 1950s. The white radicals were race-baited and red-baited before 1950: the Southern Conference disintegrated under such assaults. In their local communities radicals became ostracized and subject to the sort of economic and physical intimidation that P. D. East and Hazel Brannon Smith endured. Lower-income whites showed that they were prepared to support 'good ole boy' candidates determined to resist racial change, like the Talmadges in Georgia, rather than support New Deal-style liberals.[39]

While the conservative die may have seemed cast even before the *Brown* decision in some states, in others there were still grounds for liberal optimism after 1954. In Alabama Jim Folsom was elected to a second term by a record margin in 1954 and the two liberals, John Sparkman and Lister Hill were easily re-elected to the Senate in 1954 and 1956. In Tennessee both senators, Estes Kefauver and Albert Gore, and the governor, Frank Clement, were liberals. In North Carolina, former governor Kerr Scott was elected to the Senate in 1954 in the weeks following the *Brown* decision, despite a last-minute racial smear by his opponent. In Louisiana Earl Long secured a third term in 1955. In Arkansas Sid McMath, defeated in 1952, had the satisfaction of seeing his liberal protégé Orval Faubus elected governor in 1954 and 1956.

Yet in all these states there were racial crises before the end of 1960: mobs attempted to halt desegregation, usually successfully, in Alabama, Tennessee, Arkansas and Louisiana; the whole gamut of Massive Resistance legislation passed in Alabama, Louisiana and Arkansas, schools were closed for a year in Arkansas; North Carolina authorized local school boards to

close schools rather than desegregate and legislated for tuition grants to enable
parents to attend segregated schools. Two case-studies help to explain what
dashed liberal hopes. A study of the small number of politicians who did
not sign the Southern Manifesto indicates the idiosyncratic and personal nature
of racial liberalism and raises questions about the room for manoeuvre liberal politicians might have had in the 1950s. A study of four governors
elected in the post-war liberal upsurge suggests the paralysis and fatalism
which seemed to grip liberal politicians when they confronted the race issue.

IV

The Southern Manifesto was read to the Senate on 12 March 1956. It was a
blast of defiance at the Supreme Court for the *Brown* decision. The signatories, who constituted the overwhelming majority of southern senators and
representatives, pledged themselves 'to use all lawful means to bring about
a reversal of this decision which is contrary to the Constitution and to prevent the use of force in its implementation'. The Manifesto was the brain-
child of Strom Thurmond, but Thurmond's idea carried weight because it
was taken up by some of the South's most influential and respected conservative senators: Harry Byrd of Virginia, Richard Russell of Georgia, Sam
Ervin of North Carolina, and John Stennis of Mississippi. These leaders were
not espousing this rhetoric of defiance to appease their segregationist sentiment. Far from believing that popular sentiment was overwhelmingly in favour of Massive Resistance, they were convinced that white southerners were
insufficiently stirred up on the issue of segregation. The conservative leaders
feared that southerners were resigned to the inevitable and did not believe
that the Supreme Court and school desegregation could be halted. The first
aim of the Manifesto was therefore to act as a rallying cry to southern whites,
not to placate popular sentiment but to arouse it. Second, the leaders hoped
to enforce 'unity of action' in the South. By stirring up public sentiment,
they hoped to coerce white politicians who might be wavering in their determination to resist desegregation, in particular the five or six southern
senators who, Richard Russell lamented, were even prepared to agree with
the *Brown* decision.[40]

The success of the Manifesto in coercing wavering southerners was immediately demonstrated by the willingness of four of the most noted liberal
senators from the region – Lister Hill and John Sparkman of Alabama, William
Fulbright of Arkansas, and Kerr Scott of North Carolina – to sign. The irony
was that while conservative leaders believed that southern whites were not
sufficiently passionate in favour of segregation, moderate leaders believed
the opposite. Public opinion, they feared, was irresistibly committed to the
defence of segregation and left them with no alternative but to sign the

Manifesto. Hill was up for re-election in 1956 and in early 1956 there was certainly a racial crisis in Alabama as mobs halted the admission of Autherine Lucy to the University, blacks boycotted Montgomery buses, and the state legislature passed a barrage of anti-desegregation laws. Yet Hill, a man who believed that in all areas other than race relations federal assistance was the key to solving the South's problems, was not faced by serious primary opposition in 1956, as his political allies consistently assured him. Sparkman, a self-confessed 'TVA liberal', had been re-elected in 1954 with the highest vote ever recorded in an Alabama senatorial primary. Fulbright argued that he had to make concessions to the segregationist cause to avoid Orval Faubus replacing him in the Senate. He professed to be a 'gradualist' in matters of race relations. Yet he never attempted to campaign to build up support for gradual racial change. It was not his belief in gradualism that made him sign the Manifesto but his fatalism. Kerr Scott did, on reflection, regret signing the Manifesto and attempted too late to take his name of the list of signatories. '[H]e never went in', recalled an aide, 'for that kind of strong stuff.' But though Scott had condemned defiance of the Court, he has also announced that he did not intend to run counter 'to the majority of our people in North Carolina which is against integration'. Like the other moderates, Scott professed to favour gradual change and contended that such change would not come until white opinion accepted it. Yet he and the other liberals made no effort to lead or persuade majority white opinion to accept that gradual change.[41]

A small number of southern politicians refused to sign the Manifesto. In the Senate, Lyndon Johnson and the two Tennessee senators, Estes Kefauver and Albert Gore declined to sign; in the House one congressman from Florida, one from Tennessee, three from North Carolina and half the Texas delegation failed to add their names to the list of Manifesto supporters. Some of the non-signers – Lyndon Johnson and Sam Rayburn – were national Democratic party leaders. Some had presidential and vice-presidential ambitions. Others like Dante Fascell from Miami and J. Percy Priest from Nashville came from large urban constituencies. The Texas congressmen were to a certain extent protected by the refusal of Johnson and Rayburn to sign and by the traditional salience of economic, rather than racial, issues in the state's politics.[42]

The cases of three of the non-signatories – Albert Gore and two of the North Carolina congressmen, Thurmond Chatham and Charles B. Deane – suggest the idiosyncratic and personal nature of southern racial moderation and the ambiguous evidence of the strength of its electoral base.

Albert Gore had a different power base in Tennessee from that of his fellow Senator Estes Kefauver. The drafters of the Manifesto did not even bother to ask Kefauver to sign it; as a southerner running in the Democratic primaries against Adlai Stevenson for the presidential nomination, he had little choice but to denounce the declaration. But Gore was well regarded by his fellow southern politicians and in Tennessee was viewed as a more down-to-earth politician, more attuned to the views of his rural constituents than the national liberal, Kefauver.

Yet Gore shared Kefauver's economic liberalism: his hostility to big business, his championing of public power, and his support of progressive taxation. Gore also had national ambitions. He hankered after the vice-presidential nomination in 1956 – as indeed, did the governor of Tennessee, Frank Clement. It was said in Tennessee that year, 'in America it is possible for any man to run for president. In Tennessee they all are.' Gore had been rather less emphatic than Kefauver in his endorsement of the *Brown* decision: it was the law of the land, he stated, but the decision, he stressed, was not for immediate implementation and had taken the issue of segregation out of the hands of Congress. Gore was at pains to point out to his constituents that these views did not mean that he agreed with the decision. Gore's memory now is that he had always been 'upfront' on the race issue. He dates his awareness of the moral dimension of civil rights to his first trip from his constituency to Washington back in 1937. On the long drive from middle Tennessee he could find no rest-rooms for the black nanny who was looking after his baby to use. On that first trip therefore he had to make a long detour to stop at a cousin's house in the mountains to stay the night. Subsequently he made an arrangement with a motel in eastern Tennessee. The family and the nanny could stay, provided they arrived after dark and left before the other guests in the morning.[43]

Gore regarded the Manifesto as 'the most spurious, inane, insulting document of a political nature claiming to be legally founded I had ever seen'. It represented, he thought, an act of secession. It was 'utterly incomprehensible and unsupportable'. Thurmond approached Gore on the floor of the Senate and invited him to sign, waving the sheet with all the southern signatures in front of him and jabbing him in the chest. After Gore replied, 'Hell, no', he looked up to see that all the southern pressmen, primed in advance, were in the gallery. In Tennessee he soon heard from chapters of the Federation for Constitutional Government. As his wife's old classmate, Sims Crownover threatened, Gore faced 'almost certain defeat in 1958'. Crownover repeated a familiar theme: voters had expected Kefauver not to sign. One correspondent claimed Kefauver 'has made it clear from the outset that he would sell the entire South to the NAACP in return for a few votes' but Crownover said that voters felt Gore had 'actually betrayed the South because people felt that you were on their side'.[44]

Gore received plenty of mail to weigh against the segregationist protests. A month after the Manifesto was issued, he claimed that mail on the subject had stopped. Opponents used the race issue against him, as they had also unsuccessfully against Kefauver in 1954 and 1960. Gore's opponent in 1958,

Prentiss Cooper, specifically campaigned on the issue of the Manifesto and waved a copy of the Declaration at every opportunity on the stump but Gore, like Kefauver, fought off such well-financed challenges. He later claimed that the race issue was never as divisive in Tennessee as the Vietnam War when people would cross the road rather than shake his hand.[45]

The path of racial moderation was easier in Tennessee than in some southern states – a greater percentage of voting-age blacks were registered to vote, labour and the TVA exerted a liberalizing influence, urban newspapers in Nashville and Knoxville urged compliance with the Court. But what mattered most was that the two senators and the governor, the three leading politicians in the state, all liberals as they were in Alabama, chose, in contrast to Alabama, to seek public support for compliance with the law of the land.

That same path of racial moderation, however, proved more politically dangerous in North Carolina, a state seemingly as 'progressive' as Tennessee. Three congressmen refused to sign the Manifesto and faced immediate opposition in primary elections in the following two months. The most senior of these, Harold Cooley, had been a New Deal supporter in his youth and may even have still hankered after a vice-presidential nomination. He had assiduously maintained national political contacts as he strove to protect the state's tobacco farmers as chair of the House Agriculture Committee. He resented being presented with the Manifesto on a take-it-or-leave-it basis by the Senate. However, when faced with primary opposition, he stressed that he hated and despised the *Brown* decision and race-baited his segregationist opponent to secure victory.[46]

The conservative millionaire Thurmond Chatham and the liberal Baptist Charles Deane demonstrated two very different paths to racial moderation. Millowner Chatham and been a Roosevelt-hating member of the Liberty League in the 1930s. In 1940 he supported Republican Wendell Wilkie for the presidency. Elected to Congress on an anti-union platform in 1948, he remained a staunch opponent of unionization and of raising the minimum wage. As a student at Yale, however, in 1916 he had sat next to, and befriended, a black student in two of his classes; in the Navy in World War II he had seen desegregation in operation; on the House Foreign Relations Committee he became friendly with younger liberals, Abraham Ribicoff and Lloyd Bentsen. When the Supreme Court decision came in 1954, Chatham said that he had been expecting it. He was pleased the decision was out of the way so that America would be able to turn its attention to 'the greater problems which face us in the international sphere'.[47]

Charles Deane was, by contrast, an unequivocal liberal on domestic economic and social affairs. He had been elected in 1946 with the backing of textile and railroad unions in his Eighth District. He could be relied on by both the national Democratic leadership and by national union leaders. A devout Baptist, he was a former secretary of the state Baptist Convention.[48]

His religion and his economic liberalism led him to a liberal stand on civil rights. But there was another compelling impetus. In 1951 he had attended a play in Washington put on by Moral ReArmament, the movement for moral uplift led by Frank Buchman. The effect on Deane and his family, he claimed later, was revolutionary. His daughter sacrificed a legacy that was to pay her way through college, gave it to MRA and went to work for MRA full-time, going round the world as part of the integrated cast of a musical 'The Vanishing Island'.[49]

MRA advocated absolute personal moral standards: people imbued with those standards could resolve all the conflicts in society either in the international sphere, or in labour relations, or in racial matters. It was wholeheartedly anti-communist but did not believe that military spending could contain communism, especially in the Third World. Deane believed that America had to win the battle for hearts and minds, and that could only come from young people as disciplined in 'living the ideology of freedom' as Soviet youth was disciplined in communism. America 'had to be honest about the places where change will come if the faith of our fathers is to be fulfilled'. Deane's conviction that racial change had to come if America was to have success overseas was strengthened by a visit to Mau Mau prison camps in Kenya which brought home to him the potential black hatred for the white race.[50]

Both Deane and Chatham were defeated. In Deane's case the race issue was decisive. He had not faced serious opposition in either 1952 or 1954. No opponent filed against him in 1956 until he failed to sign the Manifesto. In every piece of campaign literature, the first two assertions by his opponent were that he would have signed the Manifesto and that he opposed race-mixing. Deane's daughter was smeared by the distribution of cropped photographs showing her at an MRA camp next to two blacks. Blacks were paid to ring up white voters and ask them to vote for Deane. A textile union leader sadly reported that his members would no longer support the congressman. As a result, an incumbent who had had powerful support in his district and had assiduously catered to his constituents' patronage and pork barrel needs found himself decisively beaten, losing the counties with the highest percentage of blacks in their population.[51]

The influence of the race issue in Chatham's defeat was harder to disentangle from local and personal factors. Unlike Deane, Chatham had faced stiff opposition in earlier primaries in 1952 and 1954. Political unknowns had run well, capitalizing on Chatham's absentee record in Congress. In 1956, irrespective of the Manifesto, he was going to face opposition from a substantial local politician, a county solicitor who represented part of the constituency that felt it had been overlooked historically in terms of congressional representation. Chatham's opponent stressed the incumbent's absenteeism, his foreign trips and his earlier support of Republican candidates. There was also a whispering campaign about Chatham's alcoholism.[52]

Nevertheless, Chatham received abusive mail as soon as he failed to sign the Manifesto, warning him that he was a 'dead duck'. The North Carolina Patriots, the state's hitherto rather quiescent version of the Citizens Council, targeted Chatham for special opposition with particular success in two counties in his district. He remained unapologetic for his refusal to sign the Declaration and ran best in high-income wards and in black wards in Winston-Salem, an early forerunner of the cross-class, biracial alliance that would foster racial moderation in southern politics in the 1960s.[53]

V

The experience of Albert Gore showed that clear moderate leadership on racial matters need not be fatal to political careers if other leaders also took that stance. The fate of Deane and Chatham, however, did highlight the segregationist potential of public opinion when state and regional leaders were not prepared to take a lead for compliance with desegregation. Conservative leaders could point to their defeats as further evidence to persuade wavering moderates that public opinion would not sustain a policy of racial moderation. The success of the efforts of southern conservative leaders to stir up what they saw as an indifferent public opinion and to paralyse racial moderates could be seen in the fatalism of four moderate southern governors in the aftermath of the *Brown* decision.

Neither Earl Long, Jim Folsom, Sid McMath nor Kerr Scott came from the region's Black Belt. They all had a basic sense of fairness and democracy that was offended by blatant injustice to blacks, in particular the callous disregard of black rights by their states' planter elites. As Earl Long pointed out to a fanatical segregationist, 'You got to recognize that niggers is human beings.' Folsom noted that 'there are sections of Alabama where a Negro doesn't stand a Chinaman's chance of getting fair and impartial justice on an equal footing with white men'. They all fought for increased appropriations for black institutions. Under Earl Long, Louisiana blacks received over half the benefits of state spending programmes, although they only constituted 30 per cent of the population. He fought for the equalization of black and white teachers' salaries. McMath in Arkansas fought for anti-lynching legislation and attempted to ensure that local blacks schools got their fair share of state funds. Kerr Scott appointed a black educator to the North Carolina state board of education, and McMath appointed one to the board of trustees of Arkansas A & M college, the first blacks appointed in those states in the twentieth century.[54]

More than anything, they all fought for the rights of blacks to vote. McMath sought to abolish the poll tax in Arkansas and enabled blacks to run for office in the Democratic Party. Folsom fought against conservative moves to disfranchise blacks under the Boswell amendment and appointed registrars who promised to register black voters. In 1954 he backed candidates for state auditor and commissioner of agriculture who also agreed to appoint sympathetic registrars. Folsom-appointed registrars became key witnesses in federal voting rights cases. In Louisiana Earl Long fought Citizens Council efforts after 1956 to purge black voters from the electoral rolls. One of his last acts as governor, behind the scenes, was to order voting rights records to be handed over to the U.S. Commission on Civil Rights.[55]

In return for their efforts, these white liberals all secured the support of black voters. They did not campaign directly for this support. Instead, they approached local leaders in the black community – the governor's chauffeur in Montgomery, a funeral director in Winston-Salem, a doctor in Little Rock, a janitor in Greenville, a college teacher in Durham – and these black leaders delivered their community's vote. Black voters recognized, as L. C. Bates, editor of the black Arkansas *State Press*, wrote of McMath's election in 1948, 'FOR THE FIRST TIME IN OUR LIFE we felt that we were voting for SOMETHING'.[56]

This assistance for their black supporters was largely within the context of segregation. When the *Brown* decision ended the comfortable notion that the separate worlds could be continued, they were constrained by their own reluctance to envisage a desegregated world, together with their sense of what their white supporters would tolerate.

Scott, McMath, Long and Folsom acknowledged that the Supreme Court decision was the law of the land. They recognized the ultimate futility of defying the Court. Folsom likened an interposition resolution to a 'hounddog baying at the moon'. It was not 1861, he said; what would the segregationists do now 'now that the Feds have the nuclear bomb'? During the Montgomery bus boycott, Martin Luther King recalled that Folsom met with the black leaders secretly and advised them to ask for the complete desegregation of the buses rather than for the first come first served segregated plan they had initially requested. Earl Long quietly supervised the desegregation of the Louisiana State University campus at New Orleans and the desegregation of the New Orleans buses.[57]

But, most of the time, they fell back on the hope that segregated schools could be maintained at the local level within the framework of the *Brown* decision. They were unable to penetrate the ritual of condescension and deference that governed their relations with black leaders and they clung to the convenient, but false, notion that black leaders were happy to continue with segregated schools. Thus they argued that there was no need for precipitate legislative action. Instead the matter should be left to men of goodwill of both races at the local level. They appeared to want segregation to continue, or, if it was to end, for desegregation to come in quietly so that it could slip by unnoticed without stirring up the flames of popular white racism. When these dreams were threatened by Massive Resistance legislation on the one hand, or determined black litigation on the other, they responded by angrily denouncing extremists on both sides, equating the Ku Klux Klan and the Citizens councils, which advocated extra-legal violence, with the NAACP which worked through the courts for the proper exercise of black constitutional rights.[58]

What the liberal politicians were not prepared to do was to build up support in their states for a realistic policy of compliance with the law of the land. They seemed resigned to the segregationist nature of public opinion. They were therefore no match for the Massive Resisters who actively strove to arouse the white public. The liberals became irrelevant as their states lurched into racial crises. In Little Rock McMath and other community leaders made no effort to mobilize community support for token school desegregation amongst the lower-income whites whose children would actually have to attend integrated Central High School. He woke up too late to the impending crisis in 1957. He was unable to prevent his protégé Orval Faubus from siding with the segregationists and was almost completely ineffectual in his belated efforts to mobilize moderate sentiment in the city. In North Carolina, in the last week of Kerr Scott's election bid for the Senate in 1954, opponents circulated as an advertisement a letter by a Winston-Salem black asking blacks to vote for Scott on the grounds of his support of non-segregation. Scott and his supporters professed outrage at this tactic, not just because of its illegality but because, the *News and Observer* argued, a 'stupid Negro' had been gullible and everybody surely knew that Scott was wholeheartedly in favour of segregation as the North Carolina way. 'I have', proclaimed Scott, 'always been opposed, and am still opposed, to Negro and white children going to school together.' Thus, in 1956 Scott not only signed the Southern Manifesto, but also backed the state's Pearsall plan which provided for local communities to close their schools rather than desegregate. As one academic sadly noted in 1956, what Scott had other liberals in North Carolina had failed to do was provide the 'leadership to persuade people that they must accept the inevitable'.[59]

In Louisiana and Alabama, Earl Long and Jim Folsom stood by helplessly as their state legislatures passed a barrage of anti-desegregation statutes. When the federal courts ordered the University of Alabama to admit black student Autherine Lucy in 1956, Folsom went on a fishing and drinking trip and could not be contacted for three days. By the time he eventually sobered up and rang his office from a pay phone in a country store, white mobs in Tuscaloosa had successfully prevented Lucy from entering the University. As an Alabama journalist noted, 'If he had been there and told the Ku Klux Klan that if they appeared he would split their heads and had the

National Guard been there the history of the state and indeed the history of
the entire South might have been different . . . But Folsom allowed the mob
to win.'[60]

It was not just the liberal politicians' failure of leadership that failed to
make white southerners understand that compliance with the Supreme Court
was inevitable, nor just the conservatives' successful efforts that persuaded
whites that the Court could be defied. The ground was cut from under many
liberals' feet by the cautious attitude of both the Eisenhower administration
and many northern liberals. Eisenhower distanced himself from the *Brown*
decision. The Justice Department developed no strategy to facilitate school
desegregation. The Supreme Court itself appeared to bend over backwards
to avoid dictating timetables of change to the white South. Leading liberal
Democrats like Adlai Stevenson strove not to antagonize conservative white
leaders. A white southerner could be forgiven for thinking that desegregation was not inevitable, that the federal government would not impose racial
change on the South. The irony was that one reason the federal government,
leading northern Democrats, and northern white intellectuals were so cautious and accommodating to the white South was the warnings of southern
white moderates and liberals themselves. They warned that precipitate federal action would simply drive the bulk of reasonable southerners into the
arms of the segregationists. Northern politicians saw the moderates as voices
of reason in the South who must be sustained if at all possible and therefore
took their warnings seriously. The southern liberals thus deprived themselves
of the one weapon that might have enabled them to convince white southerners to comply with the Court: a clearly stated determination to enforce
desegregation on the part of the federal government. Federal policy and pro-
nouncements until the early 1960s, prompted in part by liberal advice, seemed
to give southerners reason to believe that they did not have to countenance
the gradual racial change the southern liberals professed to favour.[61]

VI

It was not the gradualism of southern white liberals that was flawed; rather
it was the fact that they never spoke up for gradualism at the time. They
never attempted to campaign for, or build up support for, gradual racial
change. Southern conservatives, by contrast, mounted a righteous crusade to
convince southerners that they need not tolerate any racial change, no matter how gradual. It was the liberals' fatalism, not their gradualism, that
defeated them.

Perhaps in the long run their failure did not matter. After 1960, no southern white could dictate the timetable of racial change. Segregation collapsed
under the combined assault of the black civil rights movement from within

the region and the federal government and judiciary from outside. The southern liberals had little role to play in these changes. Few southern whites held any sway over the civil rights movement. Those who did were not the liberals but the radicals who had been so isolated and persecuted from the 1940s onwards. Clifford and Virginia Durr employed black seamstress Rosa Parks; Aubrey Williams paid for her to attend an interracial workshop at Highlander Folk School. When she was arrested for failing to give up her seat on a bus on 1 December 1955 in Montgomery, it was Clifford Durr who went down to the police station to help bail her out. It was Durr who gave the crucial legal advice to the Montgomery Improvement Association that enabled the MIA and Martin Luther King to win the momentous year-long boycott in the federal courts. Myles Horton's Highlander Folk School pioneered the Citizenship Schools that trained a new generation of black civil rights activists. Anne Braden of the SCEF counselled SNCC during its most productive years.[62]

When racial change came to their communities and states in the 1960s, it was not the liberals who played the crucial roles. The first leaders successfully to acknowledge that the collapse of segregation was inevitable were southern businessmen. They belatedly awoke to the damage to economic growth and future investment that violent resistance to the federal government was causing. They worked to persuade communities in the 1960s to take the decisive first steps towards acceptance of racial change and later worked with blacks in a cross-class alliance to elect New South governors committed to eradicating the worst excesses of the old segregated order. They were opposed by lower-income whites who followed the political model not of Jim Folsom, but of the Talmadges. In the 1960s these less-affluent whites supported candidates who combined a common man 'good ole boy' appeal with denunciations of government both as an agent of racial change and of welfare liberalism.[63]

But the old New Deal legacy did make one important contribution to the decisive racial changes that the region underwent in the 1960s. Southern radicals like Aubrey Williams and Clifford and Virginia Durr never lost faith in the Texas politician they had known as a state NYA director and New Deal congressman in the 1930s. Their confidence in Lyndon Johnson survived even when they disagreed with him about the Vietnam War. This sympathy for LBJ was not irrational. When Virginia Durr, Aubrey Williams and James Dombrowski were called up before James Eastland's Internal Security subcommittee in the 1950s it was not Virginia Durr's close liberal ally, Lister Hill, who came to their rescue but Johnson. The Majority Leader defused Eastland's assault by preventing other Democrats from accompanying the Mississippi senator to the hearings in New Orleans.[64]

The radical's faith in Lyndon Johnson was rewarded by the passage of the 1964 Civil Rights Act and the 1965 Voting Rights Act. It was perhaps the greatest irony that it was a southern liberal who finally responded to black demands and, through federal legislation, imposed immediate, not gradual, racial change on the South.[65]

NOTES

1. The author wishes to acknowledge the generous financial support the American Council of Learned Societies, the British Academy, the Newcastle University Research Committee, the North Carolina Society, the Margaret Gallagher Fund, and the Mellon Professorial Fund for the research upon which this essay draws. He also acknowledges indispensable research assistance from Carolyn Abel and Sharon Pointer.
Jack R. Skates Jr, 'World War II as a Watershed in Mississippi History', *Journal of Mississippi History*, 37 (1975), 131–42; Frank E. Smith, *Congressman from Mississippi: An Autobiography* (New York, 1964), pp. 20–2, 53, 59, 64; Dennis J. Mitchell, 'Frank E. Smith: Mississippi Liberal', *Journal of Mississippi History*, 48 (1986), 86–8; Donald Cunnigen 'Men and Women of Goodwill: Mississippi's White Liberals', (PhD dissertation Harvard University, 1988), p.560, provides a vivid example of the impact of serving in Europe on the attitude to segregation on one white Mississippian – future labour leader, Claude Ramsey. The best account of the impact of the New Deal on Mississippi is Roger D. Tate, 'Easing the Burden: The Era of Depression and New Deal in Mississippi', (PhD dissertation, University of Tennessee, 1978).
2. Smith, *Congressman from Mississippi*, pp. 66–9; Mitchell, 'Frank E. Smith', 88–90.
3. Smith, *Congressman from Mississippi*, pp.69–74; Thomas E. Williams, 'Children and Welfare in a Segregated Society: Mississippi, 1900–1970', (unpublished manuscript in the author's possession); Joanne V. Hawks, M. Carolyn Ellis and J. Byron Morris, 'Women in the Mississippi Legislature (1924–1981)', *Journal of Mississippi History*, 43 (1981), 266.
4. Smith, *Congressman from Mississippi*, pp.77–92; Mitchell, 'Frank E. Smith', 91–3.
5. John T. Kneebone, 'Liberal on the Levee: Hodding Carter, 1944–54', *Journal of Mississippi History*, 49 (1987) 154–7.
6. Kneebone, 'Hodding Carter', 159–60.
7. Turner Catledge, *My Life and the Times* (New York, 1971), p.219; Florence Mars, *Witness at Philadelphia* (Baton Rouge, 1977), pp. xiii– xiv.
8. Mark Newman, 'Hazel Brannon Smith and Holmes County, Mississippi, 1936–64', *Journal of Mississippi History*, 54 (1992), 58–67, 75–84; Cunnigen, 'Men and Women of Goodwill', pp. 581–8.
9. P. D. East, *The Magnolia Jungle: The Life and Times of a Southern Editor* (New York, 1960), pp.73, 98, 104, 121; Gary Huey, *Rebel with a Cause: P. D. East, Southern Liberalism and the Civil Rights Movement, 1953–71* (Wilmington, Del., 1985), pp. 29–58.
10. East, *The Magnolia Jungle*, pp. 134, 140–3, 149–51, 176–7; Huey, *Rebel with a Cause*, pp. 62, 73, 77, 80–1, 92–7.
11. In 'Man in the Middle: Faulkner and the Southern White Moderate', in Doreen

Fowler and Ann J. Abadie (eds), *Faulkner and Race* (Jackson and London, 1987), pp. 130–50, Noel Polk explores the implications of the way in which Faulkner distanced himself (in conversation with Malcolm Cowley) from his character Gavin Stevens 'the best type of liberal southerner'. Polk notes the characteristics of the liberal southerner which Faulkner gives to Stevens: Stevens talks about 'everything but his own failure' and is 'more interested in talking than doing'. Will Campbell, *Brother to a Dragonfly* (New York, 1977), pp. 113–21.

12. East, *The Magnolia Jungle*, pp. 197–203; Huey, *Rebel With a Cause*, pp. 106–8.

13. Hodding Carter, Interview, A-100, Southern Oral History Program, Southern Historical Collection, Chapel Hill. James Silver, *The Closed Society* (London, 1964); Jessica Mitford, *A Fine Old Conflict* (London, 1977), pp. 145.

14. Smith, *Congressman from Mississippi*, pp. 93–126, 235–300, 321; Mitchell, 'Frank E. Smith', 97–102.

15. Tris Coffin to Jonathan Daniels, 24 March 1956, Papers of Jonathan Daniels, Southern Historical Collection, Chapel Hill.

16. Virginia Durr to Estes Kefauver, 15 February 1956, Papers of Estes Kefauver, University of Tennessee, Knoxville.

17. Boyd Campbell to Tris Coffin, 3 March 1956, copy in Jonathan Daniels Papers. Tony Badger, 'The Southern Manifesto of 1956', (paper delivered at the 1993 meeting of the Southern Historical Association, copy in the author's possession).

18. Louis Daniel Brodsky, 'Faulkner and the Racial Crisis, 1956', *Southern Review*, 24 (1988), 791–807; Polk, 'Man in the Middle', 135–8.

19. East, *The Magnolia Jungle*, p. 192.

20. Huey, *Rebel With a Cause*, pp. 103–209.

21. Newman, 'Hazel Brannon Smith', 68–74.

22. Campbell, *Brother to a Dragonfly*, pp. 125–8.

23. Willie Morris, *Yazoo: Integration in a Deep Southern Town* (New York, 1971), pp. 187–9.

24. Catledge, *My Life and the Times*, p. 220; Mars, *Witness at Philadelphia*, pp. 52–3, 59, 100–204.

25. Silver, *The Closed Society*, pp. 107–33; Cunnigen, 'Men and Women of Goodwill', 174–5; Walter Lord, *The Past That Would Not Die* (London, 1966), pp. 233–48; Morris, *Yazoo*, pp. 54–5.

26. Charles Sallis and John Quincy Adams, 'Desegregation in Jackson, Mississippi', in Elizabeth Jacoway and David Colburn (eds), *Southern Businessmen and Desegregation* (Baton Rouge, 1982), pp. 243–9; Mars, *Witness at Philadelphia*, pp. 216–9; The most recent assessment of the 'New Mississippi' created by federal forces and black protest is by John Dittmer, *Local People: The Struggle for Civil Rights in Mississippi* (Chicago and London, 1994), pp. 408–30.

27. Morris, *Yazoo*, pp. 120–1. William McCord, *Mississippi: The Long Hot Summer* (New York, 1965), p.146. Donald Cunnigen argues in his study of Mississippi white liberals, 'Men and Women of Goodwill', 2, that: 'Most observers have failed to acknowledge the presence and important impact that a small group of liberal-minded whites have had on change in the region.' But Cunnigen himself is at pains to point out the caution, isolation and ineffectiveness of Mississippi white liberals before 1965.

28. Morton Sosna, 'More Important than the Civil War? The Impact of World War II on the South', *Perspectives on the American South* 4 (1987), 145. Bruce Schulman, *From Cotton Belt to Sunbelt: Federal Policy, Economic Development, and the Transformation of the South, 1938–1980* (New York, 1991),

pp. 63–112; Numan V. Bartley and Hugh D. Graham, *Southern Politics and the Second Reconstruction* (Baltimore, 1975), pp. 24–50.

29. Patricia A. Sullivan, 'Southern Reformers, the New Deal and the Movements Foundation', in Armstead Robinson and Patricia A. Sullivan (eds), *New Directions in Civil Rights Studies* (Charlottesville, 1991), pp. 81–104. Patricia A. Sullivan, *Days of Hope: Race and Democracy in the New Deal* (University of North Carolina Press: Chapel Hill, forthcoming), ch. 3.
30. James B. Gardner, 'Political Leadership in a Period of Transition: Frank G. Clement, Albert Gore, Estes Kefauver and Tennessee Politics, 1948–1956', (PhD: Vanderbilt University, 1978), pp.12, 30. Jim Lester, *A Man for Arkansas: Sid McMath and the Southern Reform Tradition* (Little Rock, 1976), pp. 8–31, 52; Edward F. Haas, *DeLesseps Morrison and the Image of Reform: New Orleans Politics, 1946–1961* (Baton Rouge, 1974), p.33; *Greensboro Daily News*, 13 June 1947; ibid., 4 May 1948.
31. Barbara Griffiths, *The Crisis of American Labor: Operation Dixie and the Defeat of the CIO* (Philadelphia, 1988); John William Coon, 'Kerr Scott, the 'Go Forward' Governor': His Origins, his Program and the North Carolina General Assembly', (MA thesis University of North Carolina, 1968), pp. 25, 33–9, 52–3, 86; Terry Sanford, interview, A-328-1, Southern Historical Collection, Chapel Hill; George Sims, *The Little Man's Big Friend: James E. Folsom in Alabama Politics, 1946–1958* (Tuscaloosa, 1985), pp. 26, 30, 33–4; Carl Grafton and Anne Permaloff, *Big Mules and Branchheads: James E. Folsom and Political Power in Alabama* (Athens, 1985), pp. 71, 74, 75.
32. Martha Swain, 'The Public Role of Southern Women', in Joanne Hawks and Susan Slemp (eds), *Sex, Race and the Role of Women in the South* (Jackson, 1983), pp.43,53; Lorraine Nelson Spritzer, *The Belle of Ashby Street: Helen Douglas Mankin and Georgia Politics* (Athens, 1982), pp. 64–87. Patricia A. Sullivan, 'Gideon's Southern Soldiers: New Deal Politics and Civil Rights Reform, 1933–1948' (PhD Emory University, 1983), pp. 245, 250–68, 280–99. *Arkansas Gazette*, 13, 26, 27 July 1948; ibid., 5, 8 August 1948; ibid., 13 October 1948; Gardner, 'Political Leadership in a Period of Transition' 51; Lester, *A Man for Arkansas*, p. 52. Michael L. Kurtz and Morgan D. Peeples, *Earl K. Long: The Saga of Uncle Earl and Louisiana Politics* (Baton Rouge, 1991), pp.129–46.
33. Hawks, Ellis and Morris, 'Women in the Mississippi Legislature', 281–2; Swain, 'The Public Role of Southern Women', 54–5.
34. Arnold Shankman, 'Dorothy Tilly and the Fellowship of the Concerned', in Walter J. Fraser Jr and Winfred B. Moore Jr (eds), *From The Old South to the New: Essays on the Transitional South* (Westport, 1981), pp. 241–52; Sara Evans, *Personal Politics: The Roots of Women's Liberation in the Civil Rights Movement and the New Left* (New York, 1980), pp. 24–37; Paul Mertz, '"Mind Changing Time All Over Georgia": HOPE Inc. and School Desegregation, 1958–1961', *Georgia Historical Quarterly*, 77 (1993), 45–51; Cunnigen, 'Men and Women of Goodwill', 244–51.
35. Mark Newman, 'Getting Right with God: Southern Baptists and Race Relations, 1945–1980', (PhD dissertation University of Mississippi, 1993), esp. pp. 108–44, 852–63.
36. Bartley and Graham, *Southern Politics and the Second Reconstruction*, pp. 24–50; Schulman, *From Cotton Belt to Sunbelt*, pp. 112–39.
37. Morton Sosna, *In Search of the Silent South: Southern Liberals and the Race Issue* (New York, 1977), pp. 140–71; John T. Kneebone, *Southern Liberal Journalists and the Issue of Race, 1920–1944* (Chapel Hill, 1985), pp. 115–74; Charles

W. Eagles, *Jonathan Daniels and Race Relations: The Evolution of a Southern Liberal* (Knoxville, 1983), pp. 121–231; Anthony Lake Newberry, 'Without Urgency or Ardor: The South's Middle-of-the-Road Liberals and Civil Rights, 1945–1960' (PhD dissertation, Ohio University, 1982), pp. 40–158.

38. Sosna, *In Search of the Silent South*, pp. 60–87, 88–104; Sullivan, *Days of Hope*, chs 1, 2; Antony P. Dunbar, *Against the Grain: Southern Radicals and Prophets* (Charlottesville, 1981).

39. James Albert Burran, 'Racial Violence in the South during World War II' (PhD dissertation: University of Tennessee, 1977); Schulman, *From Cotton Belt to Sunbelt*, p.321; Sullivan, *Days of Hope*, chs 5, 6; Thomas A. Kreuger, *And Promises to Keep: The Southern Conference for Human Welfare, 1938–1948* (Nashville, 1967).

40. Tony Badger, 'The Southern Manifesto: White Southerners and Civil Rights, 1956', in Rob Kroes and Eduard van de Bilt, *The US Constitution: After 200 Years* (Amsterdam, 1988), pp. 80–6.

41. Badger, 'The Southern Manifesto of 1956'; John Horne to Lister Hill, 20 October 1955; Tully A. Goodwin to Hill, 22 February 1956; Bart P. Chamberlain to Hill, 2 March 1956, Papers of Lister Hill, W. S. Hoole Library, University of Alabama, Tuscaloosa. John Sparkman Interview, Southern Oral History Program, Southern Historical Collection, Chapel Hill. J. William Fulbright (with Seth Tillman), *The Price of Empire* (London, 1989), p.94. Brooks Hays, *A Southern Moderate Speaks* (Chapel Hill, 1959), pp. 89–95. William Cochrane, interview with the author, September 1988; 'North Carolina's Man on the Hill' *Carolina Alumni Review*, Spring 1984, 13–14; Memorandum, John Lang, 3 February 1956, Papers of Charles B. Deane, Southern Baptist Historical Collection, Wake Forest University, Winston-Salem.

42. Badger, 'The Southern Manifesto'.

43. Albert Gore Sr to Mrs Talley, 12 October 1954, Papers of Albert Gore, Middle Tennessee State University, Murfreesboro; Gardner, 'Political Leadership in Transition', 500–670; Albert Gore Sr, interview with the author, 1 December 1990.

44. Albert Gore interview, 13 March 1976, Southern Oral History Program, Southern Historical Collection, Chapel Hill; Albert Gore Sr interview with the author, 1 December 1990; Donald Davidson to Albert Gore, 12 March 1956; Fred Childress to Gore, 12 March 1956; Sims Crownover to Gore, 19 April 1956, Gore Papers.

45. Albert Gore Sr, interview with the author, 1 December 1990; Albert Gore to Pat Hughes, 12 April 1956, Gore Papers; *Nashville Tennessean*, 13, 18 March 1956.

46. Clipping, *Henderson Times-News*, 14 March 1956; Harold D. Cooley to H.Q. Dorsett, 13 March 1956; Cooley to E. L. Cannon, 3 April 1956; Nashville (NC) speech, 7 April 1956; Henderson speech, 17 May 1956; WTVD speech; Papers of Harold Dunbar Cooley, Southern Historical Collection, Chapel Hill; *Raleigh News and Observer*, 13, 14, 17 March, 6 April, 1956.

47. Ralph J. Christian, 'The Folger–Chatham Congressional Primary of 1946', *North Carolina Historical Review*, 53 (1976), 25–53; *Raleigh News and Observer*, 18 May 1954; *Winston-Salem Journal*, 18 May 1954.

48. *Greensboro Daily News*, 2 September 1955; *Winston-Salem Journal*, 12 September 1955; Comment to the author, James L. Sundquist, 8 April 1987; John A. Lang to Charles B. Deane, 23 April 1956, Papers of John A. Lang, East Carolina Manuscript Collection, East Carolina University, Greenville, NC.

49. Charles B. Deane to Walter Lambeth, 22 October 1952; Deane to Fay Allen, 21 November 1951, Deane Papers; Charles B. Deane Jr, interview with the author, 12 September 1989.

50. Notes for schools and colleges [n.d.], Notes 22 November 1956, Deane Papers. Deane to Herman Hardison, 27 March 1956, Lang Papers.
51. Charles B. Deane Jr, interview with the author, 12 September 1989; Charles B. Deane to Mrs P.A. Wood, 28 July 1956, Lang Papers; Lewis S. Cannon to Charles B. Deane, 15 March 1956; Leaflet [n.d]; Deane to James E. Griffin, 7 May 1956; J. B. Hood to Deane, 24 April 1956; 'Pete' to Deane [n.d.]; Julius Fry to Deane, 19 June 1956; Nina Duke Wood to Deane, 26 July 1956, Deane Papers.
52. L. van Noppen to Thurmond Chatham, 8 March 1956; Ralph Scott adverts, Papers of Thurmond Chatham, North Carolina Division of Archives and History, Raleigh NC.
53. Anon to Thurmond Chatham [n.d.]; Dallas Gwynn to Chatham, 24 March 1956; I.F. Young to Chatham, 13 May 1956; Chatham to Hiden Ramsey, 31 May 1956; Chatham to Ralph Howland, 5 June 1956, Chatham Papers.
54. Sims, *The Little Man's Big Friend*, p. 165; Kurtz and Peeples, *Earl K. Long*, pp.197–9; Lester, *A Man for Arkansas*, pp. 88, 162–6; Kelly Alexander to Kerr Scott, 22 April 1949; Scott to J. S. Davis, 19 May 1949, Governors Papers of W. Kerr Scott, North Carolina Division of Archives and History, Raleigh.
55. Lester, *A Man for Arkansas*, pp. 88, 157–9; Sims, *The Little Man's Big Friend* pp. 163–5, 171; R. Jefferson Norrell, *Reaping the Whirlwind: The Civil Rights Movement in Tuskegee* (New York, 1985), pp. 73–5, 86–8; Kurtz and Peeples, *Earl K. Long,* pp. 198, 206–8; Harris Wofford, *Of Kennedy and Kings* (New York, 1980), p. 162.
56. A. H. Bryant to Kerr Scott, 6 January 1954; Joe Crawford to Kerr Scott, 11, 13, 26 January 1954; J.D. Messick to Terry Sanford, 16 April 1954; Sanford to Messick, 24 April 1954; Scott to Clark Brown, 15 June 1954, Papers of W. Kerr Scott, North Carolina Division of Archives and History, Raleigh. Sims, *The Little Man's Big Friend* pp. 167–8; *Arkansas State Press*, August 1948 (I am indebted to John Kirk for this reference).
57. Sims, *The Little Man's Big Friend*, pp.178, 183, 249; Marshall Frady, *Wallace* (New York, 1968), p.103; Kurtz and Peeples, *Earl K. Long*, pp. 200–2.
58. Lester, *A Man for Arkansas*; Sims, *The Little Man's Big Friend*, pp. 169–86; Kurtz and Peeples, *Earl K. Long*, pp. 199–200, 209–10; William H. Chafe, *Civilities and Civil Rights: Greensboro, North Carolina and the Black Struggle for Freedom* (New York, 1980), pp.48–60; Jonathan Houghton, 'The Politics of Sly Resistance: North Carolina's Response to *Brown*' (Paper given at the Organization of American Historians Convention, 11 April 1991); Kerr Scott to J.D. Thompson, 20 November 1953; W. Kerr Scott statement, 17 May 1954, Scott Papers.
59. Lester, *A Man for Arkansas*, pp. 233–5; *Arkansas Gazette*, 14 September 1957; ibid., 15 July 1958; Houghton, 'The Politics of Sly Resistance', Sylvia Ellis, 'The Road to Massive Resistance: North Carolina and the *Brown* Decision' (Graduate Paper in the author's possession).
60. Sims, *The Little Man's Big Friend*, pp. 178–82; Grafton and Permaloff, *Big Mules and Branchheads*, pp. 196–8.
61. Robert Burk, *The Eisenhower Administration and Black Civil Rights* (Knoxville, 1984), pp. 151–73; Walter Jackson, 'White Liberal Intellectuals, Civil Rights and Gradualism, 1954–1960', in this volume, pp. 98–100, 105.
62. John A. Salmond, *The Conscience of a Lawyer: Clifford J. Durr and American Civil Liberties, 1899–1975* (Tuscaloosa, 1990), pp. 174–6; Clayborne Carson, *In Struggle: SNCC and the Black Awakening of the 1960s* (Cambridge, Mass., 1981), pp.52–3; Adam Fairclough, *To Redeem the Soul of America: The South-*

ern Christian Leadership Conference and Martin Luther King Jr. (Athens, 1987), pp. 68–9; David L. Chappell, *Inside Agitators: White Southerners in the Civil Rights Movement* (Baltimore, 1994), pp. 274–5.

63. Bartley and Graham, *Southern Politics and the Second Reconstruction*, pp. 111–63; Schulman, *From Cotton Belt to Sunbelt*, p. 321

64. Salmond, *The Conscience of a Lawyer*, pp. 160–1, 200; Hollinger F. Barnard (ed.), *Outside the Magic Circle: The Autobiography of Virginia Foster Durr* (Tuscaloosa, 1985), pp. 173–4, 206, 256, 327.

65. Chappell, *Inside Agitators*, pp. 188–211, interprets the 1964 and 1965 Acts in the light of a 'vast quantitative increase in the number of white southern moderates brought into the administration's network of influence.'

5 White Liberal Intellectuals, Civil Rights and Gradualism, 1954–60

Walter A. Jackson

What assumptions did prominent white liberal intellectuals bring to the debate about civil rights in the 1950s? How did liberal anti-communist intellectuals interpret the growing militancy among African-Americans? How did these shapers of elite public opinion define the issue of civil rights in articles in major national magazines?

This essay represents an initial mapping of the public debate about civil rights among influential white liberal intellectuals from the *Brown* decision of May 1954 to the Greensboro sit-ins of 1960. Most of the figures under consideration were not participants in the civil rights movement, but they were important in shaping elite public opinion about it. Defining 'intellectual' broadly to include professors, journalists and activists who contributed to the public debate about civil rights, the essay looks at the assumptions that these thinkers brought to their analysis of developments in the area of civil rights, and how their ideas changed in response to the accelerating black struggle. In national journals of opinion such as *The New Republic*, *Commentary*, *Harper's*, *The Atlantic*, and *Partisan Review*, over 95 per cent of the articles about civil rights in the 1950s were written by whites. The discussions of civil rights in these magazines have an air of unreality, a lack of comprehension of the changes that were building up within black America. White liberal writers seldom responded to articles in black journals. The ideas of Martin Luther King did not generate a major debate in mainstream journals until the early 1960s. W.E.B. Du Bois and Paul Robeson became unpersons because of communist associations. Richard Wright's books of essays on the non-aligned movement, African liberation, and white racism generated more debate among French intellectuals than among Americans. St. Clair Drake and other Pan-African intellectuals were also ignored.

In the 1950s, the major American liberal journals of opinion addressed the civil rights issue by presenting a debate among whites on what ought to be done about a regional problem that threatened to weaken the nation and hamper the solution of more important foreign and domestic problems. This began to change a little in the early 1960s, as more African-American intellectuals were published in major journals, and white intellectuals began responding to figures like King, James Baldwin, Whitney Young, and Malcolm X. This paper will, therefore, include briefly some of the critiques that African-American intellectuals made of the white liberal mainstream.

When the Supreme Court handed down the *Brown* decision in May 1954, an ideology of racial liberalism was already in place among white intellectuals in the North. Epitomized by Gunnar Myrdal's *An American Dilemma*, published ten years earlier, this liberal orthodoxy held that the 'American Creed' required integration, civil rights, equal opportunity within the private economy, and full inclusion of blacks in American civic, economic and educational institutions. The struggle against Nazi Germany during World War II had brought American ideals into focus and imparted to the civil rights issue a sense of moral immediacy that had not been present during the 1930s.[1] The issue continued to enjoy a higher profile in the late 1940s, with the report of the President's Committee on Civil Rights in 1947, the inclusion of a strong civil rights plank in the 1948 Democratic Party platform, and President Truman's desegregation of the armed forces. But with the outbreak of the Korean War and the rise of Senator Joseph McCarthy, there was little progress on civil rights at the federal level from 1950 to 1954.

Throughout the period from 1945 to 1960, civil rights was rarely a central concern of prominent white intellectuals outside the South. Intellectuals were far more preoccupied with debates over foreign policy, civil liberties, the consumer society and mass culture.[2] Race received only passing mention in Arthur Schlesinger Jr's *The Vital Center* (1949), probably the most influential statement of post-war political liberalism.[3] Other prominent works of social criticism, such as John Kenneth Galbraith's *The Affluent Society* (1958), ignore the race question altogether. Most intellectuals of the 1950s assumed that Americans shared a basic consensus on political and social issues, and they often saw racial discrimination as the one major flaw in a fundamentally democratic national tradition.

During the 1950s, racial discrimination was perceived as a southern problem, a legacy of a backward economy. Economic modernization of the South, it was thought, would draw the region inexorably toward a society in which individuals were judged according to merit rather than skin colour. Keynesian fiscal and monetary policies, rather than extensive federal job programmes of the New Deal variety, were the preferred means of extending affluence to the poor of both races and easing the transition to modernity. Most northern white intellectuals assumed that the desegregation of southern schools and the gradual movement of poor blacks into better jobs could be managed by federal, corporate and southern elites. It would not require a new kind of politics or major innovations in economic policy. Thus it was important, for northern white liberals, to support the 'moderate' business leadership in the southern cities lest these businessmen lose control to poor whites or reactionary rural political leaders.

While liberals clearly favoured the elimination of racial discrimination from American law, they tended to conceptualize racial inequality in terms of the notion of 'prejudice', that is the study of attitudes rather than a more structurally or institutionally-based concept of racism. Thus many liberals conceived of the process of breaking down segregation in the South as an educational process, in which contact between whites and blacks in schools, restaurants, etc. would break down psychological attitudes of whites and lead to greater tolerance. Purely token or symbolic integration was of great significance, because it might lead white racists to overcome their fears and phobias, once they saw that nothing disastrous happened if one or two blacks entered a white school or restaurant. But this process, like psychotherapy, could take time.[4]

The last thing that white liberals were expecting in the 1950s was a mass movement among African-Americans in the South. Most liberals viewed politics through the lens of pluralist political theory, which held that competition among economic interest groups such as farmers, unions and various business interests provided for a stable democratic politics. It was believed that the genius of American politics lay in the diffusion of power among federal, state and local governments, in contrast to the pattern in many European countries of centralization of power in the state. With competition among interest groups as well, there was thought to be little chance for a totalitarian state to develop. A politics based on abstract idealism, religion or mass enthusiasms was seen as inherently unstable and potentially totalitarian (and of course both populism and McCarthyism were viewed in this light).[5] If you had asked a white liberal in the 1950s about 'mass movements' in conjunction with civil rights, he or she would probably have expressed fears that white resistance to desegregation in the South might lead to a right-wing extremist mass movement that could become anti-Semitic or anti-Catholic, since prejudiced people could easily turn their hostility from one target group to another. Thus liberals tended to assume that maintaining law and order worked in the interest of racial justice. Delays, tokenism, gradualism, all might be tolerated if they meant that some progress was occurring through legal means, with no chance for 'mob rule' to develop.

These theoretical assumptions were reinforced by certain practical and structural factors that bound anti-communist white liberals to mainstream institutions and piecemeal reform and insulated them from dialogue with those who of different views. First among these was the high degree of institutional racism and segregation in the universities, professional organizations, magazines and newspapers, so that black and white intellectuals rarely had an opportunity for honest exchanges.[6] Moreover, northern white intellectuals generally had contacts with white southern moderates through professional networks, and political, cultural, and religious organizations. It was to these white southern moderates that the northern liberals turned for interpretation of events in the South. The practical problem of electing a Democratic president in 1956 and 1960 also exerted a strong moderating influence on northern white liberals, since it was very difficult for a Democratic candidate to win without some southern electoral votes. Finally, anticommunist liberals of the ADA variety refused to work with progressives who joined united front organizations, so many leading white liberal intellectuals had no contact with activists associated with the Highlander Center, the Southern Conference Education Fund, or networks of local activists such as the one that sparked the Montgomery bus boycott.

In the cultural sphere, the rhetoric of white liberals was strongly universalist. People tended to assume that the cultural differences among groups were much less significant than the common American culture that united people. Liberals who combated segregationist arguments based on innate or acquired differences naturally emphasized cultural similarities between whites and blacks.

Most liberals saw the family as a fundamental institution of society that nurtures strong individuals, fosters diversity and serves as a bulwark against the state. It was assumed that much cultural change works itself out in families through the process of generational change. When Margaret Mead wrote 'We are all third generation', she meant that it generally took three generations for immigrants to assimilate to American culture. In looking at a process like school integration, many liberals assumed that it would take about three generations for blacks to assimilate to white American culture. Liberals saw the family and generational change as central mechanisms for working out problems of racial equality and reduction of prejudice. These assumptions reinforced the gradualism inherent in the liberals' approbation of piecemeal reform, suspicion of centralized authority and fear of mass movements. In the first year and a half after the *Brown* decision of May 1954, northern white liberal intellectuals and journalists were generally optimistic about the prospects for peaceful implementation of school desegregation in the South. Liberals were encouraged by the statements of many southern political leaders and school officials that they would comply with the court ruling. Most liberals envisaged a three-stage approach to desegregation, beginning with the border states, continuing to the states of the upper South, and finally reaching the states of the Deep South with large rural black populations. Successful desegregation of Baltimore and Washington D.C. schools seemed to portend additional advances farther South. Journals like *Commentary* and *The New Republic* generally refrained from chastising the South and instead ran articles on school desegregation in border state cities focusing on the nuts and bolts of implementation. Once white southerners saw that integration could occur without traumatic upheaval, it was thought, they would accept the inevitable. When the Supreme Court issued its implementation decree in June 1955, few liberals protested the 'all deliberate speed' formula. Though President Eisenhower refused to speak out in favour of compliance with *Brown*, most white liberals remained optimistic through 1955 that the momentum for desegregation would spread from the border states to the South.

Then in 1956, Massive Resistance, led by Virginia Senator Harry Byrd, spread quickly through seven states from Virginia to Louisiana. Legislatures passed laws designed to nullify the Supreme Court decision, Alabama outlawed the NAACP, and other laws were passed to repress civil rights activity. White Citizens Councils sprang up across the South, using boycotts, intimidation and ostracism to ensure conformity among whites and submission among blacks. The Klan stood ready to use violence to accomplish what state laws, local ordinances and social pressures could not. Few southern white intellectuals supported the segregationist assault on *Brown*. To be sure, there were publicists like the Citizens Council's Carleton Putnam who argued in favour of biological differences in intelligence between the races and journalists like James Jackson Kilpatrick who made a William Graham Sumneresque claim that southern folkways were so entrenched as to make school integration an impossibility.[7] But there was not really a serious intellectual debate among white southerners. What happened was that the forces of Massive Resistance intimidated and in some cases silenced the handful of white southern liberals who welcomed desegregation and the much larger number of moderates who favoured gradual compliance with *Brown*. (Of course, African-Americans had never enjoyed real freedom of expression or access to major journals and newspapers in the South, and the repression of black writers and intellectuals was much worse.) C. Vann Woodward, a southern liberal who was able to view these developments from the comfortable vantage point of Baltimore, described the Orwellian quality of political discussion in the South under the shock of Massive Resistance in 1956 and 1957: 'Words began to shift their significance and lose their common meaning. A "moderate" became a man who dared not open his mouth, an "extremist" one who favoured eventual compliance with the moderate plan of desegregation. "Compliance" took on connotations of treason. The NAACP assumed the hideous mask of Mau Mau.'[8]

For an understanding of what was happening in the South, many northern journals turned to white southern moderate journalists and intellectuals such as Ralph McGill, Hodding Carter and Harry Ashmore. These men, it was thought, represented the best in southern opinion and had the most subtle understanding of the peculiar society south of the Potomac. What did white southern moderates mean when they called for compliance with the *Brown* decision? In public, they were often deliberately vague, and spoke about the need for gradual change. They counselled white northerners to be patient. They urged the NAACP not to push ahead with desegregation suits lest they provoke a violent reaction from the immoderate whites.

When southern white moderates did get specific about compliance, their scenarios bore little resemblance to those of the NAACP. Following the late Howard Odum, they stressed that the South was a diverse region, with different customs in different areas. Thus desegregation could proceed forthwith in Appalachia and in other areas where there were few blacks. In the cities, school district lines could be drawn in such a way that segregated residential patterns would lead to largely segregated schools. The real problem, for the moderates, was in the rural areas with significant percentages of blacks. Here they hoped that 'freedom of choice' plans would mean that most blacks would voluntarily remain in black schools, even if it meant travelling by bus to a school away from one's neighbourhood. Once the *stigma* of compulsory segregation was removed, blacks would prefer to remain in black schools, according to the moderate scenario. The white moderates believed that negro principles' and teachers' vested interest in maintaining their jobs would lead them to work for preservation of black schools. Virginius Dabney quoted an anonymous Mississippian who proposed a plan to this effect: 'There would be no threats, merely conferences called by white leaders with colored leaders . . . The white spokesman would say something to the colored leaders along this line: "We don't suppose you want to send your children to the white schools," and the colored leaders would agree.'[9]

Former Virginia State Senator Benjamin Muse spoke for many southern moderates when he wrote in *Harper's* in April 1957 that 'time is needed – a very long time – before public school integration can be seriously planned in the Black Belt'. In his view, at least another generation was required to raise the educational level of black students before integration would be viable in the Deep South. In the meantime, northern liberals would have to be content with progress in the upper South states.[10] Robert Penn Warren argued for compliance with *Brown* in a series of articles in *Life* magazine, which were then published in 1955 in a book entitled *Segregation*. But in the end, he counselled that change would take time. Warren opposed 'delay for the sake of delay', but argued that desegregation would involve a gradual process of educating both blacks and whites to accept change. 'It's a silly question,' he wrote, 'to ask if somebody is a gradualist. Gradualism is all you'll get. History, like nature, knows no jumps. Except the jump backward, maybe.'[11] For Warren, the crux of the issue was for white southerners to confront their fears about blacks and to begin the process of change.

One prominent southern intellectual who took exception to the views of the moderates was the historian C. Vann Woodward, who then taught at the Johns Hopkins University and served as a consultant to the NAACP in the legal campaign against segregation. Woodward was best known in the 1950s for the powerful blow that he delivered to the mythology surrounding segregation in his book *The Strange Career of Jim Crow*, which he presented as a series of lectures at the University of Virginia in the fall of 1954. But his essays in *Commentary* magazine on the contemporary civil rights struggle also deserve a mention. In June 1956 he posed the question: 'Will the history of the New Reconstruction repeat that of the Old?' In formulating his answer, Woodward viewed the Second Reconstruction through the lens of a 1950s understanding of the First Reconstruction. Unlike the southern moderates, Woodward commended the NAACP for filing suit in 170 school districts in 17 states. But he outlined in grim detail for his national audience the elaborate strategy of Massive Resistance that was taking shape across the South. '*It is a real Constitutional crisis that we are facing,*' he warned, '*not a sham parade in ancestral costume.*'

With consummate irony, Woodward outlined the process for 'reconstructing' his native region, beginning with school desegregation in the border states, proceeding to the states of Tennessee, Arkansas and Texas, and finally, 'moving in gradually from the Southern periphery and tightening Reconstruction's hold around the die-hard states of the Deep South.' He pointed with hope to the lessening of race prejudice among the younger generation of southern whites, the support for desegregation by southern churches, and the growing resources of the black community. Southern Negroes, he observed, 'have already shown new capacities for leadership that have surprised their friends as well as their opponents.' Woodward prophesied the 'eventual doom of segregation . . . *in the long run*'. He recognized that the term 'gradualism' was anathema to blacks 'who have waited nearly a hundred years for promised rights . . .' and he claimed that he did not wish to propose any policy, merely to 'characterize a historic phenomenon'. '*Undesirable or not*', he insisted, '*gradualism is an inescapable fact and a basic characteristic of the New Reconstruction.*' Woodward's greatest fear was that northern whites would again seek a quick and easy solution like the vaguely worded Civil Rights Act of 1875 which would be thwarted by the elaborate plans of resistance, both legal and extra-legal, that were being set into motion in the South. Those tempted by 'majestic instancy', he warned, should ponder the 'unhappy history' of the First Reconstruction. 'However deliberate and halting its speed', he concluded, 'the New Reconstruction would seem to promise more enduring results.'[12]

African-American writers did not lose any time in blasting the counsels of moderation and gradualism coming out of the South. These protests were fuelled by anger over the lynching of Emmett Till in Mississippi and by the mob action that prevented the enrolment of Autherine Lucy at the University of Alabama. Roy Wilkins, the new executive secretary of the NAACP, declared that the Association expected the elimination of segregation and discrimination from American life by the one-hundredth anniversary of the Emancipation Proclamation, and the NAACP adopted the slogan 'Truly free in '63'. The journalist Carl Rowan assailed 'this cult of moderation, this enslavement to donothingism'. In the current climate of unreality in the South, Rowan charged, 'a "moderate" is any white southerner who can prove that he hasn't lynched any crippled old Negro grandmothers during prayer meeting hour.'[13]

James Baldwin pointed to the violence that often lay beneath the surface of white southern paternalism in an article on Faulkner in *Partisan Review*. Mississippi's Nobel laureate, in an interview in *The Reporter*, had been quoted as saying that he might have to leave 'the middle of the road' and take up arms against the federal government if the Yankees did not leave the white South alone to desegregate voluntarily. If it came to a confrontation, Faulkner averred, he would fight for Mississippi, 'even if it meant going out into the streets and shooting Negroes.' Although Faulkner insisted that he had been misquoted, his alleged remarks ignited a firestorm of controversy. 'Why', Baldwin asked, 'does one move from the middle of the road where one was aiding Negroes into the streets – to shoot them?' Baldwin argued that Faulkner was desperately clinging to a myth that, in the absence of federal coercion, white southerners would accord to blacks the dignity and equality that they had denied them for three hundred years. And Faulkner was not alone. Baldwin concluded that: 'the arguments with which the bulk of relatively articulate white Southerners of good-will have met the necessity of desegregation have no value whatever as arguments, being almost entirely and helplessly dishonest, when not, indeed, insane.'[14]

Rowan, Baldwin, and other African-American writers made little impact on the national debate in the 1950s, which continued to be dominated by whites. In fact, in 1956 many northern white liberals softened their criticisms of the white South in the face of Massive Resistance and the desperate cries of white southern moderates for time and patience. The diffidence of many liberals can be explained in part by their desire to recapture the White House from the Republicans in 1956. The loss of the Presidency in 1952 for the first time in twenty years had been traumatic for many liberals, and they hankered for strong executive leadership of the sort that Franklin Delano Roosevelt had provided. Adlai Stevenson, the liberals' hero, was desperate to win the South's electoral votes, and he spoke vaguely and ambiguously on civil rights during that election year. During Eisenhower's presidency, many liberals were not sure that the federal government was ready for a major constitutional crisis. With southern Democrats dominating the Congress and a weak executive in the White House, liberals feared that the federal government might not be willing to muster the degree of force necessary to defeat Massive Resistance. If a second Nullification Crisis arose, many liberals doubted that Ike was prepared to play Andrew Jackson to some Deep South Calhoun. Indeed, liberals worried that the Brown decision would meet the fate of Justice John Marshall's edict forbidding the removal of the Cherokee.[15]

Accordingly, Reinhold Niebuhr, a longtime supporter of civil rights, urged caution in responding to Massive Resistance. In Niebuhr's neo-orthodox view, ethnic particularity or 'group pride' was part of the human condition, humans were capable of great violence and irrationality in groups, and prejudice and irrational customs would yield only slowly to government measures ensuring equal rights. Reacting against twentieth-century totalitarianism, Niebuhr believed that the fanatical pursuit of utopias or abstract ideals could lead to despotism or disillusionment and a failure to achieve even modest goals. The Jacobins in the French Revolution, Radical Republicans during Reconstruction, and prohibitionists in the early twentieth century were all seen as reformers who attempted to legislate behavioural changes for which the mass of people were not ready. Niebuhr found much wisdom in Edmund Burke's concept of organic, communal change, and he argued that one had to take account of 'history', 'mores', and community attitudes in assessing the prospects for the success of school desegregation in the South. Both Niebuhr and his secular disciple, Arthur Schlesinger Jr, suggested that the gradual or 'Fabian' approach of the Vinson Court had been more effective in breaking down segregation than the Warren Court's sweeping Brown decision, which, in their view, stiffened resistance in the Deep South by attempting too much at once.[16]

In 1956 Niebuhr engaged in a delicate balancing act. He praised the Montgomery bus boycott and called on white southern Christians to prepare white public opinion for desegregation, but also endorsed Faulkner's advice that the federal government not push 'too fast' on school desegregation, 'lest the southern whites be pushed "off balance" and become subject to hysteria'. Niebuhr thought that the country had made 'steady progress in racial justice', and warned that it would 'be a calamity if this process were arrested by heedless action'. The nation's experience with 'Federal police action against recalcitrant communities in the prohibition era taught us that the power of force is limited against communities and that it tends to stiffen the resistance to the law.' He recommended that the federal government should allow individual communities to adjust their practices to the Supreme Court ruling and people of good will should 'give these organic processes of persuasion a chance to close the hiatus between the standard of equal justice and the mores of the community.'[17] Niebuhr expressed sympathy for white southern parents who feared that their children's education would suffer in integrated schools because of the 'cultural differences between the races'. He counselled prudence and admonished Christians that 'genuine love does not propose abstract schemes of justice which leave the human factor out of account.'[18]

One 'human factor' that weighed heavily on Niebuhr's mind in 1956 was the urgency of electing Adlai Stevenson president. When Stevenson angered black voters with a remark that 'You do not upset habits and traditions that are older than the Republic overnight', Niebuhr defended him. In an article in *The New Leader* in July 1956, Niebuhr admonished liberals that the moderation of Stevenson offiered more hope for Democratic victory and lasting racial progress than the more activist civil rights programme of New York Governor Averill Harriman. The eminent ethicist lectured the liberals that, 'a policy which might enlarge the "hard core" of Southern recalcitrance and arrest the promising organic growth of racial amity would be unwise and perhaps tragic. It may be politically unwise to advocate "gradualism", but it is morally wise to practice it so long as the gradualism is genuine, that is, so long as the progress is sufficiently real to give the Negro minority hope for a better future.'[19] To this, Irving Howe replied that 'Surely, one might expect something a little more forthright . . . from the foremost exponent . . . of the Protestant "crisis theology." But Mr. Niebuhr has developed a mar-vellous intellectual system . . . by which his theological right hand does know what his worldly political left hand does.'[20]

Eleanor Roosevelt, like Niebuhr, leapt to Stevenson's defence, explaining to blacks that 'Go slow doesn't mean, don't go', and she threatened to re-sign from the board of the NAACP in protest over Roy Wilkins' 'reckless' criticisms of Stevenson's statements on civil rights. Arthur Schlesinger Jr, a Stevenson speechwriter, took a more clinical view in a private memorandum to a campaign official. Schlesinger thought the trouble was Adlai's 'project-ing . . . a pervading sense of coldness about the whole problem'. The young Harvard historian suggested that Stevenson could learn from Senator John F. Kennedy how to express more emotion when making general statements about civil rights. 'If we can communicate [deep] concern, then we can remain as responsible and uncommitted as we want when it comes to policy', Schlesinger concluded.[21]

Privately, Roy Wilkins was furious at the northern white liberal intellec-tuals and journalists who 'swallowed Faulkner's line whole' and endorsed the 'go-slow line'. But publicly he remained disciplined and tactful, know-ing that he needed white liberal support in the upcoming Congressional battle over a civil rights bill.[22]

A curious notion of even-handedness appeared in the writings of northern white liberals in 1956. Taking their cue from the southern white moderates, liberals exalted the rule of law and order and sought to steer a middle course between civil rights advocates and Massive Resisters. Thus Stevenson, in a speech in Richmond, condemned equally both 'anti-Negroism' and 'anti-Southernism'. The *Christian Science Monitor* labelled both the NAACP and the White Citizens' Councils as 'extremist' groups. And the editors of *The New Republic*, in one of the more remarkable statements of the decade, re-ported that: 'Gandhi-like passive resistance, which now characterizes both the Southern defiance of the Supreme Court and retaliatory Negro boycotts, is leading toward a new national crisis of the magnitude of 1860 but whose character is only dimly seen.'[23]

Actually, *The New Republic* was one of the few liberal journals of opinion to cover the Montgomery bus boycott, an event that was greatly overshadowed in the national press by Massive Resistance. Neither *Commentary, Harper's*, nor *Partisan Review* ran a single article on Martin Luther King, the bus boycott, or the SCLC between 1955 and 1960. To be sure, *Time, Newsweek*, and *U.S. News and World Report* covered King, along with national newspapers and television networks, as Richard Lentz has shown.[24] But King's ideas would not generate extensive discussions among white liberal intellectuals until the early 1960s.[25] For an informed analysis of the bus boycott, one had to turn to Bayard Rustin's article in the pacifist journal *Liberation* or Lawrence Reddick's articles in the democratic socialist magazine *Dissent*. Irving Howe complained in 1956 that, in their appeals for moderation and gradualism, liberals were missing the significance of the bus boycott, one of the important events of the century which signalled the emergence of Negroes as 'an independent political force in the South'. But Howe's critique had little impact at the time.[26]

In September 1957 the constitutional crisis that many had feared erupted when Governor Orval Faubus of Arkansas, previously thought to be a 'moderate', sent National Guard troops to Little Rock's Central High School to prevent court-approved desegregation. After an initial period of hesitation, President Eisenhower dispatched federal troops to Little Rock to ensure compliance with the federal court's orders. The Little Rock incident had a profound effect on public opinion outside the South. It was the most dramatic confrontation between federal and state authority since the Civil War. It also crystallized for many white people in the North an issue that previously had seemed complicated, abstract, and tangled in legal argument and procedural debate. The television and photographic images of a jeering mob of white adults and teenagers surrounding black children and preventing their entrance into school were flashed around the world and provoked massive outrage. President Eisenhower rebuked Faubus for harming the international 'prestige and influence' of the United States. 'Our enemies are gloating over this incident', he reported, 'and using it everywhere to misrepresent our whole nation.' Indeed the Soviet press did devote much attention to the incident, and even after Sputnik pushed Faubus off the front pages, Radio Moscow's bulletins mockingly included Little Rock when they announced the cities that the satellite was passing over.[27]

If Little Rock contributed to a sense of international vulnerability in the Cold War, it also provided images of mob rule that evoked memories of fascism. The extensive discussion of the incident in the liberal press posed the issue as a choice between mob rule and the rule of law. The southern novelist and essayist Lillian Smith, in *The New Republic*, criticized not only the mobs in the street obstructing school desegregation but also what she called 'Mob No. 2': business and community leaders in the South who used economic and social pressures to ensure conformity with segregation. Smith also charged that southern moderates tried to censor white southerners who forthrightly opposed segregation and contended that national magazines and networks did not report on the 'hundreds of gifted, articulate white southerners ready to speak to the entire nation' about the destructiveness of segregation. A strong anti-Communist, Smith compared the attempts by segregationists and moderates to control southern opinion to Communist-style 'brainwashing', but insisted that white southern opponents of segregation were ready to break through the 'magnolia curtain' and speak to their fellow white southerners if the press would only give them a chance. Entitling her essay 'No Easy Way, Now', Smith argued that Little Rock signalled the end of any strategy of gradualism and 'moderation.' White southerners and many whites outside the South simply had to confront their irrational fears about black people and realize that those same fears were driving the mobs in the street and the institutional pressures against free discussion.[28]

Commentary magazine responded to the Little Rock mobs by commissioning an article from the nation's foremost authority on totalitarianism, the political theorist Hannah Arendt. The piece that Arendt turned in was not what *Commentary*'s editors had expected, however. To be sure, Arendt was horrified by the willingness of a substantial proportion of southern whites to tolerate 'mob rule'. But she thought it unfortunate that the Supreme Court had decided to begin the process of attacking racial discrimination with the public schools. Arendt divided human life into three categories: the political, the social, and the private. She thought that the state had an obligation to prevent discrimination in the political sphere (voting), and she favored the immediate abolition of legal prohibitions on free association in those sectors of the social sphere necessary to the conduct of business, such as public accommodations. But she considered discrimination a right in the private sphere of the home and in such institutions as private clubs and vacation resorts. The public school, for Arendt, lay very close to the private sphere. 'To force parents to send their children to an integrated school against their will means to deprive them of rights which clearly belong to them in all free societies – the private over their children and the social right to free association.' According to Arendt, it was wrong to place the burden of social change on children, subjecting them to an intense conflict between the values of their home and the values of the society.[29]

The *Commentary* editors commissioned a rebuttal from Sidney Hook, who argued that schools were indisputably a public responsibility, and that desegregated schools were essential for equal opportunity. 'By arbitrarily extending the realm of the personal and delimiting the realm of the public', Hook contended, 'the segregationists [and their liberal allies] would give those in possession of power justification to impose their way of life, subtly if possible, brutally if necessary, on any minority and (crowning irony) to do it in the name of personal freedom.'[30] Arendt withdrew her article from *Commentary* before publication, and Hook published his essay in defence of school desegregation, which did not name Arendt as his adversary, in *The New Leader*. Irving Howe finally persuaded Arendt to allow her article to appear in *Dissent* in 1959, two years after it was written, together with an editorial disclaimer and three rebuttals.

Arendt's article, however idiosyncratic, did raise some interesting issues about the boundary between the public and the private spheres, how freedom of association was to be defined in a society intent on eliminating discrimination from public life. In the 1960s, neo-conservatives would re-open the issue of the right of ethnic groups to voluntary association, and feminists would challenge Arendt's idea of a private sphere centred in the home that must be protected against the incursions of the state.[31] In the aftermath of Little Rock, however, *Commentary*'s editors did not want the discourse about the right of ethnic groups to be different and the importance of a private sphere of voluntary association as a safeguard against conformity and totalitarianism to intrude on the debate about the primary issue then before the nation: school desegregation and civil rights in the South.

Most northern white liberals differed sharply with Arendt. The extensive discussion of Little Rock in the liberal press posed the issue as a choice between mob rule and the rule of law. This embarrassing incident also provoked northern white liberals to a new level of anger and impatience with the whole strategy of allowing local officials in the South to decide when and how they would comply with the Brown decision. The Harvard historian Oscar Handlin wrote an influential critique of the strategy of gradualism in his essay, 'Civil Rights after Little Rock: The Failure of Moderation', published in *Commentary* in November 1957. Handlin declared that: 'a policy that makes moderation the highest virtue runs the grave risk of exposing itself to the pressures of extremists who keep raising the price of their acquiescence. Moderation is often mistaken for weakness, and thus becomes a standing temptation to the blackmailer. This has been the history of Negro rights since 1954.' Handlin then took aim at a number of the arguments of the southern moderates and their northern sympathizers. He pointed out that the Supreme Court had ruled that segregation was incompatible with the Fourteenth Amendment, and he insisted that the federal government could not evade its responsibility to enforce compliance with Brown in every southern school district.[32]

Handlin rejected the assumption that 'the North' had to accommodate 'the South' on this issue, writing, 'It is silly to speak of "the South" when we have in mind the whites of the South. The black southerners are also making themselves heard.' He maintained that the greatest obstacle to desegregation was not deeply-rooted southern customs but 'the unwillingness of responsible political leaders to say flatly: "Segregation must be abolished."'

Handlin insisted that 'the experience of southerners who move to the North, and the success of integration in the armed services, show that the change can be induced with relative ease'. The percentage of blacks in Baltimore and Washington, D.C., was comparable to that in most counties in Georgia, yet desegregation had occurred in those cities without serious opposition because the local leadership had lent its support to compliance. Finally, Handlin declared that 'a determined Federal government already holds powerful instruments for shaping policy and public attitudes'. Little Rock rioters should be prosecuted, the Fifteenth Amendment and existing statutes should be used to protect voting rights, and the 'great reserves' of popular support for civil rights should be mobilized. 'The only question', he concluded, 'is whether our political leadership has enough will to act.'

That was indeed the question that liberals pondered in the wake of Little Rock, and most of them saw little hope that Eisenhower would demonstrate that will. Most looked to the election of 1960 with the hope that it would produce a strong executive who would regain American leadership in the Cold War in the wake of Sputnik and provide moral leadership at home in the aftermath of Little Rock.[33]

In the meantime, very little school desegregation took place in the South in 1958 and 1959. The editors of the NAACP magazine *The Crisis* recalled the slogan 'truly free in '63' with bitter irony. Yet many white liberals found grounds for hope in the news coming out of the South. When the governor of Virginia abandoned Massive Resistance and allowed token integration, his action was hailed as a great victory. Liberals were relieved that no other southern governors seemed to be following in Faubus's footsteps, though they acknowledged that no desegregation had taken place in six states of the Deep South. In September 1959, the editors of *The New Republic* hailed 'a significant change . . . in the southern attitude. Hysteria and defiance, though still widespread, are giving way in many quarters to cool, common sense.' Future resistance would be isolated and local, not massive and regional. The editors praised North Carolina as a 'Model for the South', even though the state had only 14 black pupils in integrated schools. They admonished North Carolina to move faster 'if that state's famous Pearsall Plan of pupil assignment is to qualify as genuine gradualism . . .'[34] In December 1959, *The New Republic* summarized the optimistic view of white northern liberals in declaring: 'The South . . . may fight limited wars, but massive retaliation against desegregation has been repudiated.'[35]

Many white liberals took heart from the passage of the 1957 Civil Rights Act, which sought to combat voting discrimination in the South. The first congressional legislation on civil rights in eighty years, the act was largely ineffective because of a provision mandating a jury trial for any public official indicted for obstructing the right to vote. Liberals nonetheless saw the legislation as a harbinger of change, a sign that the power of southern reactionaries was weakening. C. Vann Woodward praised Lyndon Johnson's leadership in securing passage of the act, suggested that the southern bloc was no longer monolithic, and predicted that it would weaken further after the 1958 mid-term elections and the 1960 census reapportionment. The historian argued that it was wise that the Congress had not tried to do too much at once, had not passed a law that was unenforceable, like the 1875 Civil Rights Act which: 'thrust upon the shoulders of the Federal judiciary the whole burden of making the freedmen equal and making the whites accept the status revolution they decreed.' It was just as well that the Congress had followed the lead of the Supreme Court, which had emphasized 'gradualism, local initiative, piecemeal progress, "deliberate speed"'. If this approach did not succeed, Woodward warned, 'radical alternatives' might have to be embraced.[36]

White liberal intellectuals did not have a great deal to say about African-American political behaviour or black organizations during the late 1950s. Though some labelled the NAACP as extremist most observers by the end of the decade saw the organization as the legitimate voice of black protest. In their critique of white southern Massive Resistance and the danger of mob rule, northern liberals often praised the law-abiding nature of the NAACP, the toughness and self-discipline of the organization and its leaders. Progress in the South would be slow, and it would result from this black elite working with white southern moderate leaders. 'Negro leaders in the South are bred to patience,' *The New Republic* emphasized, 'they want the support of Southern moderates. They will not object to "going slow" once there is agreement in the South that the Court's decision will prevail.'[37] Liberals praised the new spirit of protest among southern Negroes, but saw it as an urban, middle-class phenomenon. Woodward, for example, had little hope that black voter registration would increase substantially because the mass of unregistered blacks were poor and lived in rural areas. 'Reliable studies have established beyond doubt that low-income, low-education groups, of whatever race or section, have the lowest rate of voting participation', he observed. 'It would require inspired work by able and courageous Negro leaders to awaken this group, which has never voted, into political consciousness', he continued 'and such leaders are simply not available in anything like sufficient numbers.'[38]

In February 1960, some of those missing Negro leaders appeared in Greensboro, North Carolina in the form of college students who were no longer willing to accept the liberals' framework of gradualism, modernization, reliance on NAACP lawsuits, and hopes for greater Presidential leadership. The sit-ins ignited a mass movement in black communities across the South, which continued with the freedom rides, local movements in various cities, and the March on Washington, so that by 1963, an estimated 75 000 people participated in demonstrations. SNCC members in Mississippi, Alabama and Georgia worked with local community activists in those states, to register voters, contest the control of local governments and speed the awakening of the rural masses that Woodward had thought to be slumbering only three years before. Television would open a space for the ideas of Martin Luther King that had not been present in liberal journals, and the mass movement of African-Americans in the South would challenge the political and cultural assumptions of intellectuals.

This explosion of political activity raised a number of new issues in addition to the standard agenda of civil rights demands going back to the nineteenth century. While space will not permit a full exploration of each of these issues, it is important to note them.

First, the use on a mass basis of Gandhian civil disobedience by CORE, SCLC and SNCC involved a new kind of politics not comprehended by the pluralist political theory of the 1950s. The use of direct-action tactics outside the normal political channels, the appeal to the conscience of whites, the willingness to disrupt day-to-day business and fill the gaols until demands were met, the statement of political demands in religious language all represented a fundamental departure from the interest-group politics that political scientists had analysed.

Second, SNCC, under the prodding of Ella Baker, developed a 'group-centered leadership' and participatory democracy that fuelled a successful grass-roots movement in Mississippi and other parts of the South. Closely related to this was the development of a movement culture that, for a time at least, seemed to be breaking down boundaries among people and creating a more spontaneous kind of politics.

Third, the development of alternative institutions, such as the MFDP and the freedom schools, gave to those black people who participated in them a chance to experience an alternative to the oppressive southern order.

Fourth, there was a new international context with the dramatic success of African liberation movements, which contributed to a sense of militance and impatience among African-Americans. Black nationalism was not yet a powerful ideology in the early 1960s, yet black Americans were aware of it as an alternative as a result of Malcolm X's speeches and the press coverage of the Nation of Islam.

Finally, there was a reopening of questions of economic justice, as intellectuals such as Bayard Rustin, Michael Harrington and Gunnar Myrdal presented a social democratic critique of the economic basis of racial inequality – a critique that would ultimately influence Martin Luther King in the mid and late 1960s.

This paper has suggested some of the reasons why white liberal intellectuals had difficulty in comprehending the gathering movement for civil rights among African-Americans in the 1950s. Assumptions about political pluralism, mass movements, Keynesian economics, modernization of the South, the nature of prejudice, and the failure of the First Reconstruction, all led to the view that change would be gradual and managed by elites. Institutional racism in universities, professional organizations, and journalism, together with the practical exigencies of Democratic Party politics, alliances with southern moderates, and the tenets of anti-Communist liberalism, reinforced those assumptions and isolated white liberal intellectuals from dialogue with many black intellectuals and grassroots activists of both races.

Martin Luther King gave his answer to the southern white moderates in the 'Letter from Birmingham Jail', on 16 April 1963.

> For years now I have heard the word "Wait". It rings in the ear of every Negro with piercing familiarity. . . . We have waited for more than 340 years for our constitutional and God-given rights. The nations of Asia and Africa are moving with jet-like speed toward gaining political independence, but we still creep at horse-and-buggy pace toward gaining a cup of coffee at a lunch counter. . . . I have almost reached the regrettable conclusion that the Negro's great stumbling block in his stride toward freedom is not the White Citizen's Councilor or the Ku Klux Klanner, but the white moderate, who is more devoted to "order" than to justice; who prefers a negative peace which is the absence of tension to a positive peace which is the presence of justice; . . . who paternalistically believes he can set the timetable for another man's freedom; who lives by a mythical concept of time and who constantly advises the Negro to wait for a "more convenient season".[39]

Still assembling a national coalition to press for civil rights legislation, King forebore from extending his critique to northern white liberal intellectuals in 1963. But the following year, in a debate sponsored by *Commentary* magazine, James Baldwin would be far less tactful. Baldwin termed white liberals 'an affliction' and deplored their 'missionary complex' and attitude that 'they must help me into the light', a judgement in which many African-American intellectuals would concur as the tumultuous events of the decade unfolded. I would argue that a closer look at white liberalism in the 1950s is warranted if we are to understand the gulf that opened in the mid-1960s between white and black advocates of civil rights.

NOTES

1. Walter A. Jackson, *Gunnar Myrdal and America's Conscience: Social Engineering and Racial Liberalism, 1938–1987* (Chapel Hill, 1990).
2. See Richard Pells, *The Liberal Mind in a Conservative Age: American Intellectuals in the 1940s and 1950s* (New York, 1985), chs 3, 4.

3. Arthur M. Schlesinger Jr, *The Vital Center: The Politics of Liberalism* (Boston, 1949), pp. 190, 252.

4. Jackson, *Gunnar Myrdal and America's Conscience* pp. 279–93.

5. Robert Booth Fowler, *Believing Skeptics: American Political Intellectuals, 1945–60* (Westport, Conn., 1978), pp. 47–66, 177–208.

6. On the concept of institutional racism, see Joe R. Feagin and Clairece Booher Feagin, *Discrimination American Style: Institutional Racism and Sexism* (Englewood Cliffs, NJ, 1978).

7. Carleton Putnam, *Race and Reason, a Yankee View* (Washington, 1961); James Jackson Kilpatrick, *The Southern Case for School Segregation* (New York, 1962). Kilpatrick commented on Massive Resistance in the 1950s in his editorials in the *Richmond News-Leader*.

8. C. Vann Woodward, 'The South and the Law of the Land: The Present Resistance and Its Prospects', *Commentary*, 26 (November 1958), p. 373.

9. Quoted in Anthony Lake Newberry, 'Without Urgency or Ardor: The South's Middle-of-the-Road Liberals and Civil Rights, 1945–1960', PhD thesis, Ohio University, 1982, p. 264. My discussion of white southern moderates is indebted to Newberry.

10. Benjamin Muse, 'When and How the South will Integrate', *Harper's Magazine*, 214 (April 1957), 51–5.

11. Robert Penn Warren, *Segregation* (New York, 1955), p. 65.

12. C. Vann Woodward, 'The New Reconstruction in the South: Desegregation in Historical Perspective', *Commentary*, 21 (June 1956), 501–8 cf. Woodward, 'The Great Civil Rights Debate: The Ghost of Thaddeus Stevens in the Senate Chamber', *Commentary*, 24 (October 1957), 283–91.

13. Carl T. Rowan, *Go South to Sorrow* (New York, 1957), pp. 206–7.

14. James Baldwin, 'Faulkner and Desegregation', *Partisan Review*, 23 (Fall 1956), 568–73.

15. Gerald W. Johnson, 'The Superficial Aspect: Southern Manifesto', *The New Republic*, 9 April 1956, p. 8.

16. Reinhold Niebuhr, 'The Desegregation Issue', *Christianity and Society*, 21: 2 (Spring 1956), 3–4; Niebuhr, 'A Theologian's Comments on the Negro in America', *The Reporter*, 15 (29 November 1956), 24–5; Niebuhr, 'The States' Rights Crisis', *The New Leader*, 29 September 1958, pp. 6–7; Arthur M. Schlesinger Jr, Foreword to John Bartlow Martin, *The Deep South Says 'Never'* (New York, 1957).

17. Reinhold Niebuhr, 'Notes', 28 February 1956, Niebuhr Papers, Library of Congress, Box 11, quoted in Steven Gillon, *Politics and Vision: The ADA and American Liberalism, 1947–1985* (New York, 1987), p. 94.

18. Niebuhr, 'What Resources Can the Christian Church Offer to Meet Crisis in Race Relations?' *The Messenger*, 21 (3 April 1956), 9.

19. Niebuhr, 'Stevenson, the Democrats, and Civil Rights', *The New Leader*, (9 July 1956), p. 11.

20. Irving Howe, 'Reverberations in the North', *Dissent*, 3:2 (Spring 1956), pp. 121–3.

21. John Bartlow Martin, *Adlai Stevenson and the World* (Garden City, NY, 1977), pp. 258–9.

22. Roy Wilkins, *Standing Fast: The Autobiography of Roy Wilkins* (New York, 1982).

23. 'The Passive Resistance of Montgomery's Negroes', *The New Republic*, 5 March 1956, p. 6.

114 *Walter A. Jackson*

24. Richard Lentz, *Symbols, the News Magazines and Martin Luther King* (Baton Rouge, 1990).
25. Explicitly Christian journals such as *Christian Century* would constitute an exception to this generalization.
26. Howe, 'Reverberations in the North', p. 121.
27. Harold Isaacs, *The New World of Negro Americans* (New York, 1963).
28. Lillian Smith, 'No Easy Way, Now', *The New Republic*, 26 December 1957, pp. 15–16. See also Smith, 'Words and the Mob', *Liberation*, 8:2 (November 1957), 4–5.
29. Hannah Arendt, 'Reflections on Little Rock', Dissent, 6 (Winter 1959), 45–56. See also Elisabeth Young–Bruehl, *Hannah Arendt: For Love of the World* (New Haven, 1982), pp. 308–18.
30. Sidney Hook, 'Democracy and Desegregation', *New Leader* 41 (21 April 1958): Section 2, 13.
31. On the concept that 'the personal is political', see Sara Evans, *Personal Politics: The Roots of Women's Liberation in the Civil Rights Movement and the New Left* (New York, 1979).
32. Oscar Handlin, 'Civil Rights after Little Rock: The Failure of Moderation', *Commentary*, 24 (November 1957), 392–96.
33. On the restlessness of liberal intellectuals after 1957, see Allen J. Matusow, *The Unraveling of America; A History of Liberalism in the 1960s* (New York, 1984), pp. 8–17.
34. 'Six Years Later', *The New Republic*, 7 September 1959, pp. 3–4. On the Pearsall Plan as a strategy for evading compliance with Brown, see William H. Chafe, *Civilities and Civil Rights: Greensboro, North Carolina and the Black Struggle for Freedom*, (New York, 1980), pp. 48–60.
35 'Thaw in the South', *The New Republic*, 7 December 1959, pp. 3–5.
36. C. Vann Woodward, 'The Great Civil Rights Debate: The Ghost of Thaddeus Stevens in the Senate Chamber', *Commentary*, 24 (October 1957), 283–91.
37. 'But What of the Law?', *The New Republic*, 2 April 1956, p. 10.
38. Woodward, 'The Great Civil Rights Debate', p. 290.
39. Martin Luther King Jr, *Why We Can't Wait* (New York, 1964), pp. 80–1, 83–4.

6 Rethinking African-American Political Thought in the Post-Revolutionary Era

Clayborne Carson

I

On 25 March 1957, C. L. R. James, the idiosyncratic West Indian socialist activist and writer, wrote to friends about his recent meeting in London with Martin Luther King Jr. By the time of this meeting, King was already widely known. *Time* magazine had just featured him on its cover, and the articulate, young (he was 28) Baptist preacher had already become an internationally known protest leader. The Montgomery bus boycott received almost unanimous support from Montgomery's black residents, who refused to ride buses for more than a year before the United States Supreme Court in December 1956 declared Montgomery's segregation policy unconstitutional. James, whose own writings had often stressed the radical implications of mass movements, could scarcely contain his enthusiasm and proclaimed the Montgomery mass movement to be of major historical importance. 'It was one of the most astonishing events of endurance by a whole population that I have ever heard of', he gushed in his letter.

James went on to compare King's non-violent campaign to the independence struggle in Ghana led by Kwame Nkrumah. Both movements, he argued, demonstrated the 'unsuspected power of the mass movement', a power that, according to James, radical political leaders often failed to recognize. James described both Nkrumah and King as leaders who themselves only gradually came to recognize the untapped potential of mass action. He added that Nkrumah's programme of 'Positive Action' and King's Gandhian non-violence were both spontaneous responses to masses already in motion rather than carefully developed ideologies capable of stimulating mass struggle. He concluded that the examples of Ghana and Montgomery demonstrated that Leon Trotsky and other marxist theories had been wrong in their belief that 'the proletariat needs a long experience and its cadres a long period in which they can get to understand one another and to appreciate the intricacies of politics.' Instead, James argued, the mass movements in Ghana and Montgomery serve as 'a warning to all revolutionaries not to under estimate the readiness of modern people *everywhere* to overthrow the old regime.' In particular, he insisted that Marxists needed to recognize that the use of Gandhian tactics by Nkrumah and King represented 'a technique of revolutionary struggle characteristic of our age.' James wrote that those who considered themselves to be revolutionaries would 'be making a fundamental mistake' to ignore 'the tremendous boldness, the strategic grasp and the tactical inventiveness, all these fundamentally revolutionary' that was displayed in the movements in Ghana and Montgomery.[1]

James's comments provide a useful starting point for a reassessment of Martin Luther King and African-American political militancy of the 1950s and 1960s. They remind us that the Montgomery movement was an abrupt departure in terms of mass activism from the quiescent political climate of Cold War America. Indeed, the boycott movement marked the beginning of a decade of African-American struggles throughout the southern states that were unprecedented and are still unreplicated in scale and duration.

Historical interpretations of African-American politics during the period from 1955 to 1965 have tended to emphasize the extent to which black activism of the period developed within the ideological boundaries of post-war liberalism. King, in particular, is seen as unwilling during this period to venture beyond the ideological framework of his liberal supporters. The civil rights activists of the early 1960s are depicted as far less militant than the black nationalists of the latter half of the decade. The standard narrative of the evolution of African-American politics during the 1960s portrays the black struggle as moving towards greater and greater degrees of radicalization and King as being increasingly challenged by black radicals and revolutionaries. African-American political thought, according to this widely accepted narrative, moves from the reformist, integrationist orientation of King to the revolutionary black nationalism of Malcolm X, Stokely Carmichael and the Black Panther Party. Non-violent civil rights protests gave way, it is said, to mass movements toward black liberation. Indeed, just ten years after James wrote his letter, King found himself on the defensive, under attack from black power firebrands who saw him not as a fellow radical or revolutionary but as a devotee of out-of-date policies of non-violence and integrationism.

Yet, given the rapid decline of mass insurgencies in black communities after 1968 and the continuing decline of the living conditions of African-Americans in central cities, it is time to rethink this standard interpretation. James was prescient in recognizing the radical implications of the mass black movements of the 1950s and early 1960s. The standard interpretation errs in viewing the black power movement as a revolutionary departure. To be sure, the non-violent civil rights campaigns of the 1950s and 1960s *were* seeking to bring about reform, and there *were* some black nationalist revolutionaries on the scene during the late 1960s, but the early civil rights campaigns also contained the seeds of the most significant mass movements of subsequent decades. In contrast, black power militancy of the late 1960s was either readily suppressed or transformed into forms that did not threaten to domi-nate political and economic elites.

II

Although the ideas that emerged from the African-American activism of the 1950s and early 1960s are often seen as precursors to the black power and New Left radicalism of the late 1960s, they can best be understood as the outgrowth of efforts by King, by youthful organizers of the SNCC, and other civil rights activists to create radical alternatives to both traditional black nationalism and Marxism. Once Rosa Parks's defiance of southern segrega-tion thrust King into a leadership role, he and other activists began formu-lating a strategy of social change that departed from mainstream liberalism and from the two main ideological traditions of militant African-American struggle – that is, black nationalism and Marxism.

King's alternative radicalism was constructed, first of all, on the founda-tion of social gospel Christianity, especially the African-American variant of this tradition to which his father and grandfather had contributed. Reviv-ing this tradition of prophetic dissent, King publicly criticized Cold War liberalism and capitalist materialism while also rejecting communism. Ac-knowledging in *Stride Toward Freedom: The Montgomery Story* that the works of Karl Marx had reinforced his long-held concern 'about the gulf between superfluous wealth and abject poverty', King charged that capital-ist materialism was 'always in danger of inspiring men to be more con-cerned about making a living than making a life.'[2] His version of social gospel Christianity also incorporated socialist ideas as well as anti-colonial sentiments spurred by the African independence movements.

In short, King made an important contribution to what later became known as liberation theology, which has enabled activists around the world to redefine widely held spiritual beliefs that are often used as supports for the status quo. As the Italian Marxist theorist Antonio Gramsci pointed out earlier in this century, rebels against the established social order who ignore the cul-tural dimension of insurgent struggles do so at their own peril. King under-stood that Christianity could serve either as a basis for African-American accommodation or for resistance. As a privileged insider within the largest African-American denomination, he fought an uphill struggle to transform the black church into an institutional foundation for racial struggles.

King also continued the efforts of Howard Thurman, James Farmer, Benjamin Mays, James Lawson and others to combine social gospel Christianity with Gandhian ideas of non-violent struggle. 'Gandhi was probably the first per-son in history to lift the love ethic of Jesus above mere interaction between individuals to a powerful and effective social force on a large scale', King

wrote in *Stride*. 'I came to feel that this was the only morally and practically
sound method open to oppressed people in their struggle for freedom.'[3] Under
the guidance of more experienced Gandhians, such as Bayard Rustin, Glenn
Smiley and Lawson, King came to recognize that Gandhian non-violence
represented more than simply a tactical option for oppressed people. He
became increasingly aware of the potential power of non-violent tactics when
used by militant, disciplined practitioners in close association with mass
movements. Moreover, he discerned the importance of the ethos of non-
violence as a cohesive force within the black struggle and as a spiritual
foundation for what Gandhians called the Beloved Community.

At the beginning of the 1960s, the activists associated with SNCC were
more willing than King to explore the radical implications of social gospel
Christianity and Gandhism. At the time of SNCC's founding, however, many
young black activists were drawn more to Lawson than to King. Having
tutored Nashville student activists in Gandhian principles, Lawson encouraged SNCC activists to transform the lunch-counter sit-ins into a 'non-violent revolution' to destroy 'segregation slavery, serfdom, paternalism', and
'industrialization which preserves cheap labour and racial discrimination.'[4]
Although some SNCC activists later abandoned Lawson's idealism in favour
of instrumental rather than philosophical rationales for non-violence, those
in the group continued to see themselves as involved in a freedom struggle
rather than simply in an effort to achieve civil rights reforms. Several of the
graduates of Lawson's Nashville workshop – especially Diane Nash, James
Bevel and John Lewis – were more tactically audacious than was King, who
often backed away from confrontations that lacked federal legal sanction or
were likely to result in violence.

Moreover, SNCC workers quickly moved from conventional liberalism
toward their own distinctive radicalism, which was more secular and inno-
vative than King's Christian Gandhianism. SNCC field secretaries, especially
those working with Bob Moses in Mississippi, resisted ideological conformity and derived their evolving worldview from their experiences as community organizers in the deep South. SNCC developed a distinctive style of
community organizing that self-consciously avoided the creation of new de-
pendent relationships to replace the traditional racial dependencies of southern
blacks. SNCC organizers were inspired by the example of Ella Baker, a
woman who abhorred the elitism she had encountered as a field secretary of
the NAACP and as the executive director of King's hierarchically organized
SCLC. Rejecting King's charismatic leadership style, Baker encouraged the
development of 'group-centered leaders' rather than leader-centred groups.[5]
SNCC's notion of organizing emphasized the development of grassroots leaders.
SNCC organizers often stated, and some of them actually believed, that their
job was to work themselves out of a job and that organizers should never
seek leadership positions for themselves.

SNCC's radicalism was greatly influenced by the example of activists of earlier generations. Although SNCC workers generally avoided Marxian sectarianism, they borrowed tactics and rhetoric from the dedicated Communist Party organizers who had played significant roles in southern black movements of the pre-1960 era. SNCC also borrowed from Miles Horton and Septima Clark at the Highlander Folk School in Tennessee and from the Students for a Democratic Society, although SDS was more influenced by SNCC than vice versa. Finally, during the period after 1963, SNCC borrowed ideas from Malcolm X and the black nationalist tradition, most notably concepts of consciousness-raising and institution-building.

During the first half of the 1960s, King and the college-student organizers in SNCC were, in their different ways, responsible for mobilizations of large masses of black people willing to confront white authority on a scale unequalled during the last half of the decade. These militant mobilizations compelled a reluctant federal government to enact civil rights legislation, and they established a foundation for a fundamental restructuring of African-American participation in the electoral politics of the United States.

Nevertheless, by the mid 1960s, many SNCC activists, recognizing the need to move beyond civil rights reform to address issues of poverty and political powerlessness, adopted the black power slogan. Initially, the slogan represented an extension of SNCC's organizing efforts in the deep South, but after it became popularized by Stokely Carmichael the slogan came to symbolize a sharp break with SNCC's past. Rather than continuing to develop the radicalism of the early 1960s, many black power advocates abandoned the radical perspectives that grew out of the civil rights movement in favour of racial separatist ideologies. Veterans of SNCC's earlier organizing efforts, such as Carmichael, were embittered by their experiences and abandoned interracialism and non-violence as guiding principles. As the black power proponents pursued the mirage of a successful black nationalist revolution, they also abandoned many of the valuable insights that SNCC had acquired during its years of growth.

III

The key individual in this transformation of African-American political thought was Malcolm X. Malcolm's ideological contribution to the black power era would consist largely of his bitter critique of the non-violent civil rights movement; yet ironically, at the time of his assassination in February 1965, he was seeking to forge ties with King and SNCC organizers. While a member of Elijah Muhammad's Nation of Islam, Malcolm had supported his group's policy of non-engagement, which prevented members from joining in any protest activity. Even as he fiercely attacked King's strategy of non-violent resistance, however, Malcolm increasingly recognized that the Nation offered no real alternative to black people facing vicious white racists in the South. Unlike many of his posthumous followers, Malcolm realized that the militant racial rhetoric of his years in the Nation of Islam obscured the group's accommodationism. Indeed, he knew that the Nation of Islam was not above making deals with white people when it served the leaders' interests. Malcolm later admitted that in 1961, even while he criticized civil rights activists for working with white liberals, his own organization sent him to Atlanta to negotiate a mutual non-interference agreement with the Ku Klux Klan.[6] Like early black nationalists, such as Martin Delany in the 1870s and Marcus Garvey in the 1920s, Elijah Muhammad's insistence that all whites were devils made it possible for him to reach accommodations dealing with the worst of them.

After his break with the Nation of Islam, Malcolm publicly acknowledged the radical potential of what he called the grassroots forces of the civil rights movement. Rather than attempting to supplant the radical ideas that were emerging from the grassroots, Malcolm saw the need for a convergence of those ideas and his own version of revolutionary nationalism. Malcolm's ideological transformation during the last year of his life can be traced in the remarkable range of his activities during that year. In March 1964, after leaving the Nation of Islam and establishing his own Organization of Afro-American Unity (OAAU), he immediately began reaching out to civil rights leaders he had once harshly criticized. At the press conference announcing his break with Elijah Muhammad, Malcolm announced that he was 'not out to fight other Negro leaders or organizations.' He insisted, 'we must find a common approach, a common solution, to a common problem.' Unlike many of his followers who called for unity while viciously attacking their black political opponents, Malcolm was eager to salve old wounds: 'I've forgotten everything bad that the other leaders have said about me, and I pray they can also forget the many bad things I've said about them.'

Soon afterwards, in his 'Ballot or the Bullet' speech delivered in April 1964, Malcolm sought to erase the ideological boundaries that had previously separated him from the civil rights organizations: 'The political philosophy of black nationalism is being taught in the Christian church . . . in the NAACP . . . in CORE meetings . . . in SNCC . . . It's being taught every-where'.[7] Malcolm broadened his own political perspective as a result of his tour of several African nations, including Nigeria and Ghana, following the *Hajj* to Mecca. After forming the OAAU, he sent telegrams to civil rights leaders offering to send his followers to participate in southern civil rights campaigns and 'give the Ku Klux Klan a taste of their own medicine.' During a second trip to Africa during 1964, Malcolm met with the leaders of Egypt, Tanzania, Nigeria, Ghana, Guinea, Kenya and Uganda; attended a

Cairo meeting of the OAU; and, during a day-long meeting in Nairobi with leaders of the SNCC, promized to work closely with the youthful activists.[8]

Returning to the United States, Malcolm established increasingly close links with the southern black struggle. In December 1964 he invited Fannie Lou Hamer and the SNCC Freedom Singers to be guests of honour at an OAAU meeting in Harlem. He also hosted a delegation of 37 teenage activists from the McComb, Mississippi movement. On 1 February 1965, he sent a telegram to the head of the American Nazi Party, warning, 'I am no longer held in check from fighting white supremacists by Elijah Muhammad's separatist Black Muslim movement, and if your present racist agitation of our people there in Alabama causes physical harm to Reverend King or any other Black Americans . . . you and your KKK friends will be met with maximum physical retaliation. . . .' Malcolm also sought to make amends for his previous harsh personal criticisms of Martin Luther King Jr. A few weeks before his assassination, while in Selma, Alabama, to lend support to the ongoing voting rights struggle, he met Coretta Scott King and made clear that he did not want to make her husband's job more difficult, explaining that, if whites knew that Malcolm was the alternative, 'it might be easier for them to accept Martin's proposals.'[9]

Despite Malcolm's effort to achieve an alliance of black nationalism and the civil rights movement, black power militancy after Malcolm's death was often characterized by hostility toward any black leader who advocated non-violent tactics and racial integration. Malcolm's call for liberation 'by any means necessary' became a rationale for the abandonment of militant Gandhian tactics, despite the fact that Malcolm himself came to realize the necessity of non-violent tactics as part of any sustained mass struggle. Serious ideological conflicts within the African-American political community undermined the unity Malcolm was attempting to achieve. This disunity culminated in violent clashes between militant blacks, such as the one that took place in January 1969, at UCLA, when members of Maulana Karenga's US group shot and killed two Black Panthers in the campus dining-hall. By the end of the 1960s, the rhetorical violence of many self-proclaimed black revolutionaries had been transformed into self-destructive violence that ravaged the fabric of black communities. Initially the Panthers advised blacks to 'pick up the gun', but the drug dealers of the 1970s were far better armed and more ruthless than were the black revolutionaries of the 1960s.

The decline of black militant politics during the 1970s marked the end of an era of illusory revolutionary rhetoric that obscured the simultaneous upsurge of the conservative power in American politics and of multinational capitalism as a world economic system. Although black power advocates presented themselves as revolutionaries, only the Black Panther Party was taken seriously – and then only for a brief period – as a legitimate threat by the national government of the United States. Despite their bravado, or perhaps because of it, the Panthers and other self-styled black revolutionaries were brutally suppressed through covert and often illegal FBI 'counterintelligence' programmes and deadly raids by local police forces.

Ultimately, the black power movement of the last half of the 1960s promised more than the civil rights movement but delivered less. Black Power militants talked of power yet exercised only transitory power within black communities and none outside those communities. They proclaimed that they acted on behalf of African Americans whose needs had been ignored by the civil rights leaders, but black power militancy did not prevent a rapid deterioration in the economic status of the black masses during more than two decades since the late 1960s. Black power militants talked of revolution but the veterans of the black power movement have generally found ways of accommodating to the existing white-dominated social order. After Malcolm's assassination in 1965, the black power movement adopted many of his ideas, but the lasting contributions of the black power period were more significant in the intellectual and cultural rather than the political arena. Black power militancy survives not as insurgencies but as unthreatening expressions of Afrocentrism.

While failing to produce greater power for black people, black power militancy actually led to a decline in the ability of African-Americans to affect the course of American politics. The emergence of Stokley Carmichael and H. Rap Brown as nationally known black advocates of black power prompted more effective repression once J. Edgar Hoover's FBI recognized that the black struggle could be crippled through the elimination of a few leaders. Moreover, the rhetorical violence and racism of some black militants spurred the increasing popularity among whites of 'law and order' politics. Brown, in fact, helped to create the conditions that made it possible for Spiro Agnew to transform himself from a minor Maryland politician to Vice-President within little more than a year. In the larger context of American politics, the black power controversy encouraged a conservative political trend which has led to a Republican ascendancy in national electoral politics.

IV

The Black revolution, in short, did not happen. It is no closer to reality in the contemporary United States than is the working-class revolution Marx predicted would occur in the advanced capitalist societies. The failure of black power militants and black nationalists to bring about a revolution coincided with the general decline of the revolutionary enthusiasm that seemed so strong just twenty-five years ago. Moreover, the Cold War is now over. The West won. The Soviet empire has disintegrated. The ideologues of capitalism are trumpeting their victory and some enthusiasts even proclaim not only that communism has been overcome, not only that resistance to capitalism has become unproductive, but that such resistance has become unthinkable, that history as we have known it during the past two centuries has ended, for the future will bring no revolutionary transformations, that we now live in the best of all possible worlds. In 1968, militant activists throughout the world saw themselves as part of a series of revolutionary movements that would overthrow Western capitalism and bring about a new world order. They could not have expected that the new world order would merely be a consolidation of the old.

Given the eclipse of communism and the general decline of movements of resistance to world capitalism, the leaders of the major capitalist states now look upon a world in which they face neither significant internal nor external threats. Such a circumstance could not have been predicted just twenty-five years ago. In 1968, the Soviet Union represented only the most serious of many challenges to the world-wide dominance of Western capitalism. After the Tet offensive of February of that year, the anti-colonial struggle in Vietnam would conclude in a decisive victory over the military forces of the United States. Africa was experiencing its final wave of anticolonial struggles and throughout the Third World there were insurgent movements against colonization and neo-colonialism. Moreover, many of the leading capitalist states faced significant internal challenges – from class-conscious movements usually under the banner of a dynamic New Left and from various separatist movements of racial and ethnic minorities.

Although few observers might have imagined it then, 1968 marked the culmination of an era of revolutionary enthusiasm that extended back to the American and French Revolutions of the late eighteenth century. For two centuries, militant political dissent had involved the mobilization of oppressed groups into mass movements consisting of particular classes, races and ethnicities. Revolutionaries believed that mass movements could become sufficiently powerful to capture control of a modern state, which then could be taken over by, administered by, and used for the benefit of non-elite groups – workers, the masses or, more simply, 'the people'. During the nineteenth and twentieth centuries, the Marxian vision of a working-class revolutionary movement exerted considerable influence among insurgent organizers and intellectuals but racial and ethnic nationalism had even greater popular appeal among the discontented masses. Working-class revolutions did not succeed in the advanced capitalist states that Marx had seen as most vulnerable but, when Marxian and nationalist ideas converged during the twentieth century in less developed nations and in European colonies, their popular appeal was often inexorable.

For two centuries, therefore, this apocalyptic revolutionary vision had captured the imaginations of political activists seeking to overthrow oppressive and unjust political systems. African-American or black nationalist and Pan-African versions of the revolutionary vision were similarly based on the assumption that African slaves and the descendants of those slaves constituted a potentially revolutionary force, that black people in white-dominated societies could unite in a decisive struggle against white racial domination, that racial identity was a more powerful political force than national identity as citizens of the United States.

Revolutionary mass movements of the working class or of racial minorities can now be seen as part of a revolutionary era that has concluded, never to be repeated. Yet, although we have entered a new political era, there are still reasons to hope that insights that emerged from the African-American struggle still remain relevant.

While other social movements – most notably the modern women's liberation movement – have built upon the radical ideas of the black struggles of the 1955–65 period, contemporary African-American political militancy has remained separated from the radicalism of the early 1960s. Instead, contemporary black activists seeking to challenge the status quo generally trace their ideological roots to the black consciousness movement of the late 1960s. To be sure, that movement left behind valuable insights. Malcolm and many others who identified themselves as black nationalists responded to the need for African-Americans to take pride in their history, to develop and control their community institutions and to define their own destiny. One of the limitations of the modern civil rights movement was its failure to address the need to strengthen the community institutions that were essential to its long-term success. Even so, such efforts to build strong economic, religious and social institutions should never have been the exclusive prerogative of black nationalists who combined this message with the fantasy of black separatism. The black nationalist tradition offered a rhetorical means of expressing the anger and frustration of many African-Americans but it provided no viable political strategy.

If Marxian thought no longer inspires the faith it once did and the national liberation movements of this century have exhausted themselves, what alternatives exist for the oppressed and discontented people of the world? I have suggested that African-American political movements of the modern era have provided some alternatives, but these movements have been diverse, sometimes offering radical options but also reverting to reformist civil rights efforts and atavistic cultural nationalism.

The radical options that remain dynamic or at least viable at the end of the twentieth century are not solely the product of African-American movements but are instead a combination of aspects of many different movements that have challenged European cultural domination and modern industrial capitalism from diverse perspectives. Radical variants of each of these movements have retained the ability to inspire young people during an era when the revolutionary faith of the past two centuries has disintegrated. No insurgent movement now seems likely to overthrow a modern capitalist state but some significant elements of popular dissent and rebellion continue to thrive in the midst of the capitalist victory celebrations.

The post-revolutionary radicalism that is the legacy of the black struggles of the late 1950s and early 1960s therefore draws its inspiration not from any single movement but eclectically from the creative forces within various insurgent movements. Indeed, what distinguishes what could be called the radicalism of the post-revolutionary era is that it is provisional rather than systematic, universal rather than parochial.

The more enduring legacies of the radicalism of the 1960s have been those aspects that have converged with several new currents of social change activism. These include several movements that are rarely seen as radical but which in fact mobilized and altered the consciousness of large numbers of people and produced some important insights that will doubtless inform future radical movements. One of these new social movements is the human potential movement which is in truth more of a category of movements than a coherent social movement. Human potential or, as they are sometimes called, New Age movements have drawn their insights from Freud, Asian religions, religious mysticism and meditation, drug experimentation and many other sources. Although these movements are largely individualistic and usually apolitical, they have influenced many social activists who have seen them as partial answers to the failures of the movements of the 1960s.

A second major source of radical insights has been the ecology movement which is also rarely seen as truly radical in the sense of challenging existing social structures and established political power. Nevertheless, ecological understanding has informed and will continue to inform radical activism of the future: first, because it offers a critique of modern industrial capitalism that, potentially at least, can have broad popular appeal; secondly, because it provides a set of common concerns that can bring together social change efforts that cross racial, class and national lines; and thirdly, because ecological consciousness has led to important internal criticism of the limitations of ideological awareness derived from the interests of particular classes, races, or nationalities.

A final source of radical insights for the future has been the women's liberation movement of the period since the late 1960s. Again, not all elements in the modern women's liberation movement have been radical, but the feminist critique of patriarchy has profoundly informed African-American political thought as it has informed all significant movements for social change of the past twenty years. Indeed, I would argue that feminist insights are at the heart of whatever African-American radicalism has endured since the decline of black militancy after the 1960s.

African-American feminism has incorporated the central elements of the truly radical ideas that emerged from the mass movements of the early 1960s. These include an acceptance of the notion expressed in C. L. R. James's 1957 letter that Gandhian non-violence offered a revolutionary challenge to the existing order because it provided a means for mass involvement in social change movements. Black feminist activists have also incorporated into their political understanding SNCC's approach to community organizing. The notion of organizing as the development or nurturing of the abilities of others converged with the radical feminist notion that distinctive gender-based values should be at the heart of efforts to transform society. Radical feminist political thought has also, for the most part, avoided the romanticization of revolutionary violence that stifled the development of African-American militancy during the late 1960s, offering instead the notion that political organizing involves the encouragement of enduring grassroots leadership.

What Ella Barker has called group-centred leadership avoids the egocentrism that has often distorted leader-centred, male-dominated Marxian and black nationalist politics. Such political activism is the most enduring form of political activity because it provides the best means for transmitting radical values from one generation to the next.

In conclusion, rethinking African-American political thought involves a recognition that the late 1960s did not mark the culmination of radicalism but was, rather, a brief detour that has prevented us from recognizing the true inheritors of the legacy of the black freedom struggle. Future African-American politics will no longer be strictly defined by racial identity. It will instead be defined by its ability to incorporate radical insights drawn from movements that have thrived even as black militancy has declined. Future African-American radicalism will be feminist and informed by ecological consciousness and modern insights about individual psychology; it will also draw upon older traditions of social gospel Christian and Gandhian non-violence. It will therefore be eclectic in its radicalism or it will not be radical at all.

NOTES

1. C. L. R. James to 'Friends', 25 March 1957, Martin and Jessie Glaberman Collection, Archives of Labor and Urban Affairs, Wayne State University.
2. Martin Luther King, Jr, *Stride Toward Freedom: The Montgomery Story* (New York, 1958), p.94.
3. King, *Stride Toward Freedom*, p. 97.
4. James Lawson, 'Eve of Nonviolent Revolution?', *Southern Patriot*, November 1961, p. 1.
5. Ella Baker, 'Bigger than a Hamburger', *Southern Patriot*, May 1960, p. 4; author's interview with Baker, 5 May 1972.

6. See, Clayborne Carson, *Malcolm X: The FBI File* (New York, 1991), pp. 29, 203–4.

7. George Breitman, ed., *Malcolm X Speaks: Selected Speeches and Statements* (New York, 1965), p. 38.

8. Clayborne Carson, *In Struggle: SNCC and the Black Awakening of the 1960s* (Cambridge, Mass., 1981), p. 135.

9. Coretta Scott King, *My Life with Martin Luther King, Jr* (New York, 1969; revised edn, 1993), p. 238.

Part III

Representations

7 From Shiloh to Selma: The Impact of the Civil War Centennial on the Black Freedom Struggle in the United States, 1961–65

Robert Cook

Recent works by political and cultural historians, sociologists and theologians on the thought and strategy of the civil rights movement have greatly enhanced our understanding of twentieth-century America's most vibrant social movement. Focusing particularly on the role of the black church and external influences ranging from Mohandas K. Gandhi to Frantz Fanon, such studies have highlighted the diverse cultural and ideological context in which movement leaders and organizations operated. Surprisingly few scholars, however, have investigated the way mainstream civil rights leaders used the commonplace rhetoric and mnemonic baggage of American nationalism to advance their cause. One notable exception is Alan Manis's study of civil religion in the South during the 1950s. Black and white southerners, he argues, possessed their own variants of America's civil religion which they utilized in order to pursue diametrically opposite goals in the era of massive resistance. Whereas southern white Baptists fell back on the Lost Cause and strict construction of the Constitution to defend segregation, their black counterparts in the National Baptist Convention deployed a rich array of patriotic symbols and rituals to assert their citizenship rights and depict their white opponents as un-American. This essay seeks to build on Manis's observations by investigating the impact of the Civil War centennial on the black freedom struggle during the early 1960s, a period when the tensions inherent within American cultural nationalism were exposed for all the world to see.[1]

Manis concludes his analysis in 1957. In September of that year President Dwight D. Eisenhower signed into law a joint congressional resolution establishing a national body to oversee commemoration of America's greatest catastrophe. The US Civil War Centennial Commission (USCC) received executive backing three and a half years before the one hundredth anniversary of the assault on Fort Sumter which began what southerners liked to call the War between the States. The commission was empowered to direct and coordinate all centennial activities across the nation in conjunction with similar state committees and the National Park Service (NPS), itself engaged in a costly programme to improve important Civil War sites.[2]

Commemoration of America's bloodiest conflict began in earnest on 8 January 1961, nearly a year after the student sit-ins had rocked the nation and only days before a new president, John F. Kennedy, was inaugurated. The ceremonies, masterminded by the USCC, began with a wreath-laying service at the tomb of Ulysses S. Grant in New York City. Flurries of snow whipped across the face of the attendant troops as they listened to speeches from, among others, a grandson of the great Union general, and to patriotic music played by a band from the US military academy at West Point.[3]

Other events followed in quick succession. A week-long commemoration of the founding of the Confederate government began in Montgomery, Alabama, the first capital of the southern nation, on 12 February. A glitzy centennial ball was held in Atlanta on 9 March. Hollywood star Olivia de Haviland, the original Miss Melanie, rode down Peachtree Avenue in an open-top convertible prior to a special anniversary showing of *Gone With the Wind*. In April attention shifted to Charleston, South Carolina. The Confederate bombardment of Fort Sumter was marked by a full-dress pageant through the streets and a spectacular rocket display over the ruined naval base.[4]

In July, 70 000 spectators (the bulk of them southerners) watched a re-enactment of Bull Run, the first set-piece battle of the Civil War. Some of them had paid as much as $4 for a seat in the uncovered grandstand and many were felled by the scorching heat. Those who survived the ordeal heard a narrator describe every regimental manoeuvre and cannon-shot over loudspeakers. They yelled deliriously as the boys in grey chased the Yankees from the field, just as their ancestors had done exactly a century before. Behind the grandstand serried ranks of tents offered for sale Civil War literature, souvenirs, hot dogs, soft drinks and flavoured ices. One newspaper noted that the three-day spectacular had cost 170 000 dollars to stage.[5]

While the spring and summer of 1961 marked the highpoint of the centennial, the national and state commissions established to commemorate the occasion continued to stage events at regular intervals during the early 1960s. In September 1962, the normally peaceful Maryland countryside echoed to the sound of gunfire once again as 20 000 men re-enacted the bloody battle of Antietam. The following year witnessed a battlefield mass at Gettysburg and a repeat performance of Pickett's charge, the famous assault on federal lines which had done much to seal the fate of the Confederacy.[6]

Gettysburg was also the scene of a three-day ceremony in November 1963 to mark the hundredth anniversary of Lincoln's dedicatory address at the town's military cemetery. US Secretary of State Dean Rusk reminded a local audience that Lincoln was the author of the preliminary Emancipation Proclamation of September 1862 which had declared free all slaves living beyond Union lines. A commitment to freedom, he noted with all the subtlety of a Cold War warrior, was America's main weapon in the country's fight against totalitarianism throughout the world. Interest in re-enacting the events of the past declined after this, but there was still time for a commemoration of the Confederate surrender at Appomattox in Virginia in April 1865. Around 5000 people gathered under sombre skies to watch a marine corps band play period tunes and a ceremony to mark the opening of the reconstructed court house at which the historic surrender had taken place.[7]

What, then, was the significance of these events for the ongoing struggle for black equality in the United States? One way to answer this question is to investigate the very different cultural and political agendas possessed by the important parties in that struggle: the federal government, the white South and the civil rights movement. Each of these parties espoused its own version of the American civil religion and each would attempt to use the centennial for its own ends.

While federal officials might have been forgiven for having mixed feelings about the approach of the centennial, the prospect of enticing thousands of domestic tourists to the nation's historic sites was an attractive one. Middle-class Americans during the 1950s were spending an increasing proportion of their surplus wealth on travel and the National Park Service, bulwark of the nation's heritage industry, was determined to upgrade its properties in anticipation of Civil War mania. The NPS budget for fiscal 1958 included money for the construction of a new visitors' centre and park headquarters at Gettysburg which was already receiving a million tourists every year. $100 000 were earmarked for restoration of buildings at Harper's Ferry, scene of John Brown's abortive attempt to spark off a slave insurrection in October 1859. The lure of commercial profit was thus a prime factor in the federal government's decision to commemorate the centenary.[8]

Equally significant, however, was a genuine conviction on the part of federal officials that the centennial should have an educative function. There was no pressing need to build a new visitors' centre at Gettysburg if all the government wanted to do was license entrepreneurs to sell hot dogs to trippers wandering over the battlefield. To some extent Washington was responding to public demand for information about the central event in America's development as a nation. As the southern writer Robert Penn Warren insisted in his reflections on the centennial, it was the Civil War, not the Revolution, that had laid the foundations for the superpower of the present. The conflagration of the 1860s was, claimed Warren in a faintly Lincolnian phrase, 'that mystic cloud from which emerged our modernity'. But while Americans were keen to learn more about their past in another age of acute structural change, their government was similarly determined that its citizens should be taught about the critical event in the republic's past. The problem was, what to teach them?[9]

At issue here was the very meaning of the Civil War. For a national government fighting communism abroad and cognizant of growing racial friction at home, the centennial appeared to present an ideal opportunity to remind Americans that the internecine carnage of the nineteenth century had finally brought them together after decades of sectional strife over slavery and its expansion. The central theme, which the government sought, not surprisingly, to emphasise was the very orthodox one of unity. The dead of Shiloh and the Wilderness had not died in vain; far from it – their sacrifices had saved the Union from destruction and thereby paved the way for the accomplishments of the twentieth century.

President Eisenhower signalled this message to the nation in December 1959. In a statement issued to mourn the passing of the last surviving Civil War veteran, Walter Williams of Houston, Eisenhower observed that: '[t]he wounds of the deep and bitter dispute which once divided our nation have long since healed, and a united America in a divided world now holds up on a larger canvas the traditions of liberty and justice for all.' Replicating a theme that had its roots at least as far back as Lincoln's Gettysburg Address, the president underlined his point by referring specifically to the Civil War as the War between the States and noting that with Williams's death 'the hosts of Blue and Grey who were the chief actors in that great and tragic drama a century ago have all passed from the world stage. No longer are they the Blue and Grey. All rest together as Americans in honored glory'.[10]

Members of the USCC strove to propagate the notion that there had been no losers in 1861–5; that everyone had gained as a result of sectional reconciliation between North and South. At the opening ceremonies in New York City in January 1961, the commission's chairman, Major-General Ulysses S. Grant III, insisted that the war's prime historical import lay in the fact that, 'the country was able to reunite itself after four years of strife'. Unity, then, was the overarching theme during the opening phase of the centennial, but unity was an increasingly illusory objective during America's civil rights years.[11]

Northerners and southerners had united in Congress to vote the funds necessary for a national commission to oversee the anniversary. Little controversy had been elicited by the measure – the main debate in the House of Representatives took place over the amount of taxpayers' money to be devoted to this body. Significantly it was a southerner, William Tuck of Virginia, who advocated the most liberal proposition: $100 000 per year to be spent on the commission for the duration of the centennial. Perceptive observers might have thought it rather strange that Tuck, a conservative Democrat from Southside, Virginia, and close ally of Senator Harry Byrd, should have supported federal funding on this scale. The Byrd machine in Richmond was wedded to traditional notions of careful housekeeping and states' rights and was strongly opposed to federal intervention in racial matters south of the Mason-Dixon line.[12]

Why did opponents of central government support relatively generous funding for the centennial commission? The answer lies in the Civil War's importance to the southern psyche and specifically in its centrality to the region's rearguard defence of the caste system. Although the South had lost the war, the events of 1861–5 continued to impinge heavily on the minds of white southerners long after Appomattox. For many of them, defeat in the war helped to explain why their region remained so much poorer, so much less modern, than the rest of the country. It gave them, in Robert Penn Warren's words, 'the Great Alibi'. More than that, though, the war presented southern whites with a treasure trove of military heroes – men like Jeb Stuart who had run rings around McClellan in 1862 and the saintly Robert E. Lee who had preferred to fight for his state, Virginia, rather than accept a commission in the Union army. Whereas the presentist North had begun to forget about the war by the end of the nineteenth century, southerners remained wedded to tales of derring-do and defence of the homeland throughout the opening decades of the twentieth. Advocates of a New South built on diversified agriculture and industrial capitalism repeatedly found their efforts hampered by the myth of the Lost Cause. This had been as true in the 1880s and 1920s as it was in the 1950s, but the difference was that as the centennial approached the South really was beginning to change. As the old plantation economy based on cheap labour and cotton was being replaced by a modern society grounded in agribusiness, defence plants and service industries, the economically outmoded caste system was coming under increasing attack from within and without. A large section of the white population saw their status, their culture, their identity being undermined, and they turned instinctively to their own variant of America's civil religion for psychological sustenance.[13]

The centennial, therefore, gave segregationists the perfect opportunity to celebrate what they saw as their unique heritage. The Reverend John Morris of Atlanta was quick to spot why southerners were so keen to celebrate the centennial. Sensing the amount of coverage that the latter was receiving in the local press, he noted in June 1959 that the observances would be used for 'sounding off on present-day issues more than for commemorating a bygone event. The passions that brought forth the war between Americans are not dead and will only be exploited by many who are still grieving that the South failed to win'. Exploitation was certainly the name of the game as pragmatic politicians, seeking sure-fire issues with which to mobilize the voters, fell over themselves to prove not only their opposition to integration, but also their devotion to the values for which their forefathers had died in the 1860s. Failure to do so could mean political death – hence the substantial spending ($2 million by dirt-poor Mississippi alone) by southern states on their own centennial commissions and the impressive turnout at centennial events by racist demagogues who understood the value of political theatre at a time when federal intervention was eroding their own power to maintain the caste system.[14]

The beginning of the student phase of the civil rights movement in March 1960 intensified white opposition to integration. The Confederate flag became the primary symbol of resistance to federal authority and equal rights throughout the South, and with this any hope that the centennial could be used to strengthen national unity evaporated completely. At Richmond on 4 February 1961 Governor J. Lindsay Almond of Virginia, a moderate Democrat seeking to regain lost credibility after acquiescing in token school integration in 1959, used the hundredth anniversary of his state's call for a peace conference to draw a parallel between the Civil War and the current struggle for home rule. Insisting that Virginia would continue to lead the fight for 'the preservation of the rights of the States under and through the Constitution of the United States', Almond used the anti-abolitionist rhetoric of the 1850s to condemn the activities of civil rights activists. 'It has unfortunately been the course of our history', he said, 'that men have raised false issues which could influence the minds and stir the emotions instead of exercising constructive leadership in the effort to mould common opinion in support of that which is best for the nations of the world.' Almond was not exactly advocating secession, but he was insistent that the United States could not fight communism effectively if liberal do-gooders and Negroes continued to undermine the fabric of society in the loyal South.[15]

Civil rights activists had no doubt that segregationists were seeking to deploy the centennial as a weapon in their ideological and political assault on the movement. Lawrence Reddick, a black educator close to Martin Luther King, said in April 1961 that the centennial was being used to perpetuate the Confederate 'myth'. That myth, he insisted, was 'part of the psychological and political resistance' to Negro rights and he called for the burning of all Confederate symbols. Dismissed from his post at Alabama State College for supporting student protests, Reddick insisted that the South's view of the Civil War should be exposed 'for the unhistorical romance much of it is', and he called on President Kennedy to issue 'a positive statement on the centennial, on what it means to the nation, requesting our mass media of communication to so portray it, and calling our people to so examine and honour it throughout the land'.[16]

Reddick's reference to 'a positive statement' on the meaning of the centennial indicated that civil rights advocates had their own interpretation of the War of the Rebellion. Central to this picture was the notion that the critical event of the conflict had been the North's decision to liberate the slaves. This verdict was not entirely unique to the 1960s – Frederick Douglass had striven to popularize it in the postbellum era – but the government's emphasis on sectional reconciliation frustrated African-Americans in their confrontation with the white South. Mainstream black leaders and organizations wanted the national government to take their side in this struggle, just as it had done a century before. Their basic contention was that the North's victory in 1865 had to be adjudged incomplete because southern blacks remained second class citizens. Fervently loyal and integrationist, they urged the federal government to finish the job that had been started in 1862. It was not only white southerners who welcomed the centennial as a chance to fight the Civil War all over again.[17]

Reddick's suggestion that the national media should emphasize emancipation and southern defeat fell on deaf ears. The American media were desperately worried that advertisers would boycott any programme that tried to analyse the complexities of the Civil War. There was no getting away from the fact that the conflict had involved race and that ultimately the Confederacy had suffered a devastating defeat. White southern sensibilities must not be offended and an intelligent US documentary series on the war had to wait until 1989 (and even then one of its principal guides was a silver-tongued Mississippian named Shelby Foote). Some liberal historians like Bruce Catton, author of the best-selling *Centennial History of the American Civil War*, did try to explain the sensitive racial dimensions of the conflict but in general the public appeared to be more interested in sham battles than home truths. Only the unfolding crisis of the 1960s offered progressives the chance to use the centennial to promote civil rights in the present.[18]

Conflicting objectives met head-on in Charleston, South Carolina, in April 1961. The USCC had scheduled its annual gathering to coincide with a grand re-enactment of the Confederate bombardment of Fort Sumter. Unfortunately for the Commission, ever keen to draw the most anodyne lessons possible from the war, the New Jersey state centennial commission opted to send a black delegate to the national convention. A political storm broke when it became apparent that Madeline Williams would not be accommodated with the other delegates in Charleston's Francis Marion hotel. Municipal regulations mandated segregated facilities and the city fathers were in no mood to have local customs infringed at a time when they were confronting growing black unrest in their own backyard.[19]

The New Jerseyans were furious and immediately announced that they would not be attending the national convention: *de jure* segregation was a thing of the past in the North-East and Williams was an American citizen entitled to equal treatment with other delegates. Other northern state commissions, among them New York's, then joined New Jersey in boycotting the Fort Sumter gathering. Bruce Catton, a member of the New York commission, was quoted as saying that his state 'would have been awfully hesitant to send a delegation to a place where one member was not invited. We have firm convictions about what came out of the war'.[20]

The concerted response of the northern state centennial commissions to the news from Charleston was mirrored by that of the NAACP. Frequently belittled by historians as a player in the central phase of the freedom struggle, the NAACP had long sought to use cultural nationalism as a weapon in the fight against segregation, notably by using that temple of America's civil religion, the Lincoln Memorial in Washington, to emphasize the legitimacy of black demands. Efforts by southern whites to take possession of the centennial rapidly induced NAACP leaders to contest the event. As early as January 1960 Henry Lee Moon, director of public relations, suggested that the organization should make a formal approach to the USCC 'for adequate and integrated presentation of the Negro throughout the observance'. Predictably, the attempt to segregate proceedings at Fort Sumter drew a rapid response from NAACP headquarters in New York. On 17 March the latter called on its branches across the country to promote the boycott of the Fort Sumter observances. A segregated gathering, it was averred, would be 'a betrayal of everything the Civil War was fought for.'[21]

The USCC's initial response was to stand its ground. Even a request by John F. Kennedy that all delegates to the Fort Sumter gathering should receive equal treatment was rebuffed. Bill Tuck of the USCC, no friend of the new president, issued an impassioned statement on 21 March in which he insisted that the Commission's objective was to alert Americans to the lessons gained from 'our great war of the sixties, acknowledged to have been one of the costliest of [*sic*] record and yet, from the standpoint of our American unity of today, one of the most rewarding'. The basic law under which the Commission was created, he said, gave it no power to interfere with the activities of local groups.[22]

Although Tuck's views encapsulated the commission's basic lack of sympathy with civil rights, northern liberals responded angrily to the controversy. Governors Otto Kerner of Illinois and Richard Hughes of New Jersey denounced the commission's supine behaviour as outrageous and Roy Wilkins, head of the NAACP, insisted that Tuck and his colleagues had full jurisdiction over its own meeting places and policies. Reluctant to be labelled an ally of segregation, Kennedy intervened once again, this time to insist that as a federally funded body the USCC must find a solution that would accord equal treatment to black delegates under the Constitution. This was enough for the commission's chairman, Ulysses S. Grant, who announced on 25 March that his organization would hold its meeting at the desegregated US naval station outside Charleston. The New Jerseyans then declared themselves satisfied with this compromise with even Madeline Williams suggesting that it had wrought 'a victory for the democratic process in America'.[23]

The second battle of Fort Sumter revealed a great deal about the condition of American race relations one hundred years on from the opening of the Civil War. Notwithstanding the South's crushing defeat in that conflict or the more recent actions of an increasingly radical civil rights movement, the southern caste system remained largely intact. Removing the national meeting of the USCC to a military base that was not subject to state law merely sidestepped the problem. Kennedy, of course, was well aware of this fact, but early in 1961 he had no desire to alienate the southern wing of the Democratic party by launching a frontal attack on segregation. Nevertheless he knew the significance of symbolic gestures and he was at least signalling his distaste for Jim Crow (something that Eisenhower had seldom done). The controversy was also significant not only because it highlighted the connection between the centennial and the contemporary struggle for civil rights, but also because it brought northern whites closer to the movement's interpretation of the country's past. Writing in *The Nation*, the Yale historian L. Jesse Lemisch insisted that the centennial was 'a surrender to the South' and urged Americans to 'condemn theatrics which conceal the real issues of the Civil War'.[24]

The notion, popularized by Roy Wilkins and others, that the business of the Civil War remained unfinished grew more popular by the day. As Americans enjoyed the various commemorative events of the spring and summer of 1961, the pace of domestic protest against the caste system began to quicken. In May, CORE launched its freedom ride through the Deep South – a brazen attempt to secure federal intervention on the side of the civil rights movement. Battered and bloodied by southern mobs, the riders succeeded in heightening northerners' awareness of the violence inherent in the caste system. Ex-President Harry Truman was one of the few whose consciousness was not raised by the burning of buses and pummelling of defenceless civil rights activists. Likening the freedom riders to the abolitionists who had played their part in bringing on the Civil War, he insisted that northerners should stay at home and attend to their own affairs.[25]

By this time concerns about the centennial were beginning to grow. Former US Secretary of State and South Carolina governor James F. Byrnes articulated the feeling of a growing number of southerners when he suggested that it would be impossible to relive the Civil War without reawakening many of the sectional and racial passions engendered by the original conflict. Some Americans were sickened by the spectacle of paying spectators whooping it up at Bull Run, the site of more than a thousand deaths in July 1861. The whole thing, wrote one observer, was 'a grisly pantomime' which caused the public 'to overlook those grievous imbalances and necessities in our body politic which, one hundred years ago, made the outbreak of violence a tragic but necessary preliminary to the arduous reconstitution of our society'. Responding to liberal criticism of the centennial proceedings President Kennedy appointed a black military aide to the USCC in September

1961. Shortly afterwards the centennial commission lost its two leading officials, Karl Betts and Major-General Grant, both of them victims of the adverse publicity surrounding the events at Fort Sumter and Bull Run. Kennedy then turned to one of the country's most respected Civil War historians, Alan Nevins, to head the USCC. Nevins immediately announced that there would be no basic change of policy. '[A]bove all,' he told a press conference, 'our central theme will be unity, not division . . . We shall allow the just pride of no national group to be belittled or besmirched.'[26]

Although the civil rights forces remained preoccupied with voter registration and desegregation campaigns in the Deep South, key figures in the NAACP, the SCLC and supporting white organizations were determined to exploit the centennial for their own ends. Vital to their plans was the forthcoming anniversary of the preliminary Emancipation Proclamation, issued by Lincoln as a war measure shortly after Second Manassas. Nevins announced in March 1962 that the USCC would organize a special event in Washington to mark the occasion, the first sign that the commission had begun to alter its posture even though it was not yet prepared to climb down off the fence. More important than the ceremony itself, however, was the fact that the anniversary of the Emancipation Proclamation gave the civil rights movement an opportunity to seize the centennial high ground. While the first year of the commemoration had given southern whites a chance to reassert their identity by participating in secession day parades and re-enacting the Confederate triumph at Bull Run, the second opened up possibilities for their opponents. For the fact was that in 1862 the federal government had been forced to accept the linkage between slavery and civil war by undermining the property rights of rebel slaveholders. Here then was a chance for black citizens in the mid-twentieth century to celebrate their historic loyalty to the Union and to intensify their efforts to promote reform.[27]

Martin Luther King was the most effective interpreter of the past to white Americans within the ranks of the civil rights movement. He used the nation's heritage to shame the government and the people into living up to their fine ideals. References to the glittering promises of the Declaration of Independence as well as to patriotic songs like 'America, the Beautiful' and 'The Battle Hymn of the Republic' littered his speeches. Not only did these familiar references ground him solidly in the nation's liberal tradition (making him appear less threatening to whites), but they also gnawed away at the liberal conscience by emphasizing the historic role of blacks as testers of the American dream. Combined with the violent response of segregationists to the sit-ins and freedom rides, King's eloquent attempts to blend past and present helped to shake the nation from its torpor.[28]

As the centenary of the Emancipation Proclamation approached, progressive forces across America pressed home the idea that it was time for the country to make good the promises of the Civil War era. In June 1962 Protestant, Catholic and Jewish leaders announced that they would aim to bring the moral force of the church and synagogue to bear against the problem of segregation by celebrating the formal signing of the emancipation document in 1863. The same month witnessed a call by the American Veterans Committee, a stalwart member of the Leadership Conference on Civil Rights, for President Kennedy to issue an emancipation proclamation of his own. Hopes were high among blacks and liberal whites that Kennedy would seize the opportunity to draft an executive order promoting open housing throughout the nation.[29]

It was left to King to ram this pressure home. In September 1962, nine days before the USCC was due to hold its own event in Washington, the Atlanta minister spoke at a dinner given by the New York centennial commission to commemorate the issuing of the preliminary Emancipation Proclamation. In attendance were 200 invited guests including the state's liberal Republican governor, Nelson Rockefeller. Also on hand was a draft copy of Lincoln's famous edict (the original having been destroyed in the great Chicago fire of 1871).[30]

King began his speech with a blistering description of the South as 'an autonomous region whose posture toward the central government has elements as defiant as a hostile nation'. Only the underdeveloped or primitive nations of the world', he continued, 'tolerate regions which are similar, in which feudal autocrats or military governors have supremacy over the Federal power. It is a condition unknown to modern industrial societies except our own.' Having ridiculed the persistence of nineteenth-century federalism in contemporary America, King went on to laud the Emancipation Proclamation not only for empowering blacks, but also as an illustration of federal strength. Although he conceded Lincoln's ambivalent racial views, he insisted that only truly great presidents were tortured deep in their hearts over this issue. 'No president', averred King pointedly, 'can be great, or even fit for office, if he attempts to accommodate to injustice to maintain his political balance.'[31]

Significantly, King's use of the centennial to cajole President Kennedy into a greater measure of federal intervention in the South went down well with his distinguished audience. Governor Rockefeller endorsed his views, saying that the country was fortunate that King was an advocate of nonviolence and that the struggle for equality was 'the great unfinished business before the American people'.[32]

Just how unfinished the business was became clear when the USCC found itself embroiled in yet another controversy of its own making. No sooner had it announced details of the emancipation commemoration in Washington than Bishop Smallwood Williams, president of the local affiliate of King's SCLC, announced a boycott of the event. Insensitively the commission had drawn up an all-white list of speakers for the observances scheduled to take place at the Lincoln Memorial on 22 September. Mahalia Jackson, the black soprano, was booked to perform and the Marine Corps band had been preparing to play a new work by a young black composer. The arrangements, however, clearly smacked of tokenism – too many whites on the commission were still fearful of ruffling southern sensibilities or held racist views about black capabilities. The SCLC's boycott was a clear indication that African-Americans were now demanding full equality within domestic society, not just a place on the sidelines.[33]

The new controversy led to a hastily arranged meeting between USCC members, black leaders and representatives from the justice department. The result was an agreement to seat blacks on the platform and include a black speaker in the programme. Although US Ambassador to the United Nations Adlai Stevenson was retained as the keynote speaker, the respected black lawyer, Thurgood Marshall, found his name added to the list of orators. Marshall was not the most radical black man in America by 1962, but he had a long record as a brave and effective civil rights activist and had recently been appointed a federal district judge. His inclusion in the programme was a victory of sorts for the movement.[34]

The observances to mark the centenary of emancipation have long been overshadowed by the March on Washington the following summer. Certainly, there was nothing on 22 September 1962 to match King's magnificent 'I Have a Dream' speech. Yet there was abundant evidence that the interracial, bipartisan coalition so much in evidence during the March, had begun to take shape the previous year. Spectators of both races listened attentively to the speeches before French's brooding marble statue of the Great Emancipator. Perhaps the most important of those speeches was a recorded address by the president himself. Although Kennedy chose not to mark the occasion by issuing an executive order or attending in person, he was represented by his brother Robert, the Attorney General. His words, moreover, bore the imprint of the year's civil rights struggles. Referring specifically to the abolition of 'the evil of human slavery', Kennedy went out of his way to stress that while blacks had fought tirelessly for their liberties over the past one hundred years, the task begun by his Republican predecessor was not yet finished:

> Much remains to be done to eradicate the vestiges of discrimination and segregation, to make equal rights a reality for all of our people, to fulfil finally the promises of the Declaration of Independence. Like the proclamation we celebrate, this observance must be regarded not as an end, but a beginning. The best commemoration lies not in what we say today, but in what we do in the days and months ahead to complete the work begun . . . a century ago.[35]

Civil rights activists took Kennedy at his word. Over the next nine months they redoubled their efforts to outlaw *de jure* segregation in the United States. In Mississippi workers belonging to SNCC continued their efforts to promote voter registration in that benighted state. Further east, in Birmingham, Alabama, the SCLC's campaign of marches, demonstrations and boycotts resulted in unprecedented media coverage of the civil rights movement. No American could ignore TV images of innocent black children being viciously attacked by the local white police. Kennedy himself went on air to pledge his support for the aims of the demonstrators and announced that he would be sending a tough new civil rights bill to Congress. Battles in the streets, growing sectional antagonism and decisive federal intervention in state affairs: it was, as Jimmy Byrnes had feared, like the Civil War all over again.

And in the midst of it all the centennial observances continued. The last major set-piece of the four-year heritage bonanza took place at Gettysburg in July 1963, shortly after Kennedy's dramatic address to the nation. The main event was a rerun of Pickett's famous charge against federal lines – the high water-mark of the Confederacy – but for proponents and opponents of civil rights the anniversary of the greatest battle in American history presented them with yet another opportunity to state their case. Several events preceded the battle re-enactment. Presiding over a special battlefield mass, Father Theodore Hesburgh, the president of Notre Dame University, condemned '[t]he appalling dearth of freedom for millions of Negro Americans . . .' Ex-president Eisenhower, now resident in Gettysburg, delivered a predictably conservative speech to the local fire company in which he warned against the dangers of an interventionist federal government. Lincoln, he insisted, had been a supporter of self-government, not statism. Governor George Wallace of Alabama, a man used to fighting his own sham battles with central government officials, would have agreed. He attended a wreath-laying ceremony at the monument to the Alabama dead and declared, 'This is a solemn occasion. We stand among the descendants of brave men who fought for North and South and we will stand for defence of the Constitution of the United States.'[36]

For the moment, however, the initiative had passed to the opponents of states' rights and segregation. Liberal northern politicians, responsive to the progressive shift in public opinion, descended on the Pennsylvania countryside to express their support for civil rights. Many of them did so in no uncertain terms. Governor Richard Hughes of New Jersey told a gathering at the monument to the fallen from his state that the parallels between the 1860s and 1960s were inescapable. Those northerners who had perished in the three-day battle would not rest, he insisted, until the cause for which they fought was 'liquidated'. The Republican governor of Pennsylvania, William Scranton, was less inclined to indulge his sectional prejudices, but he too predicted that in the days ahead the nation would 'be sorely pressed to learn the lessons learned at great expense during the Civil War'. Among those, he suggested, was 'the task of driving prejudice out of the human heart at least as rapidly as we are learning to drive men into outer space'. Not for the first time were white Americans beginning to conclude that the nation's moral sense had begun to lag behind the republic's technological achievements.[37]

By mid-1963 a consensus had developed around the conviction that blacks were entitled to full equality before the law. Just as the military demands of the Civil War had prompted nineteenth-century northerners to concede freedom to the slaves (as well as accept blacks into the Union army), the civil rights movement had induced their descendants to take a stand against the legal supports of the southern caste system. Just as abolitionists had sought to exploit the promises enshrined in the Declaration of Independence, their intellectual successors had used the events of the centennial to raise the consciousness of the American public in the 1960s. The civil rights movement did not have the most accurate grasp of the complexities of history, but this was equally true of the government and the white South. To some extent it did not really matter. What counted was the fact that by 1963 the movement's own version of America's civil religion had come to predominate over the orthodox and southern variants discussed above. The remarkably brave activities of movement workers and the violent response of southern whites had done most to bring about this state of affairs. However, the centennial acted as more than just a backcloth for the dramatic events of the early 1960s. In a very real sense the Civil War was part of the intellectual fabric of the civil rights crusade. By interpreting and exploiting the past as they did, black leaders like Martin Luther King and Roy Wilkins contributed to what sociologists have called the 'cognitive praxis' of the black freedom struggle.[38]

Interest in the centennial waned after 1963. There were several reasons for this. Firstly, embattled white southerners had little interest in re-enacting the kind of long drawn out offensives which had finally destroyed the Confederacy in 1864–5. Secondly, as the innocence of the early 1960s began to yield to a mood of growing cynicism, Americans in general abandoned sham battles in order to mourn the death of their own martyred president, Jack Kennedy, and to monitor the country's burgeoning military involvement in South-East Asia. By the end of 1964 they already had a body-count of their own without having to reflect on the tens of thousands who had perished in the murderous Atlanta and Wilderness campaigns. Thirdly, the civil rights movement itself found it could make less use of black civil religion by 1965. The previous year had seen angry SNCC and CORE workers rail against the failure of the federal government to protect them during the Mississippi Freedom Summer and the sell-out of southern blacks at the Democratic convention in Atlantic City. Increasingly their commitment was to a radical reinterpretation of the black experience in America, not a restatement of the old verities. 1965 saw preparations begin for the SCLC's campaign to undermine *de facto* segregation in the North. The Movement, then, had begun to look beyond Jim Crow to integrated neighbourhoods, reinvigoration of the inner cities and good, well paying jobs. There was little precedent for any of these demands in the Civil War era and, while mainstream leaders retained, for the moment, their faith in federal intervention, they made less use of the nation's plastic past to achieve their objectives.

By the time it came to commemorate the end of the Civil War at Appomattox Court House in Virginia in April 1965, little national interest in the centennial remained. One reporter at the low-key ceremony at the restored county court house noted that only around 5000 people were in attendance, mostly unrepentant whites who burst into applause when the band broke into Dixie. The same journalist found that local whites and blacks were still leading separate lives and that the former were bitter at the Johnson administration's perceived betrayal of them. A white druggist, however, insisted that race relations in the area were good. 'We've never had any trouble at all,' he was quoted as saying. 'It's only when you have the Northern agitators come in, with their Communist supporters, that you have trouble.' The black community's oldest inhabitant, Scott Palmer, a descendant of slaves, remained philosophical. Interrogated about the changes that had taken place over the past few years, he smiled toothlessly and said, 'Oh, they's about the same, about the same. Human nature don't change.' For all its achievements the civil rights movement still had a very long way to go.[39]

NOTES

1. A. M. Manis, *Southern Civil Rights in Conflict: Black and White Baptists and Civil Rights, 1947–1957* (Athens, 1987).
2. *New York Times*, 9 June 1957, X, p. 13, and 7 September 1957, pp. 1, 46.
3. Ibid., 9 January 1961, pp. 1, 23.
4. Ibid., 13 February 1961, p. 27; ibid., 10 March 1961, p. 29; ibid., 13 April 1961, pp. 1, 25.
5. Ibid., 23 July 1961, I, p. 1, 44; ibid., 24 July 1961, p. 8.
6. Ibid., 16 September 1962, I, p. 86; ibid., 30 June 1963, I, p. 39; ibid., 4 July 1963, I, p. 7.
7. Ibid., 18 November 1963, p. 47; ibid., 10 April 1965, p. 30.
8. Ibid., 9 June 1957, X, p. 13.
9. R. P. Warren, *The Legacy of the Civil War: Meditations on the Centennial* (New York, 1964), p. 46.
10. *Public Papers of the Presidents of the United States: Dwight D. Eisenhower, 1959* (Washington, DC, 1960), pp. 864–5.
11. *New York Times*, 9 January 1961, pp. 1, 23.
12. Ibid., 9 June 1957, X, p. 13; W. B. Crawley Jr, *Bill Tuck: A Political Life in Harry Byrd's Virginia* (Charlottesville, 1978).
13. Warren, *Legacy*, p. 54. The literature on post-war change in the South is enormous

but P. Daniel, *Standing at the Crossroads: Southern Life since 1900* (New York, 1986) is a useful introduction.

14. *New York Times*, 7 June 1959, IV, p. 10; ibid., 6 April 1961, p. 34.
15. Ibid., 5 February 1961, I, p. 45. On Almond's surprise conversion to token integration see J. W. Ely Jr, *The Crisis of Conservative Virginia: The Byrd Organization and the Politics of Massive Resistance* (Knoxville, 1976), pp. 122– 43.
16. Ibid., 23 April 1961, I, p. 74.
17. S. Sandage, 'A Marble House Divided: The Lincoln Memorial, the Civil Rights Movement, and the Politics of Memory, 1939–1963', *Journal of American History*, 80 (June 1993), 139, notes Douglass's attempts 'to construct a usable public memory of Lincoln' by dedicating a statue to the Great Emancipator in Washington, DC in 1876.
18. B. Catton, 'Where the Great Change Took Place', *New York Times Magazine*, 5 February 1961, pp. 11, 68–9.
19. *New York Times*, 10 March 1961, p. 29.
20. Ibid.
21. Sandage, 'Marble House Divided', pp. 144, 153– 4; H. L. Moon to R. Wilkins, 26 January 1960, General Office File, Box A76, Group 3, NAACP Papers, Library of Congress.
22. *New York Times*, 18 March 1961, pp. 1, 8; ibid., 22 March 1961, p. 34.
23. Ibid., 24 March 1961, p. 26; ibid., 26 March 1961, I, pp. 1, 72.
24. Kennedy's reliance on symbolic gestures is noted by M. Stern, *Calculating Visions: Kennedy, Johnson, and Civil Rights* (New Brunswick: 1992), p. 53; *New York Times*, 27 March 1961, p. 30.
25. Ibid., 3 June 1961, p. 18.
26. Ibid., 16 April 1961, p. 72; ibid., 29 July 1961, p. 18; ibid., 6 September 1961, p. 20; ibid., 7 September 1961, p. 31; ibid., 16 September 1961, p. 44; ibid., 14 October 1961, p. 10; ibid., 5 December 1961, p. 31.
27. As early as January 1960 Henry Lee Moon, public relations director of the NAACP, had suggested to Roy Wilkins that the organization should 'initiate steps for independend [*sic*] and large-scale celebration of the Proclamation's centennial', H. L. Moon to R. Wilkins, 26 January 1960, General Office File, Box A76, Group 3, NAACP Papers, Library of Congress; *New York Times*, 5 May 1962, p. 16.
28. On blacks as testers of the Dream see Manis, *Civil Religions*, p. 74.
29. *New York Times*, 22 June 1962, p. 10; ibid., 2 June 1962, p. 9.
30. Ibid., 13 September 1962, p. 38.
31. M. L. King, 'Address to the New York Civil War Centennial Commission, 12 September 1962', MS speech, Box 3, Martin Luther King Papers, Martin Luther King, Jr., Center for Nonviolent Social Change, Atlanta.
32. *New York Times*, 18 September 1962, p. 25.
33. Ibid., 18 September 1962, p. 25.
34. Ibid., 19 September 1962, p. 27.
35. *New York Times*, 23 September 1962, I, pp. 1, 50; *Public Papers of the Presidents of the United States: John F. Kennedy, 1962* (Washington, DC, 1963), pp. 702–3.
36. *New York Times*, 30 June 1963, I, p. 39; ibid., 1 July 1963, p. 17; ibid., 2 July 1963, p. 14.
37. Ibid., 2 July 1963, p. 14.
38. R. Eyerman and A. Jamison, *Social Movements: A Cognitive Approach* (Cambridge, 1991), pp. 120–45.
39. *New York Times*, 10 April 1965, p. 30.

8 Touchstones, Authorities, and Marian Anderson: The Making of 'I Have a Dream'

Keith D. Miller and Emily M. Lewis

On Easter Sunday 1939, when Marian Anderson sang 'America' ('My country 'tis of thee / Sweet land of liberty') from the steps of the Lincoln Memorial, the event served as both a culmination and a beginning – the culmination of a long effort to identify Abraham Lincoln as a symbol of racial equality and the beginning of a method of formalized protest that would climax when Martin Luther King Jr, delivered 'I Have a Dream' on those same steps twenty-four years later.

After the Daughters of the American Revolution had prevented Anderson from singing at Constitution Hall because of her race, First Lady Eleanor Roosevelt resigned from the DAR, and NAACP chief Walter White arranged for Anderson to perform at the Lincoln Memorial before 75 000 people. Harold Ickes, Secretary of Interior, introduced Anderson by commenting on the appropriateness of the setting: 'In this great auditorium under the sky all of us are free. When God gave us this wonderful outdoors and the sun, the moon and the stars, He made no distinction of race, or creed, or color.'[1]

As Scott Sandage explains, by scheduling the concert as a response to the controversy, 'black organizers transformed a recital of sacred music at a national shrine into a political rally.' Sandage argues that, by reinterpreting the Lincoln Memorial, the NAACP and Anderson helped revise the memory of Abraham Lincoln from that of the National Saviour to that of the Great Emancipator.[2]

Such an effort was necessary because northern white leaders had sought to define Lincoln as an icon unrelated to slavery and emancipation. When designers planned the Lincoln Memorial and commissioned a sculptor to chisel the giant statue housed inside, they envisioned their work not as a tribute to the liberator of slaves but instead 'as a symbol of national consensus, linking North and South on holy, national ground.' At the dedication in 1922 the chief planner of the Lincoln Memorial, former president William Howard Taft, gave a lengthy speech that entirely ignored the subject of

147

slavery. In another address at the dedication, President Warren Harding insisted that Lincoln 'would have been the last man in the republic to resort to arms to effect . . . abolition. Emancipation was a means to the great end – maintained union. . . .'[3]

On other occasions as well, white officials exalted Lincoln by extracting him from the divisiveness of slavery and emancipation. In 1916 President Woodrow Wilson accepted as a national site the farm where Lincoln was born. Credentialing himself, Wilson stated, 'I have read many biographies of Lincoln.' He hailed Lincoln as 'a man of singular, delightful, vital genius' and a 'natural ruler of men' with a 'great heart that seemed to comprehend all mankind.' Nowhere in his panegyric did Wilson mention slavery or emancipation. Nowhere did he even allude to the Civil War. Rather he portrayed Lincoln as a god-like figure involved in human affairs yet somehow elevated above them.

African-Americans, however, interpreted national symbols differently than did presidents. In his famous 1852 jeremiad 'What to the Slave Is the Fourth of July?', Frederick Douglass attacked slavery in part by contrasting the promises of the Declaration of Independence to the horrors of bondage. When Henry Highland Garnet denounced slavery, he invoked George Washington, Thomas Jefferson, Moses, and the Christian religion as his authorities.[4]

After slavery ended, African-American orators continue to make arguments similar to those offered by Douglass and Garnet. These later speakers contrasted the values enunciated in the Declaration of Independence, the newly amended Constitution, and the Bible to the ugly racism institutionalized in American life. Following Douglass and Garnet, these black leaders urged whites to end prejudice and hypocrisy by living up to the noble ideals of democracy and brotherhood that whites claimed to embrace. Adding Lincoln to the gallery of sanctified religious and patriotic figures whom they invoked, these orators interpreted the Emancipation Proclamation as another touchstone of democracy and freedom.

Early in this century George William Cook compared Christ's preaching to the Declaration of Independence. James Curtis and M. C. B. Mason compared Lincoln to Christ and called for equal rights. In his speech 'Abraham Lincoln and Fifty Years of Freedom', Abraham Walters praised 'the immortal Emancipator', demanded racial equality and claimed, 'Mr. Lincoln was the first to suggest to his party the enfranchisement of the Negro.' Ernest Lyon celebrated the fiftieth anniversary of the Emancipation Proclamation by evoking Lincoln and the Constitution and by describing African-American triumphs against great odds. Lyon concluded his speech optimistically: ' . . . since Right is Right and God is God, Right must ultimately prevail.' In yet another oration honouring the fiftieth anniversary of the Emancipation Proclamation, William Lewis asserted that Lincoln 'walked with God'; Lewis identified Jefferson, Lincoln and Christianity by claiming that Lincoln, in effect, declared, "'The Negro is a man'" and "'my [Lincoln's] ancient faith tells me that all men are created equal.'"[5]

During inaugural week of 1909, Francis Grimke entered his pulpit in Washington, DC, cited Lincoln, and issued a jeremiad to whites who failed to live by their expressed values: 'The secession of the Southern States in 1860 was a small matter compared with the secession of the Union itself from the great principles enunciated in the Declaration of Independence, in the Golden Rule, in the Ten Commandments, in the Sermon on the Mount.' After invoking these touchstones, Grimke protested the pattern of segregation unfolding across the South. He bemoaned the loss of the vote, rejoiced that blacks were generally 'dissatisfied' and advocated the need to struggle against 'this great evil of race prejudice.' He ended optimistically, affirming 'The right is bound, sooner or later, to triumph' and explaining 'A better day is coming; but we have got to help to bring it about.'[6]

At the consecration of the Lincoln Memorial in 1922 Robert Russa Moton, who replaced Booker T. Washington as president of Tuskegee Institute, was the only speaker to violate the careful process of crafting Lincoln's image as a national healer who stood above the issue of race. Unlike Taft and Harding, Moton dared to tie Lincoln to manumission. He hailed Lincoln as 'the great emancipator', who implemented part of Jefferson's promise that 'all men are created equal'; further, he challenged Americans to make their nation 'an example for all the world of equal justice and equal opportunity for all.' Although Moton had his say, white officials apparently won this particular battle over the memory of Lincoln. Blacks were allowed to witness the dedication of the Lincoln Memorial only from a segregated area where they sat behind white spectators – an arrangement that obviously conflicted with Moton's call for 'equal justice.'[7]

Despite their setback in contesting the image of Lincoln at the 1922 dedication, blacks continued to call for equality by appealing to sanctified touchstones and authorities. African-Americans acted on a rhetorical assumption that Kenneth Burke articulates: 'if the excommunicated would avoid the corner of negativism, he must recruit a group who steal the insignia of the orthodox.' Burke explains, 'The stealing back and forth of symbols is the approved method whereby the Outs avoid "being driven into a corner"'. By fusing their demands to hallowed emblems, blacks claimed that the American civil religion necessitated racial equality. In this argument, rejecting equal rights meant rejecting all things dear and holy.[8]

But in order to appeal successfully to the emblem of Lincoln, African-Americans first had to win the rhetorical war over what Lincoln symbolized. They did not enjoy the luxury of explaining how Lincoln intertwined his roles as National Saviour and Great Emancipator – a task that Frederick Douglass undertook in 1876 when dedicating a monument to Lincoln. No, they needed simply to define Lincoln as the emancipator – period. Then he could serve as a rhetorically useful authority and a link to connect Christianity and Jefferson's words – 'all men are created equal' – to their own situation.

Although white Americans' memory of Lincoln appears to have gradually evolved from National Unifier (in 1922) to Emancipator (in 1938), Anderson's 1939 performance at the Lincoln Memorial proved decisive in garnering massive, positive publicity that permanently associated the image of Lincoln with the theme of racial equality. She and the NAACP thereby won a decisive battle in the rhetorical contest to seize and command the symbol of Lincoln, culminating the combined rhetorical efforts of Curtis, Mason, Lyon, Walters, Lewis, Grimke and Moton. Forever would Lincoln's name be coupled with what Kenneth Burke would call the 'god-terms' of 'freedom' and 'equality.'[9]

Not only did Anderson's performance end the struggle over what Lincoln represented, it also inaugurated a stylized form of dissent in a specific location. Sandage explains:

> A standardized civil rights protest ritual evolved from the elements in Marian Anderson's concert, such as using mass rallies instead of pickets, performing patriotic and spiritual music, choosing a religious format, inviting prominent platform guests, self-policing the crowds to project an orderly image, alluding to Lincoln in publicity and oratory, and insisting on using the memorial rather than another site.[10]

Although this formalized ritual was new, it simply constituted a refined form of the same argument that Douglass, Garnet and other black orators had used before, namely criticizing whites for preaching equality and justice while practising segregation and injustice. In this refined political ceremony, not only did blacks again protest exploitation and argue from authority, they claimed the same specific authorities – Moses, Christ, Jefferson and Lincoln – that Douglass, Garnet and other African-American speakers had cited singly or in combination. And they argued from the same benchmarks – the Bible, the Declaration of Independence and the Emancipation Proclamation. Through her singing Anderson added 'America' ('My country 'tis of thee / Sweet land of liberty') to the list of touchstones.[11]

Two years after the Anderson concert, A. Philip Randolph started a March on Washington Movement, threatening President Franklin Roosevelt with a huge demonstration that would conclude at the Lincoln Memorial. Fearful of Randolph's march, Roosevelt supplied an executive order outlawing segregation in the defence industry. In 1943 Randolph organized a small band that gathered at the memorial on Lincoln's birthday and sang the spiritual 'Go Down, Moses.' Other protests followed at the site.[12]

Of course African-Americans continued to dissent in places other than the Lincoln Memorial. In 1944 a fifteen-year-old boy from Atlanta won a local oratorical contest (and qualified for a state contest) by disputing racism. His name was Martin Luther King, Jr. Whether King wrote this address, 'The Negro and the Constitution', or borrowed it from an unacknowledged and as-yet-undiscovered source, he identified himself with it and delivered it with enough conviction to win a contest.[13]

In this speech the teenage King followed familiar practices. His chief themes were identical with those of Francis Grimke. Both Grimke and King lambasted racial inequity, advocated the right to vote, applauded the black struggle for freedom, and concluded with a note of high optimism. Like Mason and Lyon, King discussed the beginning of American slavery in 1620. Like Lyon, King claimed that emancipation left blacks in a rather pitiful, undeveloped state. Again like Lyon – albeit much more briefly – King announced that African-Americans had nonetheless made important contributions.[14]

In 'The Negro and the Constitution' the young King also appealed to hallowed emblems in order to contrast America's gaudy promises to its disturbing practices. Like Grimke, King recalled the Golden Rule. Like Curtis and Mason, King identified Christ and Lincoln. Like Lewis and Moton, King incorporated Jefferson's assertion from the Declaration of Independence: 'all men are created ... equal'. Like Lyon, Walters and Lewis, King alluded to the number of years that had passed since the Emancipation Proclamation. And just as Grimke merged his voice with lyrics from the 'Battle Hymn of the Republic', King merged his own voice with lyrics from 'Lift Every Voice and Sing', sometimes known as the Negro National Anthem.[15]

In the same oration the youthful King analysed the importance of Anderson's 1939 concert:

> Marian Anderson was barred from singing in Constitution Hall, ironically enough by the professional daughters of the very men who founded this nation for liberty and equality. But this tale had a different ending. The nation rose in protest, and gave a stunning rebuke to the Daughters of the American Revolution and a tremendous ovation to the artist, Marian Anderson, who sang in Washington on Easter Sunday and fittingly, before the Lincoln Memorial.

After remarking the distinguished members of the audience and the size of crowd, King explained,

> [Anderson] sang as never before with tears in her eyes. When the words of "America" and "Nobody Knows de Trouble I Seen" rang out over that great gathering, there was a hush on the sea of uplifted faces, black and white, and a new baptism of liberty, equality, and fraternity.

Here the adolescent King associated the American Revolution, Constitution Hall, Washington, DC, and the Lincoln Memorial – where Anderson 'fittingly' sang – with the 'god-terms' of 'liberty' and 'equality.' Like the organizers who staged Anderson's concert on Easter Sunday, King skilfully fused sacred and patriotic messages, mentioning the timing of the concert on Easter Sunday and claiming that it initiated a 'new baptism of liberty.' The baptism occurred when Anderson sang 'America' and a spiritual and thereby identified patriotism and African-American culture.

Wanting his tribute to Anderson to be more than a panegyric, the teenage King transformed it into a values appeal in his protest against segregation: 'Yet [Miss Anderson] cannot be served in the public restaurants of her home city, even after it has declared her to be its best citizen.'[16]

In 1955, eleven years later, the Montgomery bus boycott catapulted King onto the national stage. In 1957, King and NAACP chief Roy Wilkins planned a Prayer Pilgrimage to the Lincoln Memorial on the third anniversary of the Supreme Court decision in *Brown* v. *the Board of Education*. On the steps of the memorial, gospel soloist Mahalia Jackson sang 'America.' Wearing his pulpit robe at that same spot, King delivered 'Give Us the Ballot', the major speech of the Prayer Pilgrimage. He urged the nation to obey the desegregation order of the Supreme Court and repeatedly implored Congress for the right to vote. He closed by referring to Moses and by quoting ten lines from 'Lift Every Voice and Sing' – the same hymn he had excerpted thirteen years earlier in 'The Negro and the Constitution'.[17]

In the nineteen years between 'The Negro and the Constitution' and 'I Have a Dream', King remembered Marian Anderson. To understand his references to her in 1963, we need to return to her 1939 performance at the Lincoln Memorial. There she helped construct her musical persona by singing 'America', an Italian aria, Schubert's 'Ave Maria', and several spirituals. By selecting 'America', she bolstered her credentials as a patriot; by choosing 'Ave Maria', she became a worthy purveyor of the finest classical music; by picking beautiful and religiously orthodox spirituals, she argued for the importance of the people who produced them. By creating her musical persona out of such disparate materials, Anderson presented herself as a loyal, black American soaked in the finest European culture.[18]

The mature King constructed his rhetorical persona in an analogous fashion. Seeking legitimacy, he carefully fixed himself within the coordinates of Christian, Euro-American moral and intellectual traditions. In an autobiographical essay, 'Pilgrimage to Nonviolence', he maintained that his ideas sprang from reading prestigious Euro-American philosophers and theologians even though he repeatedly copied the words of fellow preachers and friends to explain what he claimed to have learned from Marx and other renowned thinkers. He dotted – and sometimes saturated – his discourse with quotations from and references to Shakespeare, Jefferson, Lincoln, Thoreau, Emerson, the American Revolution, the Civil War, emancipation, *Brown* v. *Board of Education*, Moses, Christ and other biblical figures – each of whom served as an authority or touchstone that helped clarify a current situation. He garnered many of these quotations and references from books of sermons by preachers whose names he rarely mentioned.[19]

Balancing his use of Euro-American icons and history lessons, King frequently incorporated into his addresses the lyrics of spirituals, gospel songs and hymns, using them to cap several of his most important orations. Like Lyon, he highlighted his African-American identity by occasionally spotlighting outstanding black achievers who had overcome extremely formidable obstacles.

One of the achievers King chronicled was Anderson. In 'The American Dream', a sermon delivered in February 1963, he applauded her: 'From poverty-stricken conditions . . . Marian Anderson rose up to be the world's greatest contralto, so that Toscanini had to cry out: "A voice like this comes only once in a century." And Sibelius of Finland said: "My roof is too low for such a voice."'

At the end of the homily he referred to Lincoln, 'who had the vision to see that this nation could not survive half slave and half free', and quoted Jefferson – 'all men are created equal'.[20]

In 'Dives and Lazarus,' a sermon delivered in March 1963, King spoke more about Anderson. Borrowing from white preacher/scholar George Buttrick and from British preacher Leslie Weatherhead, King expounded the theme of interrelatedness, explaining the need to recognize one's dependence on others. He introduced his analysis of Anderson by talking about 'that great experience I had in reading the autobiography of Marian Anderson'. Published in 1956, Anderson's autobiography is one of only a handful of books that King ever claimed to have read after the start of the Montgomery bus boycott.[21]

After noting Anderson's autobiography, King cited Anderson as someone with a keen sense of obligation to her extraordinary mother. He devoted 342 words to detailing the enormous sacrifices that Mrs Anderson made to further Marian Anderson's education and Mrs Anderson's unlimited joy when she heard her daughter sing 'Ave Maria' and a spiritual at Carnegie Hall. Then he related Marian Anderson's gratitude to her mother. He recalled that someone had asked Marian Anderson about 'the happiest moment' in her life, inquiring,

> Was it the moment that Toscanini said that you possess the "voice that comes only once in a century"? Miss Anderson said "No." Was it the moment that you sang before Sibelius of Finland and he said, "My roof is too low for your voice"? Miss Anderson said "No". . . . What was it then? . . . "The happiest moment in my life was when I could say, 'Mother, you may stop working now.'"

Here King established Anderson's musical status by indicating that she sang

Schubert's classic 'Ave Maria' in Carnegie Hall, easily the most famous auditorium in the nation. He reinforced and upgraded that status by noting the acclaim lavished upon her by the greatest living conductor of European classical music (Toscanini) and by the greatest living composer of European classical music (Sibelius). No one could dismiss such authorities.[22]

King further explained that Anderson served as a stellar ambassador of the African-American community, one who brought spirituals to an arena where they could be savoured by the best-trained and most discriminating of musical ears. As if this were not enough, King ventured, Anderson maintained perspective on her rare fame. She was happiest when earning enough money to rescue her hard-working mother from a life of endless toil. King urged his listeners to emulate her recognition of interdependence.

King concluded by turning the whole theme of interrelatedness – including his exegesis of the parable of Dives and Lazarus and his long Anderson illustration – into an argument against white supremacy, a doctrine that denied interdependence. He thereby transmuted his Anderson illustration into a values appeal against racism, just as he had done in 'The Negro and the Constitution'.[23]

One hundred years after the Emancipation Proclamation, a few months after delivering 'Dives and Lazarus', King joined A. Philip Randolph, Roy Wilkins and other civil rights advocates in orchestrating a massive March on Washington. A galaxy of religious figures – including a Roman Catholic archbishop, the president of the American Jewish Congress, and a leader of the National Council of Churches – joined 200 000 others at the Lincoln Memorial. There they sang 'Go Down, Moses', the spiritual that Randolph's small group had brought to the same spot twenty years earlier.[24]

From the steps of the memorial, various speakers offered highly predictable values appeals in demanding strong civil rights legislation. Randolph invoked Jesus Christ. Wilkins quoted the New Testament. Moderate Whitney Young claimed that civil rights were 'constitutionally guaranteed'. Youthful militant John Lewis called for agitation 'until the Revolution of 1776 is completed.' Joan Baez sang the spiritual 'Oh Freedom'. Jewish leader Joachim Prinz cited the Pledge of Allegiance and urged action on behalf of 'the image, the dream, the idea, and the aspiration of America itself'. Walter Reuther, President of the United Auto Workers, lamented the 'moral gap between American democracy's noble promises and its ugly practices in the field of civil rights.' He added, 'There is too much high octane hypocrisy in America.'[25]

Nearing the end of the proceedings, Randolph introduced Marian Anderson, who calmed the huge crowd with a spiritual, and Mahalia Jackson, who revived everyone with an up-tempo spiritual bewailing the slaves' mistreatment and implying that justice would come.[26]

After Prinz's remarks, King's turn came. A few days earlier, he had told a friend that he wanted to give 'a sort of Gettysburg Address'. That intention was obvious when, in his second sentence, King echoed the opening of Lincoln's famous oration and alluded to the enormous statue of Lincoln gazing at his back: 'Five score years ago, a great American, in whose symbolic shadow we stand today, signed the Emancipation Proclamation.'[27]

In its structure and themes, King's 'I Have a Dream' closely resembles Francis Grimke's jeremiad of 1909. Like Grimke, King protested the loss of the vote and measured white racism against the Declaration of Independence and the Bible. Grimke rejoiced that blacks were 'dissatisfied'; King asserted that blacks 'can never be satisfied' with injustice. And, like Grimke (and Lyon), King ended with a strikingly hopeful vision based on the promises of the American civil religion.[28]

Further, as Dave Barboza observes, the form and themes of 'I Have a Dream' strongly resemble those of King's 'The Negro and the Constitution.' The major purpose of each speech is to protest racial injustice. One theme common to the orations is the need to recognize interdependence. In 'The Negro and the Constitution' King argued that slaves established 'the empire of King Cotton' that made possible the unique 'status of life and hospitality' enjoyed by southern whites. In addition he maintained that white Americans' health hinged on racial justice. Because diseases spread from blacks to whites, he argued, a 'healthy nation' was impossible as long as blacks were 'harboring germs of disease which recognize no color lines.' In 'I Have a Dream', he contended that African-Americans needed to recognize interdependence: 'many of our white brothers . . . have come to realize that their destiny is tied up with our destiny and they have come to realize that their freedom is inextricably bound to our freedom. We cannot walk alone.'[29]

Many of the same, ritualized values appeals animate 'The Negro and the Constitution' and 'I Have a Dream'. Following a pattern established (or confirmed) by Grimke, King in both orations marshalled ritualized appeals to protest an American nightmare; then he paradoxically offered hope based on the same civil religion. In 'The Negro and the Constitution' King ventured that, despite the Civil War and emancipation, 'Black America still wears chains'. In 'I Have a Dream' he used the same metaphor to describe the same nightmare: 'One hundred years [after emancipation] . . . the Negro is still sadly crippled by the manacles of segregation.' In 'The Negro and the Constitution' he objected that Marian Anderson could not 'spend the night in any good hotel in America'. In 'I Have a Dream' he decried blacks' inability to 'gain lodging in . . . the hotels of the cities'.[30]

In both 'The Negro and the Constitution' and 'I Have a Dream', he piled one racist scandal on top of another, organized each pile in parallel sentences beginning with 'We cannot', and included a biblical scale to weigh each injustice – in the first, a reference to Jesus; in the second, an excerpt from the prophet Amos. Compare:

'The Negro and the Constitution'

We cannot have an enlightened democracy with one great group living
   in ignorance.
We cannot have a healthy nation with one tenth of the people ...
harboring germs of disease which recognize no color lines ...
We cannot have a nation orderly and sound with one group so ground
   down ... that it is almost forced into ... crime.
We cannot be truly Christian people so long as we flaunt the central
   teachings of Jesus: brotherly love and the Golden Rule.
We cannot come to full prosperity with one great group so ill-delayed
   that it cannot buy goods.

'I Have a Dream'

We can never be satisfied as long as the Negro is the victim of the
   unspeakable horrors of police brutality....
We cannot be satisfied as long as the Negro's basic mobility is from a
   smaller ghetto to a larger one.
We cannot be satisfied as long as our children are stripped of their
   selfhood ... by signs saying 'For Whites Only.'
We cannot be satisfied as long as a Negro in Mississippi cannot vote....
No, we ... will not be satisfied until justice rolls down like waters and
   righteousness like a mighty stream.[31]

By the time King reached this 'We cannot' litany in 'The Negro and the
Constitution', he had already alluded to Lincoln, the Emancipation Proclamation, and constitutional amendments outlawing discrimination; he had already quoted Jefferson's 'all men are created equal'; and – in the section on
Anderson – he had already cited Constitution Hall, the American Revolution, Easter Sunday, the Lincoln Memorial, 'America' and a spiritual.

By the time he reached the 'We cannot' litany of 'I Have a Dream', he
had already echoed the Gettysburg Address; turned a Shakespearean phrase
inside out; alluded to a teaching of Jesus; and noted the Emancipation Proclamation, the Constitution, and the Declaration of Independence, which he
had quoted.[32]

Extending a metaphor for seven sentences, King used familiar benchmarks
to contend that the 'architects of our republic' had offered a 'check' that
promised freedom. 'America', he complained, 'has given the Negro people
a bad check', which kited due to 'insufficient funds'. Yet the promise of
Jefferson's Declaration is sacred and will surely be redeemed: 'We refuse to
believe that there are insufficient funds in the great vaults of opportunity of
this nation. And so we've come to cash this check.' This appeal to sterling
promises – whose realization is currently thwarted but eventually certain –

underlies the entire speech, just as it did Grimke's oration and 'The Negro and the Constitution'.[33]

Like Grimke's speech, 'The Negro and the Constitution' ended with great optimism as King blended sacred and secular appeals: 'My heart throbs anew in the hope that inspired by the example of Lincoln, imbued with the spirit of Christ, [Americans] will cast down the last barrier to perfect freedom.' Continuing 'I Have a Dream', King quoted again from the Declaration – 'all men are created equal' – and included an extended, visionary metaphor from Isaiah that reappeared in the New Testament and in Handel's 'Messiah' ('every valley shall be exalted . . .')[34]

King ended 'I Have a Dream' by borrowing, adjusting, and adding to the conclusion of a speech that black pastor Archibald Carey gave at the 1952 Republican Convention. Carey had argued against segregation by citing emancipation and appealing to Jesus, Paul, the Hebrew Bible and the Declaration. Carey began his conclusion by quoting from 'America':

> We, Negro Americans, sing with all loyal Americans:
>
> My country 'tis of thee, Sweet land of liberty. Of thee I sing – Land where my fathers died, Land of the Pilgrim's pride. From every mountainside Let freedom ring!
>
> That's exactly what we mean – from every mountainside, let freedom ring. Not only from the Green Mountains and White Mountains of Vermont and New Hampshire; not only from the Catskills of New York; but from the Ozarks in Arkansas, from the Stone Mountain in Georgia, from the Blue Ridge Mountains of Virginia – let it ring not only for the minorities of the United States, but for . . . the disinherited of all the earth – may the Republican Party, under God, from every mountainside, LET FREEDOM RING!

Compare Carey's words to those in 'I Have a Dream':

> This will be the day when all of God's children will be able to sing with new meaning:
>
> My country 'tis of thee, sweet land of liberty. Of thee I sing – Land where my fathers died, Land of the Pilgrims' pride. From every mountainside Let freedom ring!
>
> So let freedom ring from the prodigious hilltops of New Hampshire. Let freedom ring from the mighty mountains of New York. Let freedom ring from the heightening Alleghenies of Pennsylvania. . . . Let freedom ring from Stone Mountain of Georgia. Let freedom ring from Lookout Mountain of Tennessee. Let freedom ring from every hill and molehill in Mississippi. From every mountainside, let freedom ring![35]

Unlike Carey, King reached the climax of the peroration when he stated emphatically, 'Let freedom ring from every hill and molehill in Mississippi. . . .' Inasmuch as Mississippi is a low-lying state, this imagery revived the earlier metaphor of geographical transformation that King had quoted from Isaiah – 'every valley shall be exalted'.[36] Thus he brilliantly merged Biblical eschatology and the 'god-term' of freedom that, by now, was firmly identified with Jefferson and Lincoln.

King further improved Carey's conclusion by quoting a spiritual. King envisioned a day when whites would overcome the contradictions between American promise and American practice, and everyone would 'join hands and sing in the words of the old Negro spiritual, "Free at last! Free at last! Thank God, Almighty. We're free at last."' Through the word 'free', he again fused the slaves' desires with Isaiah's dramatic prophecy and the goals of Jefferson and Lincoln.

By singing 'America' and a spiritual at her 1939 concert, Anderson had similarly merged the slaves' desires with the goals of Jefferson, Lincoln and Christianity – an identification that essentially repeated the values appeals of Grimke and others. In 'The Negro and the Constitution', King remarked this identification by observing that, by singing 'America' and a spiritual, Anderson had precipitated a 'new baptism of liberty'. In 'I Have a Dream', he offered a strikingly parallel appeal.

James Cone, David Garrow, Lewis Baldwin and Keith D. Miller contend that King's religion, politics, ideas and eloquence stem from his immersion in the black church, not, as a generation of scholars has argued, from his graduate training in Euro-American philosophy and theology. Alexandra Alvarez, Robert Harrison and Linda Harrison, and Miller argue that 'I Have a Dream' reflects King's exposure to his father's folk preaching.[37]

Clearly 'I Have a Dream' sprang not only from African-American folk sermons, but also from the black oratorical (and sometimes homiletic) tradition of Douglass, Garnet, Lyon and Grimke. At her 1939 concert Anderson refined their values appeals into what became a political ritual at the Lincoln Memorial. In a speech he gave at the age of fifteen, long before he enrolled in graduate school, King offered decidedly comparable appeals throughout and analysed Anderson's concert as an example of such appeals. In 'I Have a Dream', he re-enacted the political ritual that Anderson had begun and that he had interpreted when he was fifteen.

'I Have a Dream' did not succeed despite its 'historical self-consciousness' as one critic has claimed. Instead, 'I Have a Dream' triumphed because through it King perfected the values appeals that his black predecessors (and he himself) had standardized, stylized, formalized and ritualized.[38]

'I Have a Dream' is a an acutely paradoxical oration. It is scintillating. It is incandescent. It is nonpareil. But it is also brilliantly and profoundly conventional.

NOTES

1. 'Throng Honors Marian Anderson in Concert at the Lincoln Memorial', *New York Times*, 10 April 1939, p. 19.
2. Scott Sandage, 'A Marble House Divided: The Lincoln Memorial, 1963', *Journal of American History*, 80 (1993), 136.
3. Ibid., 141; 'Harding Dedicates Lincoln Memorial: Blue and Gray Join', *New York Times*, 31 May 1992, p. 3. Covering Harding's speech, one newspaper offered the following front-page headline: 'Nationality is Supreme Chapter in Our American History, Says President', *Arizona Republican*, 31 May 1922, pp. 1–2.
4. Woodrow Wilson, 'Abraham Lincoln', in James Milton O'Neil (ed.), *Modern Short Speeches* (New York, 1923), pp. 101, 98–9; Frederick Douglass, 'What to the Slave is the Fourth of July?' in Alice Dunbar (ed.), *Masterpieces of Negro Eloquence* (New York, 1970), pp. 41–8; Henry Highland Garnet, 'A Memorial Discourse' in Dunbar, *Negro Eloquence*, pp. 558, 560.
5. George Cook, 'The Two Seals', in Dunbar, *Negro Eloquence*, pp. 383–4; James Curtis, 'Abraham Lincoln' in Dunbar, *Negro Eloquence*, p. 321; M. C. B. Mason, 'Lincoln the Man of the Hour' in Carter Woodson, *Negro Orators and their Orations* (Washington, DC, 1925), p. 542; Abraham Walters, 'Abraham Lincoln and Fifty Years of Freedom', in Dunbar, *Negro Eloquence*, pp. 558, 560; Ernest Lyon, 'Emancipation and Racial Advancement' in Dunbar, *Negro Eloquence*, pp. 461–74; William Lewis, 'Abraham Lincoln' in Dunbar, *Negro Eloquence*, pp. 409–24.
6. Francis Grimke, 'Equality of Rights for All Citizens, Black and White Alike', in Dunbar, *Negro Eloquence*, pp. 349, 350–6. For examples of similar appeals by other African-American speakers, see Robert Heath, 'Black Rhetoric: An Example of the Poverty of Values', *Southern Speech Communication Journal*, 39, (1973), 145–60.
7. 'Harding Dedicates', pp. 1,3; Sandage, 'A Marble House Divided', 141–2; Robert Russa Moton, 'The Negro's Debt to Lincoln', in Woodson, *Negro Orators*, pp. 575, 578.
8. Kenneth Burke, *Attitudes Toward History* (1937; Berkeley, 1959), pp. 223, 328.
9. Our survey of *New York Times* articles on Lincoln between 1922 and 1938 reveals a gradual, shifting emphasis from Lincoln as National Unifier to Lincoln as Emancipator. Sandage, 'A Marble House Divided', 147; Kenneth Burke, *A Rhetoric of Motives* (1950; Berkeley, 1969), pp. 275–6.
10. Sandage, 'A Marble House Divided', 152.
11. Marian Anderson, *My Lord, What a Morning* (New York, 1956), pp. 190–1.
12. Paula Pfeffer, *A. Philip Randolph, Pioneer of the Civil Rights Movement* (Baton Rouge, 1990), pp. 46–9. Sandage, 'A Marble House Divided', 153.
13. In letters to his parents the month after he delivered 'The Negro and the Constitution', King displayed an acute sensitivity to race relations and racial discrimination. Two years later he protested segregation in a letter to the editor of the *Atlanta Constitution*. Clayborne Carson, Ralph Luker and Penny A. Russell, *Called to Serve*, vol. 1 of *The Papers of Martin Luther King, Jr.* (Berkeley, 1992), pp. 111–15, 121.
14. Mason, 'Lincoln, the Man of the Hour', p. 542; Ernest Lyon, 'Emancipation', pp. 465–71; Martin Luther King, 'The Negro and the Constitution', in Carson, et al., *Called to Serve*, pp. 109–11.
15. King, 'The Negro and the Constitution', pp. 109–111; Moton, 'The Negro Debt to Lincoln', pp. 575, 579; Grimke, 'Equality of Rights', p. 349. In 'The Negro

and the Constitution' , King's words 'fac[ing] a rising sun of a new day begun' come from 'Lift Every Voice and Sing'. King merged his voice with the lyrics of 'Battle Hymn of the Republic' at the conclusion of two famous speeches, 'How Long?' and 'I've Been to the Mountaintop'.

16. King, 'The Negro and the Constitution', p. 110. According included three spirituals in the body of her famous Easter concert: 'Gospel Train', 'Trampin' and 'My Soul is Anchored in the Lord'. For an encore, she sang another spiritual, 'Nobody Knows de Trouble I Seen'. Edward T. Folliard, 'Ickes Introduces Contralto at Lincoln Memorial, Many Officials Attend Concert', *Washington Post*, 10 April 1939, pp. 1, 12.
17. David Garrow, *Bearing the Cross: Martin Luther King, Jr., and the Southern Christian Leadership Conference* (New York, 1986), pp. 90–4; Sandage, 'A Marble House Divided', 154; Martin Luther King, Jr., 'Give Us the Ballot', in James M. Washington (ed.), *A Testament of Hope: Selected Speeches and Writings of Martin Luther King, Jr.* (New York, 1991), pp. 197–200.
18. Anderson, *My Lord, What a Morning*, pp. 191–2.
19. For a more detailed account of this process, see Keith D. Miller, 'Composing Martin Luther King, Jr.', *PMLA*, 105, (1990), 70–82; Keith D. Miller, *Voice of Deliverance: The Language of Martin Luther King, Jr., and its Sources* (New York, 1992).
20. Martin Luther King Jr, 'The American Dream', Sermon (Brooklyn, New York, 10 February 1963), King Center, Atlanta, pp. 7, 14.
21. Martin Luther King Jr, 'Dives and Lazarus', Sermon (10 March 1963), King Center, Atlanta; George Buttrick, *Parables of Jesus*, (New York, 1928), pp. 128, 137–46; Leslie Weatherhead, *Key Next Door*, (New York, 1959), p. 184.
22. King, 'Dives and Lazarus', p. 12.
23. Ibid., pp. 12–15.
24. For an account of the March on Washington, see Garrow, *Bearing the Cross*, pp. 265–88. Song sheets of 'Go Down Moses' that were used at the March on Washington are available in the archives of the King Center, Atlanta.
25. John Lewis, 'Speech at the March on Washington', *We Shall Overcome*, Folkways Records, FD 5592, 1964; Joachim Prinz, 'Speech at the March on Washington', *The Great March on Washington*, Gordy/Motown Records, 908, 1963; Walter Reuther, 'Speech at the March on Washington', *The Great March on Washington*, Gordy/Motown Records; Roy Wilkins, 'Speech at the March on Washington', *The Great March on Washington*, Gordy/Motown Records.
26. Taylor Branch, *Parting the Waters: America in the King Years, 1954–1963* (New York, 1988), p. 881.
27. Garrow, *Bearing the Cross*, p. 676; Martin Luther King Jr, 'I Have a Dream', in Washington, *Testament of Hope*, p. 217.
28. Ibid., p. 218.
29. Dave Barboza, 'Dreaming the "Dream"', *Boston Globe*, 22 August 1993, p. 68; King, 'The Negro and the Constitution', pp. 109–10; King, 'I Have a Dream', p. 218.
30. King, 'The Negro and the Constitution', p. 110; King, 'I Have a Dream', pp. 217–18; Dave Barboza, 'Dreaming the "Dream"', p. 68.
31. King, 'The Negro and the Constitution', p. 110; King, 'I Have a Dream', pp. 218–19.
32. King noted the 'sweltering summer of the Negro's legitimate discontent' p. 218. Shakespeare wrote, 'Now is the winter of our discontent / Made glorious summer by this Sun of York . . .' (Richard III, Act I, Scene I). Sean Brotherson, in 'The Power of the Word: Martin Luther King, Jr.'s Speech "I Have a Dream"',

Insight, 8 (1993), 28, detects a biblical allusion in King's statement, 'Now is the time to lift our nation from the quicksands of racial injustice to the solid rock of brotherhood'. In Matthew 7:24–28, Jesus discusses the wisdom of building a house on rock versus building a house on sand. We thank Gary Hatch for showing us Brotherson's essay.

33. King, 'I Have a Dream', p. 217.

34. King, 'The Negro and the Constitution', p. 111. See Isaiah 40:04 and Luke 3:05. In addition, King's remark, 'to hew out of the mountain of despair a stone of hope', is a reference to Daniel 2:35.

35. Archibald Carey, 'Address to the Republican National Convention', in Roy Hill (ed.), *Rhetoric of Racial Revolt* (Denver, 1964), pp. 153–4; King, 'I Have a Dream', pp. 219–20. For Carey, citing mountains from various states seemed appropriate because he spoke at a convention peopled by delegates from every state. Those who listened to 'I Have a Dream' also hailed from around the nation. We thank Peter Ling for this observation.

36. We thank Suzanne Mark for this observation.

37. James Cone, 'Martin Luther King, Jr. – Black Theology, Black Church', *Theology Today*, 40 (1984), 409–20; David Garrow, 'The Intellectual Development of Martin Luther King, Jr.: Influences and Commentaries', *Union Seminary Quarterly Review*, 40 (1986), 5–20; Lewis Baldwin, *There is a Balm in Gilead: The Cultural Roots of Martin Luther King, Jr.* (Minneapolis, 1991); Keith Miller, *Voice of Deliverance*; Alexander Alvarez, 'Martin Luther King's "I Have a Dream": The Speech Event as a Metaphor', *Journal of Black Studies*, 18 (1988), 337–57; Robert Harrison and Linda Harrison, 'The Call from the Mountaintop: Call-Response and the Oratory of Martin Luther King, Jr.' in Carolyn Calloway-Thomas and John Lucaites (eds), *Martin Luther King, Jr. and the Sermonic Power of Public Discourse* (Tuscaloosa, 1993), pp. 162–78. Several scholars still attribute an important portion of King's intellectual development to his philosophical and theological training at seminary and in his PhD programme. For example, Carson et al., *Called to Serve*, p. 49, claims, 'King began to forge his own theological perspective during the fall term of his second year [at seminary]'. See also, John Patton, '"I Have a Dream": The Performance of Theology Fused with the Power of Oratory', in Calloway-Thomas and Lucaites (eds), *King and Public Discourse*, pp. 104–26 and Eugene Genovese, 'Pilgrim's Progress', *New Republic*, 206, (May 1992), 33–40. Although, as Miller argues elsewhere, King gained much in seminary from his study of sermons by white preachers, he resisted many of the ideas presented by the white philosophers and theologians whom he studied. None of their ideas and arguments had a significant impact on 'I Have a Dream.'

38. Nicolaus Mills, 'Heard and Unheard Speeches: What Really Happened at the March on Washington', *Dissent* (Summer 1988), complains, '[King] had tried too hard to write an updated *Gettysburg Address*. What emerged from his prepared text was not moral passion but historical self-consciousness', p. 285. (However, Mills asserts, the speech improved remarkably when King began speaking of his dream.)

9 Politics and Fictional Representation: The Case of the Civil Rights Movement
Richard H. King

I

Though the sources of Martin Luther King's philosophy of non-violent direct action are diverse, there is a linked set of claims at its core. It runs something like this: we are all children of God and thus have the potential to transcend boundaries of race and class, gender and culture in speaking to and understanding others. In the context of the 1960s, hostile southern (and northern) whites were to be addressed as fellow humans, capable of responding to the force of moral example and a reconciling dialogue informed by agape. The whole point of King's political theology was to begin the long work of transforming 'others' into brothers and sisters through the process of mutual self-recognition. King was not, of course, the naïf many took – and still take – him to be. The demand was not, as he repeatedly emphasized, to 'like' one's oppressor; it was rather to love him or her as a child of God.

At the time, everyone from SNCC workers to psychologist Kenneth Clark to Malcolm X expressed serious doubts about King's moral-political vision. Nor in the ensuing years have we become much more comfortable with King's commitment to non-violence and mutual recognition. Though there have been remarkable breakthroughs in South Africa, Eastern Europe and the Middle East, none of these political transformations has occurred under the aegis of King's non-violent Christian vision. Indeed, in Northern Ireland where Christianity is pervasive, the sectarian conflict has proved most intractable. Nor, though the record is less clear, have race relations noticeably improved in the United States, not at least in recent years.

In what follows I assume that something akin to King's ethic of mutual recognition should inform our efforts to come to terms with the past. There is an obligation, in other words, to 'enter into' the world of past actions and events before making judgements based on 'our' point of view alone. I also want to suggest that one of the best ways to establish a more immediate relation to the civil rights movement, is to pay more attention to the fiction that has explicitly thematised the Movement. For, it is there that one gets something like a simulacrum of the experience of the movement or at least certain aspects of it. My assumption is grounded in the wager that fiction – like history – delivers, in Raymond Carver's words, some 'news of the world'; that it has cognitive, as opposed simply to aesthetic, self-referential value; and that historical understanding may be enhanced – though never automatically – by a fictional working-through of historical phenomena. More generally, literature can inform us in the deepest sense about certain ethical and political dimensions of the way we 'are' in the world. As Martha Nussbaum has asserted, '[E]thical and social questions . . . give literature its high importance in our lives'.[1] This is not to say that a novel dealing with the Movement must tell us what should have been done or what the proper tactics or strategy here or there might have been. At its best fiction can illuminate certain dimensions of the experience of politics that otherwise might have remained hidden.

II

Though responsibility for failed mutual understanding between two groups lies generally with the more powerful of the two, this is not invariably the case. Ideally, both sides come not only to recognize the other, but also to realize something new about themselves and the nature of things. But misconceptions can flourish on both sides. I have always thought, for instance, that black Americans involved in the civil rights movement underestimated the strength of commitment needed for many whites to break with friends, parents and community to join the Movement in the South. Stokely Carmichael, for instance, too glibly assumed that when whites were expelled from SNCC in the winter of 1965–6, all they had to do was walk across town – or go back home – and take up similar work in the white community. Malcolm X, to his great credit, admitted that he had been wrong in dismissing the plaintive – and easy to mock – query from a young white women: 'What can I do to help?' Indeed, the whole assumption during the 1960s and early 1970s that white liberals, however defined, were the main obstacle to black progress and might be verbally abused at will was psychologically misconceived, politically unintelligent and morally dubious. I can understand why this scapegoating of white liberal allies happened, but still think it had little justification.

That having been said, I want to examine the notorious case where a liberal white man, novelist William Styron in *The Confessions of Nat Turner*, seemed to systematically misunderstand why his novel elicited such negative reactions from many, perhaps most, black readers. If ever a case displayed all the possibilities of interracial misunderstanding, the Styron case was it.

Two items of historical context are vital to remember here. First, the

1960s saw the rise of what was called the 'new journalism', a hybrid genre that combined fictional technique, including personal voice, with historical and/or journalistic reportage. One of its leading practitioners, Norman Mailer, published *The Armies of the Night* at just about the same time that Styron's *Nat Turner* appeared. In *Armies* Mailer spoke of the greater authenticity and historical penetration of imaginative as opposed to straight journalistic reconstruction of actual events. Later in the 1970s, novelist E. L. Doctorow would assert the inherently oppositional nature of fiction in contrast with conventional historiography: in other words, the truths of the imagination were more hostile to the status quo than the 'facts' discovered and arranged in narrative sequence by the historian.[2]

Yet to many the Styron case exemplified the way fiction could traduce the historical record and thereby contribute to the ongoing oppression of black Americans. A year after Styron's 'meditation on history' had been showered with prizes and praises from reviewers (of both races), a bitter riposte, *William Styron's Nat Turner: 10 Black Writers Respond*, appeared. A collection of polemics directed against Styron's novel, the volume offered an explosive cocktail of invective and blatant misreadings of that book. And yet it undeniably raised some extremely cogent, acute questions concerning the absence of a significant black presence in those organs and outlets – newspapers, journals of opinion and publishing companies – where books such as Styron's were reviewed and evaluated. In addition *10 Black Writers Respond* also touched on the question of whether whites were capable of writing about blacks in general and of the particular capacity of William Styron to deal with an heroic African-American historical figure.

It is crucial to recall that the ten black writers' bitter response to Styron's novel emerged just as the racial conflicts within the Movement and the society at large were increasing in intensity and the palpable frustration with the pace of social and economic change was growing apace. White workers had been expelled from SNCC, once the most integrated of movement organisations. Watts had already become a symbol, as well as a reality, of the same magnitude, but different implication, as Montgomery. Black power was on the rise.

Such was the historical and intellectual setting in which Styron was accused of reducing the heroic slave revolt led by Nat Turner to a kind of psycho-drama in which Turner, afflicted by self- and race-hatred and driven by sexual desire, slays the quintessential white virgin, Margaret Whitehead, the only act of violence he is able to carry through to completion. With this Styron seemed to have offered yet another defamatory redaction of the white racial-sexual primal scene of horror, already deeply engrained in popular consciousness by *Gone with the Wind* and *Birth of a Nation*. If that were not enough, Styron's regional origins as a southerner were mentioned repeatedly (as though it showed anything in particular), as were his dubious claims about what there was to know about Turner (not a lot, he claimed) and how much of that he knew (pretty much all of it, he asserted).

Overall, neither Styron nor the ten writers, with the partial exceptions of Vincent Harding and Mike Thelwell, emerged with much credit from the controversy. Whatever one's judgements on particular changes/omissions in Styron's novel, their cumulative effect was to transform Turner's tragedy of political action into a melodrama of sexual-racial desire (marked by a fair amount of bad writing). Styron emerged from the controversy as arrogant and insensitive. He claimed to have been faithful to the known facts, but then justified omissions of arguably historical figures – for example, Turner's wife – by appealing to the truths of 'his own imagination' and by assuming Turner's 'voice and point of view' in the novel.[3] This was the modernist deification of the imagination taken a step too far; the assumption that the artist has more immediate access to the 'truths of the human heart' than the rest of us deployed too cavalierly.

Yet the black writers often took what was no more than legend or folk-lore, at best contested stories and events, and appealed to them as though their factuality was uncontested. More seriously in the long run, they backed themselves – and those who came after them – into a literary corner by strongly implying that all representations of the African-American past should be expressed in the monumental or heroic mode. Cultural expression was to be pressed in the service of black self-improvement: the point was to find – or to construct – historical role models without flaws. Though such a mode of historical consciousness has been prominently associated with modern nationalism, it is not the dominant mode in modern historiography or liter-ary modernism. Rarely has the cause of either fiction or history been so poorly served by its champions.

In retrospect, however, the Styron affair provided a salutary lesson in the epistemology and sociology of historical retrieval. At one level, it showed how the same 'facts' about an historical figure could be deployed and narrativized for quite different effects. This should have, but didn't, lead both sides to suspect any easy distinction between fact and interpretation. The historical-political issue was not that Styron took liberties with the facts as such. Earlier fictional and biographical accounts of Turner's life had failed to mention some of the same facts Styron was pilloried for omitting. Rather, Styron imagined Turner in a way that cut against the grain of the pervasive militancy among black writers and intellectuals. On the most immediate levels, Styron was ambushed by the *Zeitgeist*. Though not without a self-congratu-latory ring to it, Styron's recent claim that his novel about Turner was 'the first politically incorrect novel of our age' has more than a grain of truth to it.[4]

Of particular interest in the Styron controversy is the rarely spoken sus-picion that white writers are incapable of doing justice to the African-American experience(s). Few people, then or now, actually say this directly and in print. In the controversy between Styron and the ten black writers, the charge was more circumscribed: because Styron was a white southerner, he was doomed from the beginning to produce a travesty of Turner's life. But the logic of the dispute pointed to the clear warning: No Whites Need Apply. Indeed, the upshot of the emerging 'black aesthetic' of the late 1960s was that African-Americans had been hoodwinked by European aesthetics and ideologies, right, centre and left. The task, therefore, was to forge a literature (and other modes of cultural expression) that drew upon the African-American and African experiences and then could be directed back to the black community without bothering with the reactions of white readers, critics or publishers.

But what sort of explanation might be advanced for this white incapacity? One possible explanation appealed to ontological or, more familiarly, biological difference. The Nation of Islam's creation story offered such a reification of racial differences; appeals to African exceptionalism functioned in much the same way. That having been said, essentialist explanations for the impossibility of communicating across racial lines have rarely been popular with, or developed systematically by, African-Americans then or now.

A second, more compelling explanation for white incomprehension posited the uniqueness of the African-American experience and its forms of cultural expression. On one level the argument from unique experience was – is – incontrovertible. That is just the problem, since it applies to every distinct people or culture, be it 'black' or 'white', 'European' or 'African'.[5] The argument from unique experience also calls into question the possibility of anthropological and historical sciences or the attempt to understand 'otherness' across space, time and cultural boundaries altogether. It begs as well the question of where African-Americans belong: in the American-European or the African culture space? Ultimately it assumes a uniformity of African-American experience that is hard to sustain, particularly in the present.

Exclusivity of experience has also been expressed in terms of proprietorship, a trope several of the ten black writers employed. Lerone Bennett referred to Styron's action of 'steal[ing] a man's life' and Vincent Harding entitled his essay 'You've Taken Our Nat and Gone'.[6] The underlying thought here is Lockean: our first property is in our own bodies and, by extension, our minds and culture. The implication is not so much, or only, that whites are incapable of writing about or understanding blacks, but whether, because of the history of white oppression of blacks, white novelists or historians have the moral (as opposed to the epistemological or legal) right to write about matters African-American. Thus the question is not 'can' but 'should' or 'may'.

An article by philosopher Laurence Thomas called 'Moral Deference' is of some pertinence here. The gist of Thomas's piece is that some peoples undergo experiences that create 'emotional category configurations' which then become 'emotional boundaries' between themselves and those who have not undergone the traumatic experiences.[7] Thomas's most general claim comes in the form of a denial that: 'there is a vantage point from which any and every person can rationally grasp whatever morally significant experiences a person might have'.[8] That is, rather than claiming too quickly to understand, much less know better, we owe what Thomas calls 'moral deference' to individuals or groups who have some unique traumatic experience. This involves 'a presumption in favor of the person's account of her experience' when that other person 'has been a victim of social injustice'.[9]

There are of course questions to be raised about Thomas's position: is it the different emotional configuration or is it having been a victim of injustice that creates the presumption of moral difference and hence deference? What does 'rationally' mean as Thomas uses it and does anyone claim that there is an important mode of human understanding that hinges exclusively on being rational in a narrow sense?

However, Thomas also rules out exclusivity claims by insisting that, 'what has to be false is that, as a matter of principle, it is impossible for anyone outside of the social category to do so',[10] i.e. understand and then 'bear witness' to what has been experienced. Thus Thomas is not asserting that because I have not undergone an emotionally traumatic experience, I can never understand or speak with insight about someone else's. Rather, authoritative understanding should not be assumed too easily.[11]

Although he does not mention the Styron case, Thomas's article supplies us with an appropriate label for the Styron problem: above all, his was a failure of 'moral deference' or, perhaps 'tact', if using that term of etiquette is not taken as a trivialization. The upshot is that, while white Americans can write about the African-American experience, they should do so only after considerable thought and care. They must in short 'earn' that right. But the opposite is true as well: blacks must take the trouble to understand the 'white' culture they think they know so well.

Though I am inclined to accept Thomas's basic argument, Stephen Carter has voiced, in another context, a certain doubt about the viability of such a position. The danger, claims Carter, lies in assuming that victimhood confers some sort of unique value: 'For nothing about value or authority ought to turn on who has suffered more. Our suffering might have marked us and it is surely a fact of history that we must never forget, but it is not a symbol of special worth'.[12]

Carter would agree with Thomas that African-Americans are a category of people with a unique 'emotional category configuration', but deny that any 'special worth' or deference is due them. On Carter's account, what the victim of injustice does with that experience determines whether she or he is worthy of moral deference. Moreover, since American blacks are not a morally or experientially homogeneous category, one cannot assume that, in the case in hand, every African-American is due this deference.

History is replete with victims who became executioners, oppressed peoples who turned into oppressors once they gained power, using their former victimhood as warrant for outrageous action and giving lie to the notion that being a victim entails superior wisdom, virtue or compassion. This was a 'fact' of which Martin Luther King and Robert Moses were well aware. As a Christian, King assumed that unearned suffering in the context of the Movement was redemptive, a position that sounds closer to Thomas's than Carter's position. And yet Thomas does grant that the victim must also present his/her case responsibly and that moral deference does not necessarily foreclose criticism.

Finally, however we evaluate the whole controversy between Styron and the ten black writers and whatever attitude the novelist or historian should bring to his or her material, the Styron case demonstrated the dangers, more than the opportunities, of a fictional as opposed to historical rendering of the past.[13] The controversy was to scare off white novelists from writing about the Movement or black figures for a good long time. Indeed, I'm not sure whether any white novelist has focused on the Movement as specifically African-American or, dealt directly with slavery in a work of fiction since the Styron affair.

III

In the meantime, however, there have been a good number of novels dealing with the civil rights movement, in striking contrast with the paucity of Hollywood films that have taken the movement as its focus.[14] (Contrast the number of civil rights films or novels with the number of films and novels about the Vietnam War.) Two observations are also relevant here: most of the novels which deal with movement experience are written by women; the vast majority of them are also composed by African-Americans. The latter is, I suppose, statistically and ideologically predictable; the former is much more of a puzzle.

Here I want to look briefly at three political novels dealing with the Movement or some dimension of it: Ernest Gaines's *A Gathering of Old Men*; Alice Walker's *Meridian* and Rosellen Brown's *Civil Wars*. The point will be to see what we might learn about/from the Movement that is underemphasized in its historiography and more generally how fiction might further the mutual self-recognition of, and between, the races. I will not pretend to cover every aspect of the three novels but will read them primarily as political novels; ones dealing with political ideas and action as well as with a political community or movement.

Gaines's *Gathering* has a deceptively simple feel to it. The novel is organized around a staged confrontation between a small black community in south-western Louisiana and the local sheriff named Mapes. At issue is who has killed Beau Boutan, one of the sons in a large Cajun clan. The sheriff's task is to get a confession from the black perpetrator and put him in jail before the Boutan clan comes looking for revenge and lynches the man who killed Beau. After having been instructed to bring their guns by Candy Marshall, a young white woman whose family owns the land they work, the 18 black men, and a few black women, gather at the house of Mathu, the leader of the black community. Candy's plan is to have everyone, including herself, confess to killing Beau. In the course of the confrontation with Mapes, we learn the stories of several individual lives and ultimately a kind of moral history of the community emerges. In a manner reminiscent of Faulkner's *As I Lay Dying*, the narrative is constituted by several voices, and the effect in the novel is to create the reality of community.

Despite its somewhat fable-like quality, the world Gaines creates has a certain complexity to it. The time is the mid-1970s; technology has already transformed the tenants' relationship to the land; and most of the young people have gone north or moved to the cities. Nor is the confrontation simply a racial one. In the three-tiered social structure, there are the well-off Anglo landowners like Candy's family; the Catholic Cajuns who serve as an intermediary class that runs the plantations but resents the power and status of the Anglos; and the blacks who work the land as tenants or small landholders. The twist to the plot is that, though everyone thinks that Mathu has killed Beau, it is Mathu's son Charlie who has done it. The novel ends with shootout between two riff-raff attached to the Boutan family and the old black men, with Mapes eventually siding with the blacks. At a public trial they are all exonerated.

Two themes of *Gathering* illuminate crucial aspects of the civil rights Movement: the formation of a political community and the centrality of self-respect in that transformational ethos. The two aspects reinforce each other: becoming political results from a set of self-respecting choices and in turn creates a new collective entity of which the black men and women can be proud.

Gaines's novel is a kind of 'narrative of commitment' in which the community in formation – not an individual – is the central character.[15] The outlines of the emerging community become discernible through the talk back and forth among the blacks, Mapes and Candy in front of Mathu's house on the day of the murder. In that place and from that talk, a political space is created out of the various dimensions of the southern black experience. The process of speaking in public recalls the religious talk of testifying and witnessing, of call and response, so central to the black religious community. But the scene in Mathu's yard also resembles an open-air courtroom where the white world is put on trial and its misdeeds remembered by the various black men who testify to the past indignities visited upon them and their families by the Boutans. Finally, Mathu's yard becomes a battleground in which a risk of life is entered into and courage is demonstrated. Again, what Gaines depicts in *Gathering* is the transformation of an oppressed social community into a self-conscious political community prepared to talk and act together in public for the first time.

By 'political' I refer to the newly-found capacity of the community to take responsibility for itself, to be self-determining and thus move from a passive to an active stance. The crucial transformational moment comes when one of the black men says to their friend and protectress, Candy, that they have to talk amongst themselves without her present. Candy reveals the paternalistic side of her concern for them when she responds, 'I'm protecting them like I've always protected them'.[16] But to be self-determining, the black community must not only overcome its fear of the Boutans who physically intimidate them but also forego Candy's protective role. She has only their best interests at heart – as she of course construes those interests. Interestingly, sheriff Mapes does come to understand what is happening to the black community and the individuals in it.

The other crucial dimension of the new political community is the sense of self-respect that manifests itself. As one character says early on: 'Anytime we say we go'n stand up for something, they say we crazy . . . Give a old nigger like me one more chance to do something with his life.'[17] Later, Mathu points up the moral dimension of the self-respect when he says 'A man got to do what he think is right, Sheriff . . . That's what part him from a boy'.[18] And finally just before the final shootout, Mathu, a kind of political Lucas Beauchamp, thanks the old black men who have risked their lives to protect him: 'I felt the same way that man [sheriff Mapes] did out there feel about y'll . . . But I was wrong . . . Hate them [the whites] 'cause they won't let me be a citizen, hated y'll 'cause you never tried'.[19] Thus though the time of the novel is the mid-1970s and there is no civil rights organization in sight, *A Gathering of Old Men* does give us a kind of allegory of a community organizing itself and the acquisition of self-respect.

Gathering is not without flaws. The concluding violence and the exoneration are hardly convincing in realistic terms. It is a resolutely male novel in that the chief characters, except for one, are men and their mode of confrontation is potential, and then actual, violence. People who live in such a 'culture of honor' need no lessons from Frantz Fanon or the Black Panthers about the importance of facing down the oppressor, through violence if need be. There are other novels about movement days, such as Thulani Davis's recent *1959*, which focus on the politicization of a black community. But Gaines's *A Gathering of Old Men* represents the logic of the process with a clarity that is complex and moving as well. It does a dangerous thing –

makes us sympathize with violence – yet wagers that we can and should understand that as well.

Still fairly close in time to the Movement in which she had played a part, Alice Walker in *Meridian* dramatizes the internal complexities of the life-trajectory of Meridian Hill, a young black girl from rural Georgia, as she is liberated, psychologically and politically, by the Movement. Most importantly, the novel illuminates several important aspects of the Movement: first, the various motivations propelling activists into the Movement and the complexities of living a political life in it, as well as how people, whose life had been devoted to the Movement, functioned after it had run its course. Early in the novel, but late in the story, Meridian says: 'What you see before you is a woman in the process or changing her mind.'[20] We don't know what she is changing into, but her self-description should alert us to the novel's status as a kind of African-American *Bildungsroman* in which political action constitutes the curriculum and the pedagogic method.

Meridian begins after the Movement has collapsed and there is an aura of loss about it. Walker moves easily among several registers in the novel: an 'other' surreality breaks through occasionally, while *Meridian* is rarely afraid to take up abstract ideas (the meditations and debates on violence are particularly compelling). Chapters do not follow one another in a tightly linked way; the novel is episodic, made up of different 'takes' on the experience of engagement in, then disengagement from, the Movement. In contrast with *Gathering*, the third-person narrative voice generally foregrounds Meridian as the moral and emotional centre of the novel, though Truman Held, one-time lover, betrayer and then friend, and Lynne, a white woman for whom Truman leaves Meridian and then in turn abandons, play prominent roles.

If *Gathering* is about the emergence of a political community, then *Meridian* is about its dissolution. Neither the narrator nor any of the characters tries to generalize about the causes of its dissolution. But the reader can't help feeling that the complex and tortured triangular relationship between Meridian, Truman and Lynne is meant to point up an internal dynamic that tore the Movement apart. Hidden away inside the narrative of public events and historical oppressions, what brings these three characters together yet drives them apart is not just politics: it is also an explosive mixture of race and sex. Once Walker recreates the Movement split along such lines – and she is working some of the same territory as Styron – we realize just how simplified the constitution of Gaines's political community really is. We are hardly conscious of sexual rivalries or gender divisions in *Gathering*. The men and women are too old and the women hardly present anyway.

Meridian also illustrates the disadvantages, as well as advantages, of using fiction to understand or illuminate the Movement. By convention the historian is charged with exploring the causes of a certain phenomenon, in this case the fragmentation of the civil rights movement. Various factors are assessed and put into the balance; complex judgements are delivered; and qualifications are made. Yet most novels, *Meridian* included, do not attempt this sort of rounded judgement as such. Characters *within* the novel may try to explain what has happened, but rarely does the novel itself deliver such an explicit judgement. As mentioned, *Meridian* can be read to suggest that the decline of the Movement was essentially determined by self-destructive, internal conflicts rather than larger historical and social forces. But however inadequate such as 'internalist' explanation may be, *Meridian* does at least confront the issue of sex and race, while mainstream historiography/ historians still lack the language, or perhaps the will, to handle the agonizingly personal, racial and sexual confrontations that *Meridian* insists were at the heart of the Movement.[21]

Walker *is* relentless. Truman wants Meridian to 'Have my beautiful black babies'.[22] But he then takes up with the blonde-haired Jewish student, Lynne, by whom he has a daughter. After their relationship founders and the daughter has been murdered, Truman uses his art to celebrate blackness, particularly embodied in black women. Yet all the while, as Meridian discovers, he is bedding down with a southern white girl. Thus Walker creates a portrait etched in acid of the pseudo-black militant artist as make-out man, a fickle narcissist who talks black but sleeps white. As can happen in Walker's fiction, if there is a villain, it's likely to be a black man not a white one.

Walker also constructs Lynne on the borderline between plausibility and caricature. At times scathingly, at other times sympathetically, rendered, Lynne is fascinated by the poor black southerners she meets. (She has also been disowned by her northern Jewish parents for having taken up with Truman.) Her fascination – and naiveté – is shown in the way the narrator presents Lynne's attitude toward black southerners: 'To Lynne, the black people of the South were Art'. The narrator continues: '. . . to her, nestled in a big chair made of white oak strips, under a quilt called The Turkey Walk, from Attapulsa, Georgia, in a little wooden Mississippi sharecropper bungalow that had never known paint, the South – and the black people living there – was Art.[23] It should be difficult for any right-thinking academic or intellectual to read this passage without an acute sense of embarrassment. Walker has nailed Lynne (and us) for our fascination with the effects of poverty and a pre-modern style of life, as long as we don't have to experience them ourselves.[24] The oppressed, particularly if very young or very old, are interesting, exotic, authentic in the way 'we' aren't. What Truman and Lynne share, for all their differences, is an attraction to, and fascination with, 'otherness', without any respect for the circumstances that have created that otherness. Their attitude is dangerous to themselves and others precisely because it dehumanizes through desire rather than through obvious cruelty.

The reverse side of this aestheticizing of the other is the psychologically excruciating rape of Lynne by one of Truman's friends, Tommy Odds. One of his arms has been amputated after an attack by whites and Odds forces Lynne to have sex with him by playing on her white guilt. The full meaning of the slogan 'the personal is the political' is revealed in the sexual relationship par excellence. As Truman ruminates: 'By being white, Lynne was guilty of whiteness . . . was it possible to be guilty of a color?' Or, he continues: 'Was it because she was a white woman' whose mere presence was an invitation to get black men killed.[25] As Odds later says to Truman: 'She ain't been fucking you, she's been atoning for her sins.'[26] Odds is of course a less polished, more honest, version of Truman himself, playing on white racial guilt and cultivating his blackness to work his will.

Finally, there is Meridian. Not only is she in the process of changing her mind, but as Truman thinks to himself: 'no matter what she was saying to you, and no matter what you were saying to her, [she] seemed to be thinking of something else . . .'[27] Indeed, there is a great vagueness about Meridian as a character. Having escaped the prison house of motherhood and marriage and survived the Movement, Meridian is still engaged in a one-woman community organizing/voter registration project, along with serving as a moral mentor for Lynne and Truman who make pilgrimmages to see her. Because she seems to have opted for the Buddhist solution – the diminution of desire – she takes on the status of guru. In the end she is as close to Lynne as to Truman. Indeed, *Meridian* can be read as a novel about the growth of women's self-awareness in the wake of the collapse of the civil rights movement: the former historically – and almost logically – emerges from the latter.

Yet Meridian's experience in the Movement remains central to her self-understanding. It has clarified her thoughts about violence and what her role in any future struggle might be. Most disturbing for her about the Movement is the creation of a party line which all members are required to parrot, just as her mother and respectable opinion tried to bring her into line as a daughter and young mother. As she says: 'I've always had trouble telling the "correct" thing from the "right" thing. The right thing is never to kill.'[28] Thus political movements, even the civil rights movement, create ideological straitjackets and demand a willingness to sign over one's independence of mind. Whatever role Meridian will end up playing, perhaps that of the people's poet who 'sings from memory songs they [the real revolutionaries] will need once more to hear', it will be one that is 'right' rather than 'correct' because she has chosen it.[29]

Like Walker's *Meridian*, Rosellen Brown's *Civil Wars* is a novel of grief and loss and, more significantly, one of the few novels to explore the significance of the Movement for its white participants. Its two central characters, a married couple named Teddy Carll and Jessie Singer, are representatively paired. A southerner, Teddy was disowned by his family for joining the movement and has only gradually re-established a tenuous *modus vivendi* with them. Jessie is a red-diaper baby, the daughter of New York Jewish,

Old Left parents. Having originally come to Mississippi as a volunteer, she was swept off her feet by Teddy and they got married. However, the time of the novel (1979) finds the two living in Jackson, Mississippi, where Teddy is frittering his life away selling textbooks, a captive of his own morally heroic past, while Jessie is in the process of realizing that they must some-how make a break with what their life has become: 'Teddy and she were what they once were, not even what they were today; surely not what they were doing.'[30]

They have reached a point where they can no longer live on past reputa-tions (brave civil rights workers) and desires (black and white together). We learn that Teddy was almost killed when he was run off the road by hostile whites and that he is now 'rusting with disuse'.[31] In the midst of all this, Teddy's sister and brother-in-law are killed in an accident and the Carlls must assume responsibility for raising their son and daughter, along with their own two children.

Not a lot happens in *Civil Wars*; nothing much does during an extended period of mourning. The 'action' consists largely of trying to work through the loss of political commitment and the dereliction of self once organized around that experiences. Jessie remembers when 'everything was political'[32] in the positive, exhilarating sense. Echoing Lynne's thoughts on 'black peo-ple as Art', Jessie remembers thinking when she first arrived in Mississippi: 'There was a kind of glamour to such poverty in photographs; if it had texture, that became the grittiness of art, uncompromising vision, good matte paper.'[33] At the time, Teddy's personal and sexual charm lay in his ability to link the personal and political:

> most of them [other women] would have been astounded by the change of focus from their bodies to the body politic. All his charm lay in that surprise, in the breadth of his passions.[34]

The Movement time was the golden time when, above all, the public and private, the political and personal, coincided rather than worked at cross-purposes.

Jessie also remembers the emotional costs to Teddy of rejection by his own family. Clearly his deep personal investment in the Movement as his true 'home' and 'family' are explained by the prior loss of original home and family. But it has also produced in him an internal censor, an over-whelmingly politicized super-ego, which prevents his responding fully to their present dilemma:

> there were things she could dare to think and say that, having said them as a bigoted child, Teddy could never say again . . . But Teddy had a list, a little bit like the Pope's index and just as futile to appeal, of forbidden topics and general thematic areas which he made clear caused him distress.[35]

This is a far cry from the Teddy whom Jessie remembers arguing with his black Movement comrades, trying to explain the white southern hostility to the Movement.

> White folks are my people. (It cost him something to say ... because he hated so many of them to the bottom of his bowels ...) Maybe not human in our terms. But human enough in theirs ... I'm not talking Klan. I'm talking just folks, and when they die they still get buried with honor and people still grieve for them just as if they were human. It's a pretty good facsimile. They don't have to stop and give it a human thought until they *want* to.[36]

He continues by contrasting these 'normal' southern whites with the white volunteers whom veteran black workers often scorned: 'So don't shit on the ones who stop and think. They choose that. They elect to do it. They can afford to, and you and your folks can't'.[37]

Clearly Brown's perspective illuminates the different psychologies of political commitment that brought white and black people into the Movement. For many whites the experience of Freedom Summer jerked them out of the expected trajectory of their lives and forced them to make life-defining choices. Put another way, black civil rights workers certainly met a certain resistance from the black communities they were attempting to organize and their families might object to the danger involved in the movement, but the black community *did* fundamentally support the movement. This was much more rarely the case with white volunteers whose families and communities often deeply disapproved of what they were doing to the point, as both *Meridian* and *Civil Wars* make apparent, of disowning or casting them out. Indeed Doug McAdam's *Freedom Summer* makes the point that, though white Movement volunteers did not succumb to the 'big chill' and generally remained committed to the values, in one form or another, that took them to Mississippi in the first place, 'they have paid for this lifelong commitment with a degree of alienation and social isolation that has only increased with time.'[38]

Second, Teddy's emphasis upon choice is crucial, for he is identifying what differentiates a life of moral nullity from one of moral imagination. Hannah Arendt's point about Adolph Eichmann was not that he was cruel or vicious, but that he lacked some essential moral capacity or imagination and that the 'lesson' we should learn from the Eichmann phenomenon was always 'to think what we are doing'. Similarly, Teddy suggests, though the average white southerner seemed to be living a normal life, the white southern sense of the 'normal' failed to equip most white southerners with the moral self-awareness to change their and their region's lives.

But that was what Teddy had done in the Movement days. The horrible irony is that fundamental choices he made in those heroic times hardened

into counter-productive, personal dogma. He cannot – and dare not – keep
making the same kind of choice over and over again. Yet he persists in
doing so. The power of Brown's book is that she won't allow Teddy and
Jessie's difficulty to be just a private marital tragedy or just a failure of
personality. Indeed, what Jessie sees happening in her own marriage has
happened in her parents'. As a young girl, Jessie's father disappeared period-
ically on Party assignments; as a result her parents gradually became es-
tranged. Jessie, says the narrator, could never forgive his 'final inattention'.[39]
Mother and father, female and male, private and public, introspection and
action: the old dichotomies keep turning up and ensnaring succeeding generations in their repetitive patterns. Though Jessie's is the narrative authority in the novel, the novel allows us to see that she too is haunted by the
ghosts of old family patterns and may be culpable in the demise of her
marriage and family. But, again, what is happening is not just the outcome
of frailities of two decent, brave people. They have been permanently scarred
by history itself: 'it had come to her with astounding clarity, in one of their
sloughs of depression, that the ebb of political movements is not so much
ideological as it is physical. That exhaustion, body and soul weariness, ought
to be the name of the villain that undoes progress, preempts choice.'[40] All
the choices, all the personal assessment of credit and blame, look quite different
in such a light.

Much later in the novel, the Carlls have bought a home in a new neighbourhood, but Teddy scarcely shows his face there any longer: 'There was
public time – at a sufficient distance it was called history – and there was
private time that beat like a small hot heart inside the body of that history . . . You couldn't escape the public part, you were in it and it in you.
But you could escape the private apparently: Teddy could by vanishing . . .'.[41]
Or Teddy thinks he can. But he is wrong, for he refuses to make the distinction between public and private, past and present, that must once more be
drawn. After a flood has inundated their new neighbourhood, he returns to
his family too late to really help. He finds that Jessie has resolved not, this
time or ever again, to begin the repetitive cycle again. Teddy once more
loses his world.

Whose fault is it – theirs or history's? How should people like Meridian
or Teddy and Jessie keep going? Neither *Meridian* nor *Civil Wars* offers
easy answers, or any answers at all. It is no answer to say that it is up to the
individual *or* to claim that history calls men and women against their own
personal wishes and must be heeded. Whatever the case, these last two novels
in particular reveal something crucial to the historical consciousness, particularly of the American Left since the 1960s: the amount of mourning
work yet to be done, of losses to be worked through. Only then can what
was begun in the 1960s – the process of bridging the gap between black and
white – be taken up again. Not so that differences can be effaced or so that

they can be fixed in concrete; but so that the essential work of mutual recognition can continue.

If this seems a daunting task, the old Jewish story of the man who was assigned to sit at the gate of the village and wait for the coming of the Messiah may offer some consolation. When the man complained to the village elders that his pay was too low for such a momentous task, they responded: 'You are right. The pay is low. But consider: the work is steady.'

NOTES

1. Martha Nussbaum, 'Perceptive Equilibrium: Literary Theory and Ethical Theory' in Ralph Cohen (ed.), *The Future of Literary Theory* (London, 1989), p. 58.
2. See E. L. Doctorow, 'False Documents' in Theodore Solotaroff (ed.), *American Review* (New York, 1977), pp. 215–32. Albert Stone, *The Return of Nat Turner: History, Literature and Cultural Politics in Sixties America* (Athens, Ga., 1992) is an often interesting but tendentious account of the controversy from the 1960s to the present. Stone is so dismissive of Styron that his defence of the ten black writers comes to seem suspect after a while. In addition he dismisses any historiographical treatment of slavery, past or present, that fails to fit the approach that considers slave culture above all else a form of resistance. For a good antidote to Stone, see Seymour Gross and Eileen Bender, 'History, Politics and Literature: The Myth of Nat Turner', *American Quarterly* (October 1971); pp. 487–518 which is both more tolerant of Styron and sceptical of the ten black writers, without becoming a shill for either.
3. Stone, *Return of Nat Turner*, pp. 8, 11.
4. Quoted in Ian Parker, 'The Great American Depressive', *Independent on Sunday Magazine* (17 October 1993), p. 14.
5. See Kwame Anthony Appiah, *In My Father's House* (New York, 1992) for a forceful challenge to the view that cultures are, can or should be hermetically sealed off from one another.
6. See Lerone Bennett, 'Nat's Last White Man', in John Henrik Clarke (ed.), *William Styron's Nat Turner: Ten Black Writers Respond* (Boston, 1968), p. 5, and Vincent Harding, 'You've Taken Our Nat and Gone', ibid., pp. 23–33.
7. Laurence Thomas, 'Moral Deference', *Philosophical Forum*, XXIV, 1–3 (Fall–Spring 1992–3); 241.
8. Ibid., 233.
9. Ibid., 243, 234.
10. Ibid., 241.
11. Oliver Sacks tells of the remarkable experience of watching Robert De Niro trying to enter the world of the encephalitics who were depicted in the film, *Awakenings*. The first time De Niro was to appear before the cameras in his role, Sacks asked one of the patients with whom he could communicate to indicate how De Niro was doing. During the filming the patient turned to Sacks and simply nodded her head a couple of times: De Niro had got it right. *Awakenings* (rev. ed; London, 1990), p. 386.
12. Stephen Carter, *Reflections of an Affirmative Action Baby* (New York, 1991), p. 209.

178   *Richard H. King*

13. It is another question whether the novelist and/or the historian should automatically aim for moral deference. The problem with the idea of moral deference is that it can easily slip into a kind of uncritical attitude towards individuals or groups who are especially marked by oppression. Yet, there just is a difference between writing about the experience, traditions, cultures with which one feels most comfortable and those that are somehow 'other'. Nor is there any reason to think that novelists *per se* are better at grasping the 'other' than historians. And yet . . .

14. In her *Down from the Mountaintop: Black Women's Novels in the Wake of the Civil Rights Movement, 1966–89* (New Haven and London, 1991), Melissa Walker takes up nine novelists and discusses the way their work reflects the effects of the civil rights movement. The book is a useful compendium but offers little more than plot summaries and thematic discussions. Her contextual judgements are often highly reductive.

15. 'Narrative of commitment' is an alternative to Robert Stepto's ideas of 'narratives of ascent' and 'narratives of immersion'. See Robert Stepto, *From Behind the Veil* (Urbana, 1979).

16. Ernest J. Gaines, *A Gathering of Old Men* (New York, 1984), p. 174.

17. Ibid., pp. 36, 38.

18. Ibid., p. 85.

19. Ibid., pp. 181–2.

20. Alice Walker, *Meridian* (New York, 1976), p. 25.

21. Hayden White's work in general has addressed this matter of the limits of the rhetoric of history. A closer look at the kind of education and professional training which American historians receive might also be in order.

22. Walker, *Meridian*, p. 11.

23. Ibid., p.13.

24. This attitude is by no means confined to white people thinking about black people. The history of the reception of James Agee and Walker Evans, *Let Us Now Praise Famous Men*, as well as Agee's complex ruminations and Evans's classic photographs, exemplify this same 'aestheticization' of the other.

25. Walker, *Meridian*, p. 137.

26. Ibid., p. 164.

27. Ibid., p. 14.

28. Ibid., p. 188.

29. Ibid., p. 201.

30. Rosellen Brown, *Civil Wars* (New York, 1985), p. 18.

31. Ibid., p. 27.

32. Ibid., p. 246.

33. Ibid., p. 240.

34. Ibid., p. 31.

35. Ibid., p. 14

36. Ibid., pp. 42–3.

37. Ibid., p. 41.

38. Doug McAdam, *Freedom Summer* (New York and Oxford, 1988), p. 232.

39. Brown, *Civil Wars*, p. 164.

40. Ibid., p. 83.

41. Ibid., p. 353.

Part IV

Comparisons

10 The Limits of America: Rethinking Equality in the Changing Context of British Race Relations

Tariq Modood

I

Most people would agree, but for the fact that it is rarely commented upon, that despite the various differences that exist between the leading theorists and commentators of British race relations, most of them share a paradigm. They work within an Atlantocentric model and focus on the historical experience of the Atlantic rim.

This is true of the two founders of the British sociology of race relations, John Rex and Michael Banton. Rex brought an understanding of 'race' based on a South African experience and, while he generalized it to include all situations marked by severe conflict and exploitation, his empirical studies of British immigrant community developments described the situation in terms of a black–white polarity.[1] Banton's approach has been more historical and so has explicitly brought out the differences in the various race relations situations in different times and places but has been based on the Atlantic rim.[2] More recently, a 'cultural studies' or 'racism discourse' approach has emerged. Its starting point was a focus on the moral panic about young Afro-Caribbean males and mugging and other crimes, theorized as the essential relationship between the British criminal justice system and the non-white (conceived of course as 'black') population.[3] In the work of its most distinguished exponent, Paul Gilroy, while 'black' continues to be argued for as a socio-political category capable of being meaningfully embraced by British Caribbeans and Asians alike, the content of 'black' has increasingly been freighted with Afro-diasporic culture with no attempt made to show whether and how this has relevance for Asian peoples in Britain or how and why they should make the black experience their own.[4] Indeed, his latest work with its eloquent and bold argument that 'blackness' is necessarily a product not just of white domination and the resistance of the oppressed but also of a dialogue with European modernity, makes explicit its Atlantocentricity. The Atlantic focus also permeates all British anti-racist politics, above all in

181

the subsumption of Asians into a political blackness and is revealed in Peter Fryer's 'engaged' history of 'black' people in Britain which despite the usual prefatory remarks about Asians as an integral part of black Britain devotes less than twenty of its six hundred pages to them.[5]

What is meant by an Atlantocentric model is the conceptualization of the black–white relationship in the Atlantic rim as the paradigm of race relations. The historical core of this model is the slave-trade triangle, and the modern political core consists of the US civil rights movement, anti-apartheid, the urban and equal opportunities programmes that arose in response to riots and the prospect of social breakdown in the inner cities. In this way the Atlantic triangle could be said to be widened from Liverpool–West Africa–Virginia to London–Soweto–Los Angeles. As such it represents, of course, a valuable political force with much to its credit. Yet the conceptualization of British race relations in Atlantocentric terms, even if it once seemed plausible, is currently faced with two problems. The first is the non-Atlantic character of the majority of non-white Britons. According to the 1991 Census two of the three million people in Britain of non-European origins have origins from outside the Atlantic triangle, above all from the Indian subcontinent. They bring with them cultures, solidarities, communal authorities, aspirations, enmities and memories, including a colonial relationship of subordination which is quite different from the Atlantic pattern. The second flows from the first. Events outside the Atlantic world, outside of its intellectual and political frame are now impinging on domestic British race relations – in fact, more so than race-relations events within other parts of the Atlantic area, are affecting Britain. Khalistan, Kashmir and Khomeini; the Gulf War, the destruction of the mosque at Ayodha and the fate of multiculturalism in Bosnia have a greater influence on British race relations than the fortunes of the ANC in South Africa or Jesse Jackson or the riots of Los Angeles. In March 1989 the chairman of the influential US congressional black caucus brought a large delegation to London to support the launch of a parallel organization at Westminster; it has sunk without a trace. The Ayatollah Khomeini without leaving Tehran was able to inspire, and possibly fund, the creation of a 'Muslim Parliament' in London launched in January 1992, which has repeatedly been able to capture the media headlines and, for better or for ill, colours majority–minority relations in the UK.

The event which made Khomeini's influence in British politics possible was of course the Rushdie affair. The working-class Asian Muslim anger over *The Satanic Verses* and the ensuing crisis clearly constitutes one of the major events of British race relations. Yet, as the Iranian revolution was to the CIA and the invasion of the Falklands to British military intelligence, so Muslim anger has been to British anti-racism. It is barely intelligible, let alone predictable, within British anti-racist perspectives. Throughout the 1980s, of the nine non-white groups identified in the Labour Force Survey, Pakistanis and Bangladeshis (virtually all Muslims) have suffered the highest rates of unemployment, have the lowest number of educational qualifications and the highest profile in manual work; and this is true in each respect not just for women but also men, and not just for the middle-aged (the first generation) but also the young. They have had the most adverse impact from immigration laws and rules, they have the worst housing and suffer from the highest levels of attacks on person and property. If a racial underclass exists in Britain, here it is. Why should this most socially deprived and racially harassed group bear all this, and yet explode in anger on an issue of religious honour? Why should this anger take place in Britain rather than France, Germany or America where the number of Muslims is greater, hostility against them no less and their condition much worse in the two European countries? The fact that the available theories of race look like non-starters in answering such questions is a serious drawback to any claims that they are adequate interpreters of social reality in contemporary Britain.

II

Why is there this difficulty, this inability to understand and explain such key events? The central concept of the Atlantocentric perspective is *racial dualism*: being white or not is the single most crucial factor in determining the sociological profile and political dynamic of any non-white group.[6] This may have been true of some societies once, and it may be true of some societies today. It probably was never true of Britain and it certainly is not true of it today. British racial politics were clearly influenced by American precedents; Martin Luther King Jr and Malcolm X both visited Britain before their murders and were a source of inspiration and emulation; wittingly or unwittingly they may have contributed to the impression that the racial divide that had shaped their politics existed also in Britain. The two countries however are very different and the British race relations situation is one which is characterized by the complex class structure of the country and an ethno-religious pluralism of recent origins which is still taking shape.

Everyone would readily agree that the migrants to Britain and their descendants, coming from different parts of the British colonial world, consist of a heterogeneity of geographical origins, nationalities, religions, languages, cultures, customs and so on. To take just those from the Indian subcontinent as an example: they are from three major countries (Pakistan, Bangladesh and India; not to mention those who came via a generation or two in East Africa); have three principal religions (Hinduism, Sikhism and Islam); and have at least five languages and literatures (Punjabi, Urdu, Hindi, Bengali and Gujurati). Nevertheless, it has been widely assumed by sociologists and egalitarians that the heterogeneity amongst non-whites was more than compensated for by two powerful commonalities. Firstly, that the ethnic minorities shared a similar economic position: they were disproportionately working-class or even formed a distinct underclass. Secondly, they were equally shaped by racism. In order to expound my view that British race relations are characterized not by a dualism but a pluralism I need to address both these points.

There is some truth in each of these two points but the first was true for only a limited period of time and even then in only a qualified way; the second has been interpreted too simplistically. The economic commonality argument was largely true during the period of immigration and early settlement, the 1950s to the 1980s. The need in Britain was for cheap, unskilled labour to perform those jobs in an expanding economy which the natives no longer wished to do, and the bulk of the immigration occurred in response to this need. The immigrants brought limited skills (including very little English in the case of Asians), virtually no capital, often did not plan to settle in Britain and were therefore willing to enter British society at the bottom. This, however, was not true of the East African Asians who were business people and administrators in an English-speaking context and were allowed to enter Britain under sufferance (sometimes with some material capital as well as their human capital) as political refugees in the late 1960s and early to mid-1970s, and constituted about 10 per cent of the non-whites. Even in the period in which the economic commonality argument was largely true, if researchers had attended more closely to aspiration, hours worked, money saved, the purchase of property, self-help amongst kinsfolk, the emergence of self-employment, acquisition of educational qualifications, they would have been able to see that different groups were using different survival and advancement strategies and that divergence in socio-economic positions was probable. Instead, sociologists focused on racial discrimination and disadvantage, believing that no significant social mobility was possible without major state intervention, and interpreted all trends in the most pessimistic light (often sincerely, sometimes perhaps politically) and systematically minimized economic divergences within the minority population. Thus, for example, the first major study of Asian self-employment, a remarkable phenomenon of resourcefulness by those who were being let down by the failing manufacturing industries, dismissed it as an economic dead-end, unprofitable activities which could not survive.[7] Yet, from virtually nil, Indians had achieved by 1990 the number of millionaires proportional to their population size. The first national survey to register the beginnings of an educational-economic divergence amongst minorities glossed over it, as in its title, *Black and White Britain*.[8] When entry into higher education was monitored for ethnicity and revealed that most minorities were not under-represented and some were significantly over-represented, expert writers were still publishing predictions of uniform under-representation.[9]

There is now strong evidence from several sources, notably the annual Labour Force Survey and the 1991 Census that the diversity between the minorities in terms of educational qualifications, occupation and social class, self-employment, unemployment, home ownership (not to mention household size and structure, endogamy and age distribution) is considerable; more than between whites and non-whites taken as aggregate wholes.[10] Moreover that some minority groups (Indians, Chinese and possibly Africans) have or are developing a socio-economic profile which is better than that of the white population, while some groups (Bangladeshis, Pakistanis and Afro-Caribbeans) continue to be over-represented amongst the less qualified, the manual workers and the unemployed, though even between these groups there are significant differences, not least of gender. I offer three tables of statistics from the 1991 Census to illustrate my argument against racial dualism. Table 10.1 shows that of those in employment Whites and Black-Caribbeans have a very similar class distribution, as do Black-Africans and Indians – the latter pair enjoying a more advantaged position. The best position is occupied by the Chinese and Asian-Others, and the worst of all by the Bangladeshis. Of course as each social class band is extremely broad, it is possible that the non-white groups are disproportionately at the bottom of each band and are very likely over-represented in the professional and managerial categories due to the large number of shopkeepers. Moreover, a credible picture requires us to compare also the levels of unemployment, presented in Table 10.2.

Table 10.1 Percentage of employed in social class by ethnic group, 1991 Census

	W	B–C	B–A	I	P	B	A–O
Professional	5	2	9	9	6	5	10
Managerial	29	26	28	28	22	13	27
Skilled non-manual	24	24	23	23	18	20	25
Skilled manual	21	22	13	16	25	26	22
Semi-skilled	15	19	17	21	24	32	10
Unskilled	6	7	10	3	5	4	3

Key

W   White
B-C   Black-Caribbean (includes 'Black-Other' of Caribbean origins)
B-A   Black-African
I   Indian
P   Pakistani
B   Bangladeshi
C   Chinese
A-O   Asian-Other

Source: Ballard and Kalra, *The Ethnic Diminsion of the 1991 Census: A Preliminary Report*, (Manchester, 1994).

Table 10.2   Percentage of unemployed men by ethnic group, 1991 Census

White	10.7
Black-Caribbean	23.8
Black-African	28.9
Black-Other	25.5
Indian	13.4
Pakistani	28.5
Bangladeshi	30.9
Chinese	10.5
Asian-Other	14.2

Source: D. Owen, *Ethnic Minorities in Great Britain: Economic Characteristics*, (Warwick, 1993).

In the case of rates of male unemployment we do have a dualism.[11] But it is not a racial dualism. Whites, Chinese, Indians and Asian-Other have employment rates within the range of 10–14 per cent, while all the other groups have rates within the range of 24–31 per cent. This means that the rates of unemployment do confirm the advantageous class position of the Chinese, Asian-Other and Indians; but seriously qualify that of the Africans and the Caribbeans; and reinforce the initial disadvantaged picture of the Bangladeshis and Pakistanis. Table 10.3 presents the figures on those with degrees, diplomas and other higher educational or higher vocational qualifications. There we have not a dualism but a tripartite banding with the Africans and Chinese roughly twice as numerous as the Whites and Indians, who in turn are twice as numerous as all the others.

Table 10.3   Percentage holding higher qualifications then A-level by ethnic group, 1991 Census

White	13.4
Black-Caribbean	9.2
Black-African	26.5
Indian	15.0
Pakistani	7.0
Bangladeshi	5.2
Chinese	25.8

Source: *The Sun*, 24 January 1994.

It can be seen, therefore, from these three tables that broadly speaking Indians and Chinese are now on a par if not perhaps doing better than Whites and that if there is a dualism in employment in Britain it is not a *colour* dualism.

III

A further thing that these tables show is that the non-white groups, with the possible exception of the Chinese and Asian-Other, are perhaps not doing as well in employment terms as might be expected in terms of the qualifications they hold. The most dramatic case of this are the Africans, twice as many of whom have a higher qualification compared to Whites, and yet well over twice as many African men are unemployed compared to white men. It may be suggested that regardless of their *position* in the occupational hierarchy all or most non-white groups are in a lesser position than they objectively should be and that the cause for this is a blanket racial discrimination. This in fact brings us to the second point that I said I needed to consider in order to argue against racial dualism. There is some truth in the view that despite their differences non-white groups suffer from racism, although, it has been argued, the Chinese do not seem to be a target.[12] I believe, however, that it falls far short of racial dualism for two reasons. One is that it has only a limited effect on outcomes: the character of ethnic communities, structural inequalities created by class processes affecting whites and non-whites alike, even the unequal geographical development of the British economy in the 1980s which has benefited Indians in the South-East but has been devastating for Pakistanis in the North, are critical and probably singly but certainly in combination have a greater determining effect on outcomes than does race.

Secondly, racial discrimination is not a unitary form of disadvantaging because not all non-white groups are discriminated against in the same way or to the same extent. Colour-racism may be a constant but there are other kinds of racism at work in Britain. *Direct* discrimination depends upon stereotypes and there are no stereotypes about 'blackness' as such: the stereotypes are always about specific groups or quasi-groups ('Jamaicans are lazy', 'Asians don't mix', 'Muslims are fanatical', etc.). Hence, different groups will be affected differently, and some groups can become or cease to be more 'acceptable' than others. White people have in surveys always stated more prejudice against Asians than Afro-Caribbeans and this is now rising especially amongst the young.[13] Moreover, stereotypes, like all social generalizations, allow for counter-examples, so that individuals of any group who are able to demonstrate, for example in an interview, that they are a counter-example to the stereotype, will receive less unfavourable treatment. *Indirect* discrimination depends on policies and practices which (unintentionally) disproportionately disadvantage one group compared to others. Groups whose language, religion, customs and family structures are most different from the white majority norm, will experience the most disadvantage and exclusion. Just as colour-blind class discrimination can be a form of indirect racial discrimination, so membership of a minority community can render one less employable on the grounds of one's dress, dietary habits or the desire to take leave from work on one's holy days rather than those prescribed by the custom and practice of the majority community. This direct and indirect discrimination, taken together, constitutes 'cultural-racism' (in contrast to colour-racism) and is targeted at groups perceived to be assertively 'different' and not trying to 'fit in'.

It is this form of racism that is least acknowledged, debated or repudiated (sentences beginning: 'I am no racist but . . .' are most likely to be expressions of cultural-racism) and is not properly outlawed (the courts have deemed discrimination against Muslims to be lawful) and yet is the racism that is on the increase, has the greater impact upon Asians and is an important cause of the rising levels of racial violence in Britain and Europe. One way to understand this rise is to see it as a backlash to the emergence of 'public ethnicity'. Minority ethnicity, albeit white ethnicity, has traditionally been regarded in Britain as acceptable if confined to the privacy of family and community and if it did not make any political demands. In association with other socio-political movements (feminism, gay rights, etc.) which challenge the public–private distinction or demand a share of the public space, claims are increasingly made today that ethnic difference is not just something that needs 'mere' toleration but needs to be publicly acknowledged, resourced and represented. Thus there is a vague multiculturalism as a policy ideology and it has perhaps contributed to a new ethnic assertiveness, so that many of the race relations conflicts today (for example, the Honeyford affair, the Rushdie affair) arise out of a demand for public space, for public respect and public resources for minority cultures and for the transmission of such cultures to the young. Yet, because our racial equality legal and policy framework is premised on colour-racism, there is no clear view from any part of the political spectrum (except perhaps from the nationalist Right) as to what extent these political demands are justifiable, especially in relation to religious communalism, and how cultural-racism should be tackled. In many ways prejudice and antipathy against ethno-religious groups poses a challenge the seriousness of which has yet to be appreciated. For not only is there a challenge to recognize and oppose 'cultural racism', but, additionally, a challenge to the taken-for-granted secularism of the multiculturalists and indeed of British public life. While a secular framework need not necessarily be insensitively hegemonic, contemporary secular multiculturalists are unaware of the contradictory signals that they are sending out. For a multiculturalism which states that public recognition of minority cultures is essential to equal citizenship, when combined with a denial of an equivalent public recognition of religion, can only convey the message that religious identity has and ought to have less status than other forms of group identity.[14] Why should it be the case that groups proclaiming themselves to be 'black' are to be empowered and given distinctive forms of political representation, but equally disadvantaged groups that mobilize around a religious rather than a colour identity are to be discouraged? While such questions are not answered, non-white religious groups may rightly complain of double standards.

IV

It should be clear that the diversity under discussion is important not just in the experience of racism, in what constitutes racism, but also in resisting racism and in the mobilization of oppressed groups. For we need a concept of race that helps us to understand that an oppressed group feels its oppression most according to those dimensions of its being which *it* (not the oppressor) values the most; moreover, it will resist its oppression from those dimensions of its being from which it derives its greatest collective psychological strength. This point can be llustrated by reference to Muslims once again. They hardly ever think of themselves in terms of colour or in terms of race as defined by anti-racists. And so, in terms of their own being they feel most acutely those problems that the anti-racists are blind to; and respond weakly to those challenges that the anti-racists want to meet with most force. For this reason, and because of their own racism, Muslims cannot easily, confidently or systematically assume the moral high ground on the issue of colour-racism; their sense of being and their surest conviction about their devaluation by others comes from their historical community of faith and their critique of 'the West'. Authentic anti-racism for Muslims, therefore, will inevitably have a religious dimension and take a form in which it is integrated to the rest of Muslim concerns. Anti-racism begins (or ought to begin) by accepting oppressed groups on their own terms (knowing full well that these will change and evolve) not by imposing a spurious identity and asking them to fight in the name of that. The new strength amongst Muslim youths, for example, in not tolerating racial harassment, owes no less to Islamic reassertion than to metropolitan anti-racism: people do not turn and run when something they care about is under attack. The racist taunt 'Rushdie' rouses more self-defence amongst Muslims than 'black bastard!'.[15]

People often ask, why has Britain not had a US-style civil rights movement? Is it just the absence of impressive leadership of the quality of Martin Luther King Jr? I think it is for more fundamental reasons, one of which makes far more sense once we break out of the Atlantocentric frame. Consider this example of certain social dynamics where a South Asian perspective offers explanatory and policy insights. The example is directly to do with political identities or mobilizing identities.

Diagrams 10.1 to 10.4 represent schematically the political situation at four time-periods. Diagram 10.1 represents the situation before the arrival

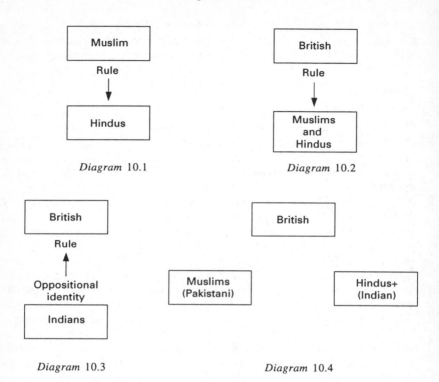

Diagram 10.1

Diagram 10.2

Diagram 10.3

Diagram 10.4

of the British in India, when Muslims ruled over Hindus. Diagram 10.2 represents the situation when the British ruled India. Diagram 10.3 depicts a later time when the nationalist movement attempted to create a unified oppositional identity of Indian. The last diagram shows the failure of that movement with the assertion of a Muslim identity by the majority of Muslims, leaving some Muslims and other minorities grouped around a Hindu+ identity, a majority Hindu grouping aspiring to transcend sectarian divisions. The point of the example is that an oppositional identity depends upon emotionally welding together a disparate population; to do so one must draw upon the traditions and beliefs of the oppressed, especially in a way that is readily communicable to the ordinary mass of people. Where the relevant population embodies one or more major historical cleavage, the task is difficult. The mobilization of the Indian masses required an appeal to past Hindu glories, to Hindu symbols and customs, in short to a form of Hindu nationalism. But the beating of that drum led through group competition and a 'me-too-ism' to a rival oppositional identity, a Muslim nationalism and eventually the creation of Pakistan, which, too, the more populist it had to be, that is to say the more it had to mobilize mass action, the more religious it also became in rhetoric, imagery and so on. If the matter could have been left to an Anglicized Indian elite, communal passions would not have been aroused; but the politics of anti-imperialism required the mobilization of the masses and the political struggle had to be couched in terms that made sense to the masses and could elicit their support and sacrifices.

There are four lessons or insights relevant to Britain in this story. First, in the Atlantic model it is assumed that the form and the extent of the racist and imperial domination is such that it erases the diversity amongst the dominated or at least makes the diversity politically insignificant. The South Asian experience is that this emphatically is not the case.

Second, as the development of an Indian oppositional identity was confused with Hindu nationalism, so it is not surprising that the development of a contemporary British 'black' (i.e., non-white) oppositional identity was confused with the development of a black ethnic pride (African roots) movement, and triggered off other ethnic assertions such as 'Asian', 'Muslim' and so on, and reduced a political 'black' to an ethnic blackness.[16]

Third, in the Atlantic model the ethnicity in question is a political ethnicity; not exclusively political, but that is its core, and this is reflected in symbols, agenda, choice of leaders, themes in literature etc. For South Asians the primary identity is a religious one.

Fourth, for black Americans and Afro-Caribbeans in Britain all the cultural, political and ideological resources are and have been focused on opposition to exclusion, subordination and discrimination; on the reaction to a dominant 'Other' and the right of entry into the dominant system. For South Asians, especially the Muslims, there is the historical fact of ruling and an ideology of rule, and the minority communities of these traditions in Britain have structures of authority which they may wish the wider society to acknowledge, as well as to allow entry into that society.

Despite the hegemony that it has enjoyed for the last three decades the Atlantocentric model is less than helpful in Britain, and is now under challenge in the United States too. There is a new multiculturalism, an emphasis on ethnic diversity rather than racial dualism within a politics of difference as found, for example, in Iris Marion Young's, *Justice and the Politics of Difference*.[17] We can no doubt learn something from it, although any formulation of pluralism and of equality which does not feature Muslims is less than helpful in Europe: Young's long list of oppressed groups never mentions Muslims, yet the racialization of Muslims, who form two-thirds of all non-white people in the European Union, is now at the heart of European race relations. Of course, there are those on both sides of the Atlantic who criticize Muslims and others for organizing (as in the Indian example) along religious lines to press for civil rights. In my view this is just a secular prejudice though one which is found in much anti-racist thought and practice.

For a liberal society is no more pro or anti political mobilization on the
basis of religious affiliation than it is on the basis of class or race or gender. What destroys liberal citizenship is if any one of these collective modes
always trumps the others: if people come to inhabit any one of these collective modes to the exclusion of the others such that deep social divisions are
formed and the free criss-crossing association of individuals necessary for a
common citizenship is difficult. The individualism associated with post-
modernism, again present in a radical form in Young's political philosophy
of resistance with its prioritization of individual autonomy, is too destruc-
tive of communities and is certainly not a necessary price for racial equality
let alone an undisputed end in itself.[18]

In western Europe Muslims and many others see ourselves as establishing
new communities in old countries, that is to say in a context of long-estab-
lished on-going traditions, cultures and nationalities. A framework for racial
equality therefore which ignores the realities of ethno-religious communities
and a plurality of nation-states, and of how these two sets of entities can be
harmonized with each other, is a non-starter in Western Europe. Moreover,
given the nature of the most prominent forms of racism in Europe, where
hostility to lighter-skinned Maghrebians and Turks can be greater than to
culturally-integrated and darker-skinned Africans and Caribbeans, some notion like cultural-racism must be a precondition of effective anti-racism. If a
suitable British or European perspective on race and equality can be developed – and I am not an unqualified optimist – then it may be that it will
offer Americans an example of a society that goes beyond racial dualism
and embodies some of the principles of a liberal pluralism.[19]

NOTES

1. J. Rex, *Race Relations in Sociological Theory* (London, 1970); J. Rex and R.
   Moore, *Race, Community and Conflict: A Study of Sparkbrook* (London, 1967);
   J. Rex and S. Tomlinson, *Colonial Immigrants in a British City: A Class Analysis* (London, 1979). John Rex's more recent work (e.g., J. Rex, *Ethnic Identities and Ethnic Mobilization in Britain* [Warwick, 1991]) is much more sensitive
   to ethno-religious differences so he probably no longer conceives of British race
   relations in terms of a black-white relationship. He has not yet, however, attempted to reconcile his theoretical perspective with his latest work (though see
   J. Rex, 'The Role of Class Analysis in the Study of Race Relations – A Weberian
   Perspective', in J. Rex and D. Mason (eds), *Theories of Race and Ethnic Relations* (Cambridge, 1986), for perhaps a start).
2. M. Banton, *Racial and Ethnic Competition* (Cambridge, 1983).
3. S. Hall et al., *Policing the Crisis* (London, 1979); M. Keith, *Race, Riots and
   Policing: Lore and Disorder in a Multi-racist Society* (London, 1993).
4. P. Gilroy, *There Ain't No Black in the Union Jack* (London, 1987); P. Gilroy,

The Black Atlantic: Modernity and Double Consciousness (London, 1993).

5. T. Modood '"Black", Racial Equality and Asian Identity', *New Community*, 14, 3 (1988), 397–404; T. Modood, 'Political Blackness and British Asians', Sociology, 28, 4 (1994); P. Fryer, *Staying Power: The History of Black People in Britain* (London, 1984).

6. Not all sociologists who work within an Atlantic historical framework accept racial dualism. Banton has argued that the view of eminent American social scientists such as Talcott Parsons and Carl N. Degler that racial dualism is a precondition of anti-racism is a form of American ethnocentrism (M. Banton, *Racial and Ethnic Competition*, pp. 61–71).

7. H. Aldrich, T. P. Jones and D. McEvoy, 'Ethnic Advantage and Minority Business Development', in R. Ward and R. Jenkins (eds), *Ethnic Communities in Business: Strategies for Economic Survival* (Cambridge, 1984), pp.189–210. For a critique, see T. Modood, 'The Indian Economic Success: A Challenge to Some Race Relations Assumptions', *Policy and Politics*, 19, 3 (1991), 177–89 [also in. T. Modood, *Not Easy Being British: Colour, Culture and Citizenship* London and Stoke on Trent, 1992]).

8. C. Brown, *Black And White Britain* (London, 1984).

9. T. Modood, 'The Number of Ethnic Minority Students in British Higher Education: Some Grounds for Optimism', *Oxford Review of Education*, 19, 2 (1993), 167–82.

10. T. Jones, *Britain's Ethnic Minorities* (London, 1993); R. Ballard and V. S. Kalra, *The Ethnic Dimensions of the 1991 Census: A Preliminary Report* (Manchester, 1994).

11. I am confining my analysis to male unemployment, as female employment is considerably complicated by ethnicity: for example, the very low levels of Pakistani and Bangladeshi women who make themselves available in the formal labour market, or the fact that the position of a Black-Caribbean woman is so much better than that of Black-Caribbean men in relation to White women and men respectively. For these reasons male unemployment is a much better indicator of racial inequality and disadvantage.

12. Y. Cheng and A. Heath, 'Ethnic Origins and Class Destinations', *Oxford Review of Education* (1993), 19, 2, 151–66.

13. K. Young, 'Class, Race and Opportunity', in R. Jowell et al. (eds), *British Social Attitudes, The 9th Report*, (Aldershot, 1992).

14. T. Modood, 'Establishment, Multiculturalism and British Citizenship', *Political Quarterly*, 65, 1 (1994), 53–73.

15. T. Modood, 'British Asian Muslims and the Rushdie Affair', *Political Quarterly*, 61, 2 (1990), 143–60 [also in J. Donald and A. Rattansi (eds), *Race, Culture and Difference* (London, 1992)].

16. Modood, '"Black", Racial Equality and Asian Identity'; Modood, 'Political Blackness and British Asians'.

17. I.M. Young, *Justice and the Politics of Difference* (Princeton, 1990).

18. B. Parekh, 'Decolonising Liberalism' in A. Shtromas (ed.), *The End of Isms?* (Oxford, 1994), and 'Cultural Diversity and Liberal Democracy', in D. Beetham (ed.) *Defining and Measuring Democracy* (London, 1994).

19. T. Modood, 'Ethic Difference and Racial Equality: New Challenges for the Left', in D. Milliband (ed.) *Reinventing the Left* (Cambridge, 1994).

11 British Responses to Martin Luther King Jr and the Civil Rights Movement, 1954–68

Mike Sewell

I

The significance of race relations in Britain increased steadily between the Montgomery bus boycott and the assassination of Martin Luther King Jr. Large numbers of immigrants arrived from South Asia, Africa and the Caribbean. For example, Caribbean immigration grew rapidly after the McCarran Act of 1952 virtually ended coloured immigration to the United States. By 1961 there were 172 379 West Indian-born people in the United Kingdom.[1] The period also witnessed a wave of decolonization. Trouble in South Africa and then Rhodesia injected race-related issues into the political agenda. In the same month as King's assassination, the government published a White Paper on the extension of the 1965 Race Relations Act. Days later, Enoch Powell spoke out vehemently on immigration, giving the issue a new prominence.

British responses to the African-American freedom struggle could not be viewed apart from the issues of race relations that were demanding more and more attention. A slogan such as 'black power' might have a specific American meaning, but in British ears it resonated with fresh images of Mau Mau and other independence struggles or the use of the same slogan at home. This paper will sketch some of the connections between British and American race relations that grew between 1954 and 1968 and suggest that the significance of the civil rights movement in British eyes was intimately connected to the ascending salience of race issues in Britain.

II

A broad consensus underlay British responses to both King and the movement for which he so frequently served as a representative symbol. The press, from the *New Statesman* to *The Economist* and from the *Daily Herald* to *The Times*, praised 'the integration leader'. Gains for the civil rights movement were progress. Setbacks were defeat. Even on the right of the political spectrum, the *Daily Mail* was generally supportive of the broad goals of the American civil rights movement.[2] The sympathetic consensus frayed over the prospects for integration beyond the eradication of Jim Crow, perhaps as a result of growing fatalism about the issue in a British context, as marked by Powell's speech. The demands of more extreme nationalist and separatist leaders and organizations on both sides of the ocean from the middle sixties also strained British sympathy.[3]

British commentators placed American developments in a global context, the better to understand and explain them to an audience that had no direct experience of that country and its racial mores. Britain's imperial experience conditioned the way that British writers perceived the situation in the United States, as did the context of the Cold War. These two trends were related to the third. Little British commentary treated the race issue in the United States as a uniquely *American* matter. The points of reference and comparison that occurred to Britons, as to Martin Luther King himself, were global: the dilemma of race relations seemed universal and not national. American exceptionalism was downplayed and the view expressed that race was the great issue facing the world. *Race*, the journal of the Institute of Race Relations, first printed in 1959, exemplified this global perspective. During its first decade it carried articles on race relations in the Americas, Polynesia, Europe, the Caribbean, Asia and Africa, as well as theoretical pieces. The editor's introduction stressed the multiracial nature of the Commonwealth and turmoil in Africa:

> In an age when international conferences are the fashion, those of Bandung, Cairo and Accra are among the most significant. The relations between white and black Americans are headline news on both sides of the Iron Curtain and on our own doorstep we have the sombre events of Notting Hill to remind us that there is a coloured community in our midst.[4]

In 1963, Denis Brogan claimed in *The Spectator* that the 'rising tide of colour' was increasing in importance all over the world, be it in the challenge to white imperialism or to white supremacists in the United States. He praised L. E. Lomax's *The Negro Revolt* and commented on Birmingham, Alabama, in a discussion that emphasized the unity of the global race issue rather than singling out the United States as exceptional.[5] A cartoon in a popular newspaper depicted a black colossus striving to rise whilst Lilliputian figures representing Verwoerd, Bull Connor and the Bristol Bus Company strove to hold him down.[6] The *Daily Herald*, at the time of the March on Washington, juxtaposed the USA, which had stepped 'peacefully forward', and South Africa, whose story remained one of 'bitterness'. A subeditor included the following headlines: 'Continents Linked by Racial problems . . . The March of Freedom . . . At the Feet of Lincoln'.[7]

In 1961 *The Times* used the word *zareba* to describe the Jim Crow South. *Zareba* is a Sudanese word for stockade of fortified camp. The colonial experience provided a vocabulary for the explanation of the situation in the United States.[8] Africa was a prism through which British commentators filtered African-American news the better to understand and explain it. This may have been a product of British journalists and scholars in the 1950s and 1960s having cut their teeth in Africa and Asia. James Cameron knew India better than America. Sheila Patterson, author of *Dark Strangers*, was expert on southern Africa. Their experiences conditioned their understanding of events across the Atlantic. Gandhian influence was quickly noticed by British commentators.[9] King's espousal of an overtly Gandhian approach to challenge the white supremacist status quo in the South necessarily evoked the original use of such tactics against British authority. It was, however, possible to mitigate such potentially painful memories. *The Times* opined in November 1964 that King's task was harder than that of his role-model in that he had to force himself to love Bull Connor or George Wallace.[10] In such ways could a post-imperial sensibility be massaged while still sympathizing with the cause of racial equality in the USA.

British comment emphasized links between anti-colonial nationalism and African-American aspirations. This was true of the presence of Thurgood Marshall as a legal adviser among Kenyan negotiators in London in 1959.[11] It was also the case when H. Rap Brown's bodyguards at a New York press conference in 1967 sported caps bearing the words Mau Mau. The reference was to a New York gang, but *The Times* chose to highlight them in a photograph and caption.[12] The gang's association with a movement whose reputation was for violence against whites, even if the vast majority of its victims were black Kenyans, is itself interesting. Links between the global colonial and post-colonial issue of race relations and the situation in the United States were commonplace. *The Times* in March 1960 proclaimed a 'New Wind [sic] in the South':

> The new winds are blowing not only over Africa but all round the globe. The Negroes now engaged in the Southern United States on a non-violent campaign of resistance to racial discrimination may well have learnt something in method from GANDHI's tactics in Natal and afterwards in India; they may perhaps have been encouraged by the example of orderly protest set a few years ago in the bus boycott at Johannesburg. In object they clearly seek recognition of the partnership of races which is the declared aim for the Central African Federation and elsewhere. But they are also trying to carry a stage farther a process of liberation which has fashioned their own country.[13]

Perceptions of the American freedom struggle were influenced by Macmillan's statement on white rule in Africa as well as being understood as part of an American process.[14]

British commentators also viewed the civil rights movement, opposition to it and the attitude of successive administrations in the context of the

Cold War. East–West competition for the friendship of emerging nations added urgency to British comments about the situation in the United States. In 1955, for example, it was noted that the meeting of the ILO had become a forum for condemnation of the United States on the race issue.[15] A Foreign Office official commented that events in Little Rock were 'a present for Communist propaganda in Asia and Africa'.[16] Reports from the British embassy in Washington (routinely circulated to the colonies and to British representatives in newly independent states) and the marginalia appended by the officials betrayed significant concern for the damage done to the Western cause by Jim Crow. In November 1956, Harold Caccia emphasized that in the eyes of millions in Africa, India and Asia, the United States 'must stand or fall' by the validity of its stated ideals.[17]

Others similarly perceived global ramifications to the persistence of Jim Crow. The Labour Party Conference in 1958 passed an emergency motion urging Alabama's governor Jim Folsom to commute the death sentence of a condemned black man. The message sent to the governor stressed the widespread British concern over the fairness of southern justice and the opportunity such cases gave to critics of the West to denounce the United States for hypocrisy.[18] This theme occurred repeatedly in British press commentary on civil rights during the Eisenhower and Kennedy administrations. In October 1961 *The Times* commented on King's visit to Britain:

The insistence of the non-white races everywhere on a full measure of social respect and acceptance is one of the explosive forces of our time; the ground swell of Negro unrest and protest in America is part of it. If the United States is to hold its position of world leadership, it must, as its wiser leaders know, have its own racial house in order. It must develop and use to the full the talents of all its citizens working together. Thus political necessity reinforces social conscience in impelling America towards full integration; but human prejudice works the other way, class and colour lines reform almost as fast as they are erased, and nobody knows how much time, leadership and political change will be needed. What is vital is that the United States should move, and be seen to move, tolerably fast in the right direction.[19]

Leader writers and journalists emphasized these points repeatedly.[20] Sometimes the focus was Africa, sometimes it was broader, but the message was consistent. Support for civil rights was predicated on the assumption that this was a wise diplomatic move as well as morally just. The British press gave particular coverage to Dean Rusk's May 1963 speech. The secretary of state did little more than reiterate what northern moderates (and the British press) had been saying for years. That he was a southerner gave the speech all the more impact, but the coverage devoted to it reflected the importance the British gave to rectifying the propaganda advantage that they perceived accrued to the Soviets.[21] The Cold War provides the key to understanding many British responses to the civil rights movement.

III

British perceptions were anything but static. Colin MacInnes, writing in 1963, characterized British reactions to the race issue at home as fitting into three stages: self-congratulatory insouciance, panic and rejection, and resigned resentment.[22] The model is loosely applicable to shifts in British perceptions of events in the United States. The evolution of British responses to King and the movement began with a complacent assumption that race problems in the United States were alien. There was even smugness in British carping about the limits to American democracy that the civil rights movement high-lighted. As the global race question was more and more posed at home, concerns about the possible model represented by American race relations grew. This was the prominent subtext to laments about the killing of King in April 1968. By then another trend was evident. Rioting, the emergence of the black power movement and the increased shrillness of debate over racial matters in Britain stimulated fatalism.[23] This conservative, resigned tend-ency drew sombre lessons from America that focused on riots, extremism and racial tensions.

In the 1950s and early 1960s there was confidence that the USA was different from Britain. Patterson commented that the 'proper comparison is not with Durban or Little Rock' but with the British past or, maybe, with New York Puerto Ricans.[24] After trouble in Notting Hill in 1957 it was denied that the incident had been a racial one and that a misperception of it as such might harm relations with the new commonwealth. A sociologist wrote to *The Times*: 'What needs to be clearly set on the record for the benefit of the citizens of Bulawayo, Pretoria and Little Rock – whose com-ment has been forthcoming – is that there is no widespread hostility towards coloured people in Britain.'[25] A letter to *The Times* from a West Indian stressed that Britain was different. Afro-Caribbeans were different from Alabamian blacks because the races in Britain trusted each other.[26]

Problems, however, seemed to be mounting in Britain. The 1960s saw parallel debates about immigration restriction and legislation against racial discrimination. Fenner Brockway tried for years to gain support for his anti-discrimination bills, but it was not until the mid-sixties that circumstances turned in his favour. Race became more salient in British politics for dom-estic as well as international reasons. Election campaigns in Smethwick and elsewhere spawned such slogans as: 'If you want a nigger for a neighbour, vote Liberal or Labour', further raising the profile of worsening (or more prominently bad) race relations. Grants were awarded for the academic study of British race relations and the results suggested that discrimination was on the increase or had previously been underestimated.[27] Allegations of colour bars in places of work and recreation increased and denials by white employers and others were looked at more sceptically.

By 1966 the sense of urgency was growing. Authoritative studies such as the *PEP Report* were crucial to raising awareness of the extent of discrimination in Britain.[28] Recognition took the form of articles in the press on 'the Dark Million' and the 'sensitive condition' of race relations.[29] The 1966 Reith lectures were devoted to global race relations. The Junior Minister at the Home Office with responsibility for immigrant affairs, David Ennals, warned that laws must be strengthened to prevent the racial violence sweeping American cities from spreading to Britain. He still emphasized the differences in scale between British and American race relations problems. Nonetheless, he argued that the government wished to act to prevent any possibility of similar occurrences.[30]

There was a clear trend towards a view that America's present might be Britain's future. There had been harbingers such as a Foreign Office minute on how London's immigrant neighbourhoods were coming to resemble the northern cities.[31] In 1963, the *New Statesman* was disconcerted to hear complaints about discrimination reminiscent of the American South.[32] But the fight against Jim Crow did not lend itself to easy British parallels, nor did the integrationist struggle between 1954 and 1963 present issues in such a way that an American model seemed immediately relevant to the complacent British whose minorities were only just becoming large enough to demand attention.[33]

Violence in America's cities transformed the situation. After Watts the *Spectator* warned that if nothing was done this might be Britain's future.[34] The question 'could it happen here?' was asked with greater and greater urgency. James Cameron had suggested in the *Daily Herald* in 1963 that 'This Can't Happen Here – YET' over coverage of events in Birmingham. Cameron noted that Britain was 'pretty lucky' with 'our Negroes', but stressed that events in Notting Hill, Bristol, St Helens and Nairobi, in the last of which British troops stood accused of beating up Kenyans, suggested that complacency was misplaced. The key difference between 'them' in the American South and the British was that 'they' had more Negroes. What 'they' were up to in Tennessee or Alabama 'we' were up to at home on a smaller scale.[35]

Rioting gave particular urgency to this new strand of comparisons. It focused attention on the discontents of minorities at home and drew forth a near-unanimous call for preventive measures, especially anti-discrimination legislation. The riots that followed King's assassination prompted the press to highlight the need to pre-empt the possibility of anything similar ever happening in Britain. *The Times* and other journals were critical of the new Race Relations Bill for not going far enough and they criticized Tory opposition to it.[36] Later in the month, the chief London correspondent for the *New York Times* was commissioned to discuss: 'What Britain can learn from America . . . once hope of being part of the society is lost, the victim may almost inevitably turn against it in nihilist fury. The lesson of America is that the public commitment to prevent discrimination came too late. Britain still has a little time, if politicians will lead.'[37]

A third stage of British responses was apparent by 1968. It challenged the sympathetic, liberal view that had had the field to itself before the mid-1960s. Racial problems were increasingly described as unavoidable, the lesson being that it was best to minimize problems by restricting immigration and even repatriating immigrants rather than trying to outlaw discrimination or encourage integration. Even the article just quoted began by (mis)quoting Eisenhower on how laws could not change men's hearts. The idea that integration could be achieved had drawn the following sceptical comment from a diplomat in Washington in 1962 on:

> The danger that lies in the natural revulsion to miscegenation. As one authority on race relations said recently, in the end the problem comes to this 'would you like your daughter to marry a Negro?' The same expert points out that there is no scientific evidence for the belief that intermarriage has any harmful effects: nonetheless it is a strongly held belief . . . For an effectively integrated society seems impossible while such irrational prejudices remain strong.[38]

A Foreign Office official commented: 'I agree: in the end it is surely illusory to go on talking about multi-racialism and at the same time to deny miscegenation. The two are indivisible.' The more right-wing press, for example the *Daily Mail* in 1965, reinforced scepticism in articles asking 'Can Integration Work?'[39] As the debate on the immigration restriction gathered momentum, advocates of stricter controls used the failures of integration in the USA as a warning of what continued mass immigration could produce in Britain. Peregrine Worsthorne suggested in the *Sunday Telegraph* in June 1963 that integration was a chimera.[40] The more liberal James Cameron responded that this reaction to violence in the United States was sad and that such a resigned logic must be resisted.[41]

This fatalist strand reached a new prominence in Enoch Powell's speech of 20 April 1968. The report of the speech in *The Times* began with his use of the classical image of the river Tiber foaming with much blood:

> He went on: 'That tragic and intractable phenomenon which we watch with horror on the other side of the Atlantic but which there is interwoven with the history and existence of the States itself, is coming upon us here by our own volition and our own neglect.
> Indeed, it has all but come in numerical terms, it will be of American proportions long before the end of the century. Only resolute and urgent

action will avert it even now . . . the word "integration" summed up a dangerous delusion suffered by those wilfully or otherwise blind to the realities.'[42]

The headline over *The Times* leader comment was 'An Evil Speech'. The editor thought it 'almost unbelievable' following the violence consequent to the assassination, 'that any man should be so irresponsible as to promote hatred in the face of these examples of the results that can follow.'[43] Condemnation was widespread. David Pitt, Chairman of the Campaign against Racial Discrimination, told a CARD memorial meeting for Martin Luther King that the speech was 'shameful', Humphrey Berkeley MP recalled Oswald Mosley. The Chairman of the Birmingham Coordinating Committee Against Racial Discrimination wished the speech referred to the Attorney General as incitement to racial hatred. Nicholas Scott, Conservative MP for Paddington South, said Powell was assuming the mantle of Governor Wallace and thought his 'emotional bigotry' would make matters worse.[44] The MP for Cambridge, David Lane, wrote to deplore Powell's speech.[45]

On the other hand two Tory MPs wrote to stress that racial strife was the product of militant minorities that provoked a white backlash, 'especially in our crowded cities among those having to share the problems of integration at a grass roots level.'[46] They characterized racial antipathies as 'one of the facts of international life', linking the USA to South Africa, Guyana, Canada, Cyprus, Palestine and Malaysia to support the claim. Similar problems in Britain were the fault of unrestricted immigration which should be stopped and repatriation initiated. The Bill giving the RRB strong enforcement provisions was an attempt 'insolently to curtail individual liberty'.[47] Resignation to the 'fact of international life', as seen when the vice-president of Eastern Area Young Conservatives welcomed the speech for bringing the issue 'into the open', (claiming that there had always been and would always be racial prejudice) became more apparent as anti-immigration and anti-Race Relations Bill sentiment introduced a dose of fatalism, partly derived from American models, into debate.[48] A new stage had been reached in British race relations and perceptions of events across the Atlantic.

IV

Direct responses to Martin Luther King Jr and the freedom struggle included a number of especially prominent themes. To British observers race was not just a Southern problem. Journalists, scholars and diplomats noticed tensions in the north as well as the south. Whether it was Levittown or Chicago in 1957 or New Jersey in 1962, where residents were perplexed by a CORE school campaign against their *de facto* segregation, the British pounced on evidence of the national scope of American racial unrest.[49] Support for

George Wallace in Wisconsin in 1964 was held to denote the widespread prejudice there as well as in the South.[50] This perception of northern, urban racial problems may have been connected with the perception that Britain's problems would be more like those of the north than the south. It nay also have reflected a desire to score points off the United States at a time when American anti-colonialism still rankled. Certainly when African and Asian diplomats experienced discrimination or Ralph Bunche in New York experienced discrimination it was closely reported.[51]

The British were persistently critical of the Eisenhower and Kennedy administrations for timidity in the face of hard choices. A post-Suez *Schadenfreude* pervaded diplomats' reports on the Eisenhower administration's inaction. Reports on the situation in Little Rock in 1957 suggested that the president had acted belatedly and had created problems for himself through delay in taking a lead on the issue.[52] A Foreign Office official minuted that it was 'tough for Mr E' but he should have acted sooner.[53] *The Times* commented sympathetically on black leaders' requests that Vice-President Nixon should spend as much time with them as he did with foreign leaders.[54]

Kennedy fared no better:

PRESIDENT KENNEDY's appeal against further 'provocation' is difficult to understand. The 'freedom riders' are doing no more and no less than has been done by others in this now established pattern of organized, peaceful assertion of rights built up by the bus boycott of 1956, the more recent lunch-counter 'sit-ins', the careful boycott of certain shops, and the organized registration of Negro voters. They add up to a remarkable display of discipline and maturity, and demonstrate one clear way the battle will be won. Although victories so far have been limited they have been sufficient to provide confidence in slow but steady progress and to win a great deal of respect and sympathy ... It is clearly difficult for the President to be facing MR KHRUSCHEV next month carrying the burden not only of Cuba but now of Alabama, too. There is however, a redeeming difference in the Alabaman situation which he could use to his advantage [through] the restrained conduct of the Negroes and the determination of the Federal Government to help them.[55]

James Cameron deplored the way liberal, bourgeois Mr Kennedy tolerated the actions of a barbarous and savage, if small, minority. He called on the president to show the same resolution as in the missile crisis in upholding the law and facing up to the 'fascists' of Birmingham and Oxford whose actions were reprehended by the vast majority of Americans.[56] When Johnson responded to the movement's pressure in 1964–5 *The Times* compared his turning away from global to national injustices favourably with the attitudes of his predecessors.[57]

British sympathies can be seen in the language used to describe American events. In 1960 *The Times* linked the cause of the sit-in movement with Abraham Lincoln, praising 'studious' blacks for persevering in protest despite 'the vulgar exhibitionism of the Ku Klux Klan . . . again inciting to brutality . . . These Negroes have very neatly put their adversaries in the wrong.'[58] The movement was characterized as peaceful, restrained, disciplined, dignified, non-violent, steadfast, orderly, a crusade. Its opponents were stubborn, bitter, reckless, wily, vicious, a violent mob, rabble rousers. Filibusters were devious freebooters, Southern juries were notorious, Governor Ross Barnett was characterized by his 'bleak defiance' and Mississippi whites in 1964 were 'unsavoury', whereas James Meredith was 'steadfast' and black protest in 1963 was 'orderly and dignified.'[59] James Cameron commented on the behaviour of the 'medieval gauleiter called Theophilus Eugene (Bull) Connor'. This was of a piece with other evocations of Nazi Germany in British comment on the Deep South.[60]

In 1965 the behaviour of southern whites was still a matter for disapprobation in the British press. A parallel theme emerged in disapproval of rioting and, especially, the black power slogan and the rise to prominence of the Nation of Islam and Malcolm X. One of the first such criticisms came in March 1961 in a piece about the Black Muslims.[61] By 1963 Jon Lewis and SNCC were described as 'impatient'. In May 1964 *The Times* contrasted 'militant' SNCC to 'urbane' SCLC. Discussion of Adam Clayton Powell's exclusion from Congress reinforced negative stereotypes of black behaviour. *The Times* recalled John Wilkes in an editorial that compared Powell unfavourably to Julian Bond.[62] Riots were regarded as 'an outburst of despair' and interpreted as products of the neglect of the urban African-American population.[63] But they were increasingly condemned alongside reminders that this was the result of allowing race relations fester. Lessons for Britain were never far from the surface.

There was a pronounced British tendency to denounce the extremists on both sides. White supremacists were lampooned in 1959 for banning a children's book featuring a rabbit 'family' in which one parent was black and the other white. In 1967 there was a similar treatment of calls for the banning of black and white minstrel shows from British television.[64] David Ennals stressed that American white supremacism had led to the rise of black power radicalism.[65] White illiberality was condemned and held up as an object lesson of what should not be allowed to happen in Britain if black extremism was to be avoided. Extremists deserved each other. In particular, black power was segregation in reverse: 'Negroes in Quest for Own Apartheid.'[66] This idea was present in a diplomat's comments in the 1956 Lucy case and a profile of Georgia Senator Richard Russell that linked the Citizens' Councils and the NAACP as polarizing forces in the South.[67] James Cameron thought it axiomatic that a fanatic like George Wallace produced in response an extremist like Malcolm X, reinforcing his wish to keep in mind the millions in between.[68] The desire of the Nation of Islam and American Nazis for the total separation of the races were connected in *The Times* after Malcolm X's assassination. It compared him unfavourably to King and noted similarities between his and Barry Goldwater's approach to politics.[69] A 1965 article on American extremism described Joe McCarthy, the Klan, Goldwater, the John Birch Society, the Citizens' Councils and the Nation of Islam.[70] *The New Statesman* called Bull Connor and Papa Doc 'brothers under the skin' and *The Economist* asked 'Just How Many Like Stokely?'. It noted the tendency for the assassination of King to help extremists of both races.[71]

Despite occasional hesitations, the campaign in the courts received generally sympathetic coverage into the 1960s at a time when more direct forms of action were not as readily understood or condoned.[72] As awareness grew, British reactions demonstrated the effectiveness of non-violent direct action protest as a way of thrusting the issue into the limelight and eliciting a sympathetic white reaction. This is clear from the peaks and troughs in British coverage, the 'pictures worth a thousand words'[73] from such protest as Birmingham or Selma and through myriad comments about particular events or circumstances. Again the three-stage process may be discerned. Complacency about the efficacy of the legal process; shock and alarm that it was not effective, combined with sympathy for the protests of the 1956–65 period; revulsion at the violence of the post-1965 rioting and black power agitation.

King was the hero. He was the 'integration leader' at a time when doubts as to the merits of integration were scarce.[74] He was characterized by *The Times* in June 1963 as near the centre of the political spectrum and in July 1964 as 'the outstanding leader of Negro opinion'.[75] A piece on the *Atlanta Constitution* identified the city as the home of Martin Luther King.[76] King was taken, along with other prominent blacks described in an article entitled 'Room at the top for U.S. Negroes', as 'indicative of the vast American Negro potential'. The list was said to have been chosen 'at random' but included mainly moderates, mainly men and mainly political and business figures. Interestingly, Ralph Bunche was described as 'perhaps the best known American Negro today'. King appeared alongside the first Negro judge, the head of Howard University Medical School and Ethel Waters.[77] After King's assassination the *Daily Mirror* carried a photograph of a vicar washing a black child's feet and quoted him as saying: 'I thought that some token action was needed to express sorrow at the tragic death of Luther King.'[78]

All this suggests that the apotheosis of King in 1968 in the British press was perhaps not so marked a contrast with what had come before, as Richard Lentz suggests it was in American news magazines.[79] British depictions of King were less complex because there was no direct British stake in the events described well into the 1960s. Attitudes to American discomfiture were of a piece with Graham Greene's satire on American moral superiority in the character of Alden Pyle in *The Quiet American*. By the 1960s there was a desire to see King's method's succeed. If they did there was hope for the successful integration of the 'dark million' into British society. If he failed the message for Britain was not an attractive one. Criticism of the movement's more radical elements carried a parallel message. Either way, between 1954 and 1968 mainstream identification with American racial liberals grew significantly.

V

British racial liberals developed links with the civil rights movement. King's 1961 visit provoked editorial musings on the situation in the USA (including some shrewd predictions) *and* British race relations.[80] British complacency was punctuated by concern either when there was trouble in Britain or when outside events such as this provoked it. By 1968 there were warnings in calls for American-style legislation (*The Sun* called it 'civil rights legislation') that British race relations stood at 'the eleventh hour'.[81] Criticism of the 1965 Race Relations Act was frequently couched in terms of its failure to go far enough along American lines. CARD (established after King's 1964 visit and mimicking American nomenclature) and the Race Relations Board were the most prominent agencies pressing for such a course. In 1967–8 those calling for Britain to heed the lessons of the USA included Home Secretary Roy Jenkins in a speech to the Institute of Race Relations and Mark Bonham Carter, reporting on an extended trip there for the RRB that: 'American experience had shown that the problem will not solve itself. It has been assumed that Negroes would be successfully integrated like the Irish or the Poles but this has not happened.'[82] A conference at Ditchley Park of British and American figures from government, universities and politics met to discuss the issue and heard that the situation in Britain was going the same way as the United States.[83] The Home Office brought over Roger Wilkins from the Justice Department for consultations.[84]

Canon Collins, a leading light in CND and the Christian Action Movement, sponsored King's first visit to London to preach in St Paul's Cathedral. He also led the movement to create a King Memorial Fund in 1968. CND borrowed liberally from King's ideas and rhetoric as well as sharing much of his philosophy of non-violent protest. Just as King had stimulated the creation of CARD, so Malcolm X's visit brought him together with some of his British 'disciples' such as Michael de Freitas or Michael X.[85] Stokely Carmichael visited British black power activists. The ideas and rhetoric of radical British advocates of racial equality owed much to their American mentors. A black power conference in 1968 concluded that the way forward was to demand action from a panicky society just as CARD or SCORE (established in 1964 among Oxford students, who, like CARD and the

Birmingham Co-ordinating Committee, chose a name which bespoke their US influences) had learnt techniques for claiming rightful attention from complacent society through direct action protests.

The strategy, language and songs of British protest after 1960 were strongly affected by American examples. The tactics of SCORE were directly influenced by the American example discussed at its founding conference in 1964. The sit-in and demonstration became staples of agitation. There was a bus boycott against a colour bar in Bristol in 1963.[86] There were sit-ins against colour bar cafes and marches against housing discrimination. In 1961 *Varsity*, the Cambridge students' newspaper, reported plans for a civil disobedience campaign against the wearing of gowns in the form of a march of un-gowned students all risking a fine of six shillings and eight pence.[87] Easter 1968 provided a marker for the extent to which the nature of British protest had developed under American and other influences. The press commented on marchers protesting about the Bomb, King's death, Rudi Dutschke's deportation, Rhodesia and Vietnam, led in protest songs (many of them American) by Julie Felix.[88]

More tangible Anglo-American links included Hull University's creation of a grant for Wilberforce College students in May 1961.[89] A Welsh church donated a window to a bombed-out church in Alabama.[90] Coventry invited a banned Alabama biracial youth group to continue its discussions there.[91] In 1963 British minority groups petitioned the US ambassador about the situation in Birmingham, Alabama.[92] These were just a few of the gestures of support for the civil rights movement emanating from the United Kingdom. King's visits marked the highpoints of connection. His *Face to Face* interview with John Freeman on BBC television and his preaching in St Paul's had a direct influence. Visiting London on his way to collect the Nobel Peace Prize, he warned of the need actively to address race issues and denounced moves to restrict immigration. He held a press conference directly after preaching at evensong in St Paul's. King's sermon to a packed congregation was described as 'spellbinding' and was reported at length. Responding to questions, he discussed British race relations, caste in India, world peace, called for Britain and the United States to put strong pressure on South Africa and reiterated that 'pragmatic non-violence' was the way forward. He also stressed that the doctrine of black supremacy was as great a danger as that of white supremacy and played down its American strength.[93]

We should not, however, leap to the conclusion that the American influence was the sole one. West Indian pressure groups such as the NCCI developed strategies that echoed British tradition, anti-colonial nationalist agitation and life in immigrant areas of British cities. Events in South Africa and India had a profound impact. Such figures as Trevor Huddlestone were active in the United Kingdom after fighting racism in South Africa, and the Anti-Apartheid Movement became a leading British vehicle for organized anti-racism. King himself was consistently portrayed as a 'disciple of Gandhi' and it was recognized how much consumer boycotts and other methods of protest owed to South Africa and India.[94]

Opponents of racial equality made parallel connections. Southern supremacist literature found its way to like-minded types in Britain. Dagenham racists claimed to have formed a Klavern, a sub-division of the KKK; the racist leader Colin Jordan had good links with American Nazi leader, George Rockwell. Rockwell and Klan chief, Robert Shelton, were both denied entry to Britain to attend racist gatherings.[95] The extent to which there was a backlash combining the issues of immigration restriction, lament for passage of empire, opposition to governmental efforts to legislate against discrimination and informed by American ideas may be worth investigation.

Nationalist groups in Wales, Scotland and Northern Ireland were also inspired by the civil rights movement. To Welsh nationalists, King and the movement were powerful role-models in their revival in the 1960s and beyond.[96] The vocabulary of rights denied was used by those fighting linguistic discrimination. The merging of cultural identity with political aspiration saw the rhetoric of 'we shall overcome' as well as some of the tactics of the freedom struggle imported into Celtic nationalist agitation. The Northern Ireland Civil Rights Association, formed in 1967, staged marches, used the songs of the American movement and employed its tactics. It attacked a system of gerrymandering, unequal treatment by law enforcement agencies, employment and housing discrimination and ethno-religious bigotry. By provoking confrontation, NICRA succeeded in grabbing British attention for the first time in decades. Government action from the centre to force change over wishes of local majority provoked antagonism not dissimilar to Southern laments for home rule. One veteran of NICRA recalled:

> It started off [with legal cases] but when people were watching the American civil rights movement they wanted marches. They thought discrimination was just as bad in Northern Ireland as it was in America. Certainly they were hearing about jobs and listening to Martin Luther King and seeing the police beating people, they wanted marches.[97]

There were, of course, obvious differences between the two movements. Traditional Irish imperatives were strong, while the model of the National Council for Civil Liberties in mainland Britain was also influential. It remains worth investigating how far Colin MacInnes's model of complacency, urgency and resignation may be applicable to attitudes towards Northern Ireland as well as reactions to ethnic polarization at home and in the United States.

While this demonstrates again that we should not overestimate the impact of the civil rights movement in Britain, it is clear that it provided a new vocabulary and ways of articulating protest. Initial complacency about race was replaced by a debate about how to prevent the situation developing along American lines. It was asked with mounting urgency whether the American dilemma was becoming a British one. By 1968 the debate was at full pitch around what lesson should be taken from the US experience. Liberals wanted action on American lines against segregation and discrimination, to avert disaster. More conservative figures argued that such action was useless and used American lessons to derive very different conclusions. Race tensions were a universal given, a fact of life, and stopping immigration, repatriation, and tough rather than soft government stances were the solution. Both sides felt that the 1968 legislation would be futile. But there was no consensus on whether to extend it further. The disagreement is still to some extent unresolved as are perceptions of the significance to Britain of the American experience.

NOTES

1. Sheila Patterson, *Dark Strangers* (London, 1963), pp. 47–8, 66, 359.
2. J. Mossman, 'On Trial Before the World Today: Man's Inhumanity to Man', *Daily Mail*, 28 August 1963, p. 6 described opponents of the March on Washington as 'fanatical', demonstrators as 'proud' and 'dignified'.
3. See leader comment, *Daily Mail*, 17 August 1965, p. 1 that, 'This way lies Los Angeles'. The same newspaper also carried proportionally more descriptions of favourable reaction to Enoch Powell's 1968 speech than most.
4. 'Editorial', *Race*, 1, 1 (1959), p. 2.
5. Denis Brogan, 'The Rising Tide of Colour', *Spectator*, 7 June 1963, p. 726.
6. Cartoon, 'The Volcano', *Daily Mail*, 7 May 1963, p. 8. For the reference to Bristol, see note 32.
7. 'U.S. Steps Peacefully Forward', *Daily Herald*, 29 August 1963, p. 2. See also *The Times'* series 'The Black Man in Search of Power', that placed the US struggle amid a global survey, March 1968.
8. Leading article, 'Negro Rights', *The Times*, October 1961, p. 11.
9. For example, 'Freedom Walkers', ibid., 3 May 1963, p. 12 compared civil rights marchers favourably to CND.
10. 'Man in the News', ibid., 15 October 1964, p. 10, and 'Luther King Wins Nobel Prize', ibid., p. 12, greeting the news of the Nobel Peace Prize award.
11. 'Mr. Civil Rights', profile, ibid., 28 March 1960, p. 8, claimed he was 'chiefly known in Britain' for this.
12. 'Negro Revolution', ibid., 8 August 1967, p. 4.
13. Leading article, 'New Wind in the South', ibid., 29 March 1960, p. 13; see also 'Winds of Change over the Chicago Campus', ibid., 6 January 1962, p. 11.
14. Report on Martin Luther King's press conference, ibid., 31 October 1961, p. 5 including his remarks in London about African change helping change in America; leading article, 'Limited Victory', ibid., 13 May 1963, p. 13 on how change in Africa was fuelling black impatience; 'Black and White in Washington, D.C.', ibid., 27 August 1963, p. 9; leading article, *Spectator*, June 1963, p. 723 on

how the British and South African governments should note events in Washington relating to a universal problem; 'The Race War', *New Statesman*, 11 November 1963, p. 476; 'Contintents Linked By Racial Problems', *Daily Herald*, 29 August 1963, p. 2.

15. Leading article, 'Progress, Even If Slow', *The Times*, 8 June 1955, p. 7.
16. Minute by R. Parsons on Sir H. Caccia to Foreign Office, no. 111, 20 April 1959, Public Record Office, London, (PRO) FO371/139808.
17. Caccia to Selwyn Lloyd, 14 November 1956, no. 373, FO371/120377; he returned to the theme in April 1959, no. 11 to FO, FO371/139808, suggesting how much the freedom struggle in the US had learned from Africa.
18. 'Labour Party Plea For U.S. Negro', *The Times*, 23 September 1958, p. 6.
19. 'Negro Rights', leading article, ibid., 30 October 1961, p. 11.
20. For example, ibid.; 'Spread of Anti-White Extremism', ibid., 10 March 1961, p. 12; leading article, 'Limited Victory', ibid., 13 May 1963, p. 13.
21. 'Mr Dean Rusk Denounces Colour Discrimination', ibid., 29 May 1963, p. 9.
22. C. MacInnes, 'The New British', *Spectator*, 7 June 1963, pp. 729–32.
23. Leading article, 'Black Power on the Campus', *The Times*, 18 May 1967, p. 11, which condemned Carmichael; or Stephen Jessel, 'Black Power Prophet', ibid., 19 July 1967, p. 10, whose sub-editing included the captions 'Violence is Just' and 'Uncompromising Against Whites'.
24. Patterson, *Dark Strangers*, p. 18.
25. Dr B. Wilson of Leeds University, letter in *The Times*, 5 September 1958, p. 11.
26. Letter from H. Humphries, *The Times*, 18 October 1962, p. 13, responding to dire warnings in a letter from N.S. Chamblee of Birmingham, Alabama.
27. For example the Nuffield Foundation funded a major project in 1963, as Philip Mason put it, to take a long look at the Midlands before they became like Harlem, 'Long Look at Colour Question', *The Times*, 27 September 1963, p. 13.
28. 'Immigrants Face A Filter' and leading article, 'By Race and Colour', *The Times*, 18 April 1967, pp. 3, 9, for a summary and discussion. See also the book version, W. W. Daniel, *Racial Discrimination in England* (London, 1968), produced at the request of the National Committee for Commonwealth Immigrants and the Race Relations Board.
29. 'The Dark Million' series of articles in *The Times*, 18–29 January 1965.
30. 'Ennals Warning On Race Violence', *The Times*, 25 July 1967, p. 2.
31. Comments on Sir H Caccia to Foreign Office, no. 62, 4 March 1957, FO371/126719.
32. See, 'Colour Bar: Bristol Fashion', *New Statesman*, 10 May 1963, pp. 708–10, on how the refusal of unions and management to allow black workers into public areas 'for fear of adverse reactions from customers' prompted a boycott.
33. British minority responses merit a separate study. There is not the space here to do more than suggest the potential of this area for investigation.
34. 'After Los Angeles?', *Spectator*, 20 August 1965, p. 223.
35. James Cameron, 'This Can't Happen Here – YET', *Daily Herald*, 8 May 1963. p. 8; the *Daily Mirror* warned in its leader comment on 8 April 1968, p. 2, that 'it really *could* happen here.'
36. 'A Chance to Do Better', leading article, *The Times*, 10 April 1968, p. 11; also, 'Race Myths Keep Colour Issue Smouldering', ibid., 16 April 1968, p. 6; ibid., letters of 17 April 1968, p. 11; Ian Trethowan, 'Tory Dilemma over Race Bill', ibid., 18 April 1968, p. 10; leading article, 'Intolerance' and letters, ibid., 19 April 1968, p. 11. Also 'Race, Tories and the Law', *Spectator*, 19 April 1968, p. 513.

37. 'What Britain Can Learn from America', *The Times*, 22 April 1968, p. 11.
38. Mr Greenhill to Foreign Office, no. 1824/62, 19 November 1962, FO371/16243 and minute by Mr Quantrill.
39. Barry Norman asked six minority leaders with a variety of views, 'Can Integration Work?', *Daily Mail*, 20 August 1965, p. 6.
40. 'Their Turn Now', *Sunday Telegraph*, 2 June 1963, p. 14. The article characterized racial divisions as 'seemingly insoluble', and linked African and American black militancy.
41. James Cameron, 'Alas Kennedy Is No Lincoln And Nkrumah Is No Uncle Tom', *Daily Herald*, 5 June 1963, p. 6.
42. 'Mr Powell Filled with Forebodings', *The Times*, 22 April 1968, p. 2.
43. 'An Evil Speech', *The Times*, 22 April 1968, p. 11; the front covers of both *The Economist*, 27 April 1968, and *Spectator*, 26 April 1968, used the phrase 'dangerous nonsense' about what the latter termed a 'notorious speech'.
44. 'Mosley Speeches Recalled', *The Times*, 22 April 1968, p. 2, summarized reactions.
45. 'Deplorable Speech', Letter in ibid. p. 11.
46. 'White Back-lash', letter from Sir Frederic Bennett; 'Infringement of Freedom', letter from Mr Gilbert Longden, ibid.
47. Ibid.
48. 'Mosley Speeches Recalled', op. cit.
49. 'Anti-Negro Crowd', *The Times*, 21 August 1957, p. 8, and 'Pennsylvania Township Faces the Racial Issue', 23 August 1957, p. 6; Lord Hood to Foreign Office, no. 287, 11 December 1957, FO371/126719 and minuted comments on other cities; 'School Segregation Storm in New Jersey', *The Times*, 8 February 1962, p. 11; see also Alistair Cooke's criticism of northern double standards in *America Observed* (London, 1987), pp. 82–6.
50. 'When South Meets North', *The Times*, 7 April 1964, p. 11 and 'Way up in Wisconsin', leading article, 9 April, p. 13.
51. 'Apology to Indian Ambassador', *The Times*, 24 August 1955, p. 6; 'Discrimination in Washington DC, ibid., 25 May 1961, p. 10; 'Insult to African Diplomatists', ibid., 6 June 1961, p. 10; 'U.S. Delegate "Gashed With Glass"', ibid., 29 September 1964, p. 10; on Bunche, see 'Controversy Over A Club Colour Bar', ibid., 11 July 1959, p. 5 and 'Club's Gesture to Dr Bunche', ibid., 16 July 1959, p. 5.
52. Sir H. Caccia to Foreign Office, no. 493, 13 September 1957, FO371/126719.
53. Minute on despatch AU1823/7 of September 1957, FO371/126719.
54. 'Travel Dilemma Faces "Nixon Africanus"', *The Times*, 12 March 1957, p. 8; leading article, 'America in Africa', ibid., 8 April 1957, p. 9.
55. Leading article, 'Freedom Riders', *The Times*, 23 May 1961, p. 11.
56. Cameron, 'This Can't Happen Here – YET', op. cit.
57. 'A Heave for Civil Rights', *The Times*, 18 March 1965, p. 13, 'Appomattox and After', ibid., 9 April 1965, p. 15; but see also the biting denunciation in a cartoon published 19 July 1967 of the neglect of blacks by the administration for the Vietnam War.
58. 'New Wind in the South', *The Times*, 29 March 1960, p. 9.
59. 'Hostility to Negro Student', *The Times*, 12 January 1963, p. 6.
60. Cameron, 'This Can't Happen Here – YET'; 'Negoes in the Charming South', *The Times*, 10 June 1954, p. 9, commented on the 'Hitlerite' southern whites' arguments; in 1962 the atmosphere in Mississippi was described as 'somewhat totalitarian', in, 'After the Battle of Ole Miss', ibid., 9 October 1962, p. 11.
61. 'Spread of Anti-White Extremism', *The Times*, 10 March 1961, p. 12.

62. 'Not The End of The Battle', *The Times*, 3 March 1967, p. 13; 'U.N. Envoys Honour Georgia Negro', ibid., 22 January 1966, p. 7 noted the support of UN envoys for Bond over his exclusion from the Georgia Legislature and for King.
63. Leading article, 'Outburst of Despair', *The Times*, 23 July 1964, p. 11.
64. 'Tale of Black And White Rabbits', *The Times*, 23 May 1959, p. 6; 'Nursery Book Banned', ibid., 15 September 1956, p. 6; leading article, 'Rabbits and Politics', ibid., 24 September 1956, p. 9; 'One Little Pig Was Black', ibid., 2 June 1959, p. 10; 'BBC Asked to Ban TV Minstrels', ibid., 19 May 1967, p. 3; leading article, 'The Wrong Target', ibid., p. 11.
65. 'Ennals Warning on Race Violence', *The Times*, 25 July 1967, p. 2.
66. 'Negroes in Quest For Own Apartheid', ibid., 5 March 1968, p. 8.
67. Sir Roger Makins to F.O., AU1822/1, 16 March 1956, FO371/120377; 'Man in the News', *The Times*, 1 March 1960, p. 8.
68. Cameron, 'Alas Kennedy Is No Lincoln . . .'
69. 'After Malcolm X', leading article, *The Times*, 23 February 1965, p. 13; also 13 May 1963, p. 13; 'Limited Victory', ibid.
70. 'American Forms of Extremism', ibid., 24 June 1965, p. 13.
71. 'Alabama's Bull', *New Statesman*, 10 May 1963, p. 701; *The Economist*, 13–19 April 1968, p. 16, compared Carmichael unfavourably to King.
72. See, leading article, 'Another Step Forward', *The Times*, 22 November 1962, p. 13 in which the legal strategy was described and the agency of blacks themselves asserted as crucial to the movement's success.
73. The phrase occurs in 'Alabama's Bull', op. cit.
74. 'U.S. Bans Discrimination in Housing', *The Times*, 22 November 1962, p. 11; a leading article the same day was headed 'A Step Forward', ibid., p. 13.
75. 'The American Negro Giant Awakes', *The Times*, 10 June 1963, p. 13 and 'National Guard Moves In', ibid., 28 July 1964, p. 8.
76. 'Newspapers of the World', *The Times*, 31 March 1965, p. 11.
77. 'Room At The Top For U.S. Negroes', *The Times*, 28 March 1961, p. 11.
78. 'One Small Gesture', *Daily Mirror*, 13 April 1968, p. 1.
79. Richard Lentz, *Symbols, News Magazines and Martin Luther King*, (Baton Rouge, 1990).
80. 'Negro Rights', *The Times*, leading article, 30 October 1961, p. 11.
81. 'The Black Man in Search of Power' 6, *The Times*, 16 March 1968, p. 8; also comments by Professor R. Rose, Visiting Professor at Leicester University, ibid., 1 March 1965, p. 7; *Sun*, 8 and 10 April, 1968, commented that there was a little time left before it was too late for such legislation to work; see also *Spectator*, 20 August 1965, p. 223–4.
82. Reprinted in *Race*, vol. 3, no. 3, 1967, pp. 215–232; 'US Race Laws as British Model', *The Times*, 1967, p. 2; also Bonham Carter's letter, 'Integration by Way Of Law', ibid., 18 May 1967, p. 11, RRB annual reports and his 'Measures Against Discrimination', *Race*, 9, 1, 1967, pp. 1–24. Bonham Carter's letter appeared next to a leading article evoking Nazism in its denunciation of Black Power and Stokely Carmichael.
83. 'British Race Relations Worse', *The Times*, 5 December 1967, p. 3.
84. 'Negro Expert's Guidance', *The Times*, 14 July 1967, p. 3.
85. The word 'disciples' was used in 'Can Integration Work?', *Daily Mail*, 20 August 1965, p. 6, just after the Watts riots.
86. 'Bus Boycott By West Indians', *The Times*, 3 May 1963, p. 11; ibid. 6 May 1963, p. 8; ibid., 7 May 1963, p. 5; leading article, 'Industrial Colour Bar', ibid., 7 May 1963, p. 12; also 'Colour Bar: Bristol Fashion', *New Statesman*, 10 May 1963, p. 708.

87. 'Planned Disobedience', *Varsity*, 4 November 1961, p. 1; 'Look No Gowns', ibid., 11 November 1961, p. 1; 'Gown Protest', letter from organizers and editorial comment, ibid., p. 4.
88. 'The Bomb, MLK, Rudi Dutschke', *Sun*, 16 April 1968, p. 6.
89. 'Hull Grant for U.S. Negro Students', *The Times*, 13 May 1961, p. 8.
90. 'Gift from Wales to Bombed Church in Alabama', *The Times*, 5 June 1965, p. 7.
91. 'Alabama Youth Meeting', *The Times*, 5 October 1961, p. 6.
92. 'Petition to U.S. Ambassador', *The Times*, 14 June 1963, p. 12; there was also a march, see, '400 Marchers', ibid., 2 September 1963, p. 6.
93. 'Dr King's Racial Warning to Britain', *The Times*, 7 December 1964, p. 6.
94. 'Fresh Impetus For An Old Crusade', *The Times*, 15 March 1960, p. 9; 'Man In The News', ibid., 15 October 1964, p. 10 and news item on King's Nobel Prize, ibid., p. 12.
95. 'Ku Klux Klan Warn Councillor', *New Statesman*, 27 November 1957, p. 6; Despatch of 10 May 1957, no. 1824/9/5Y on the Ku Klux Klan FO371/126719; when the *Spectator*, ('After Los Angeles?', 20 August 1965, pp. 223–4), commented on the Watts riot, it expressed fear of an incipient KKK in the Midlands. See, also, 'Home Office Ban Entry of Nazi Delegates', *The Times*, 2 August 1962, p. 10; 'Inquiry on Visit By U.S. Nazi', ibid., 7 August, p. 8; 'Home Secretary Bans Klan Leader', ibid., 16 June 1965, p. 12; ibid., obituary for George Rockwell, ibid., 26 August 1967, p. 12.
96. I am grateful to Adam Fairclough for this information.
97. Quoted by R. Munck, 'The Making of the Troubles in Northern Ireland', *Journal of Contemporary History* 27, 1992, p. 217.

12 Non-violent Resistance to White Supremacy: A Comparison of the American Civil Rights Movement and the South African Defiance Campaigns of the 1950s

George M. Fredrickson

During the 1950s and early 1960s non-violent protesters challenged legalized racial segregation and discrimination in the only two places where such blatant manifestations of white supremacy could then be found – the southern United States and the Union of South Africa. Comparing these roughly contemporaneous movements and looking for connections between them may give historians a better perspective on the recent history of black liberation struggles in the two societies, while at the same time providing social scientists with material that should be helpful to them in their search for a theoretical understanding of social and political movements aimed at overthrowing established racial or ethnic hierarchies.

The ANC's 'Campaign of Defiance against Unjust Laws' in 1952 resulted in the arrest of approximately eight thousand blacks (including Indians and Coloureds as well as Africans) and a handful of whites for planned acts of civil disobedience against recently enacted apartheid legislation. The campaign did not make the government alter its course, and it was called off early in 1953 after riots broke out in the wake of non-violent actions in the Eastern Cape. Repressive legislation, making deliberate transgression of the law for political purposes a serious crime in its own right, made the ANC wary of again attempting a nation-wide campaign of civil disobedience, but it could not prevent the Congress and other black or interracial organizations from protesting non-violently in other ways and refusing generally to cooperate with the regime in its efforts to erect barriers between blacks and whites in all aspects of life. School boycotts, bus boycotts, non-cooperation with the programme of removing blacks to new townships, and mass marches to protest efforts to force African women to carry passes were among the actions of the mid-to-late fifties which the ANC led or supported. In 1960, the Pan-Africanist Congress – a militant faction that had recently seceded from the ANC because of its objections to the parent organization's policy of cooperating with the congresses established by other racial groups as well as to its relatively cautious approach to mass action – launched a campaign of civil disobedience against the pass laws that ended with the massacre of 69 unarmed protesters at Sharpeville. Chief Albert Lutuli, president-general of the ANC, showed his sympathy for the Sharpeville victims by publicly burning his own pass, and the one-day stay-at-home which the Congress called to register its solidarity with the PAC was well supported. But the government quickly suppressed all public protest, and both the ANC and the PAC were banned and driven underground. After Sharpeville, non-violent direct action no longer seemed a viable option for the liberation movement, and in 1961 some ANC leaders, in cooperation with the South African Communist Party, inaugurated the era of armed struggle by establishing a separate organization to carry on acts of sabotage against hard targets.[1]

The non-violent phase of the American Civil Rights Movement began with the Montgomery bus boycott of 1955–6 and culminated in the great Birmingham, Mississippi, and Selma campaigns of 1963–5. Viewed narrowly as an attack on legalized segregation and disfranchisement in the southern states, the movement was remarkably successful. It led to the Civil Rights Acts of 1964 and 1965, which effectively outlawed Jim Crow and assured southern blacks access to the ballot box. It becomes immediately apparent therefore that an obvious and fundamental difference between the two movements is that one can be regarded as successful in achieving its immediate objectives while the other was a conspicuous failure.[2]

Fully explaining success or failure obviously requires an assessment of the context – what each movement was up against and what outside help it could expect in its struggle. But before looking at such limiting or favouring circumstances, the movements themselves have to be described and analysed in an effort to compare the resources and capabilities that each brought to the confrontation with white power. Furthermore, it would be mechanistic and historical to ignore the possibility that movements emerging at about the same time and involving people who in both instances defined themselves as black victims of white oppression may have influenced each other in some direct and important way. We need to know what they shared or had in common and how they differed – in ideology, organization, and leadership. What do similarities and differences in political thought and behaviour as well as in social and cultural characteristics tell us about the situation of black people in these two racist societies during the 1950s and 60s? What role, if any, did internal differences play in determining the success or failure of non-violence?

Somewhat surprisingly, little evidence has come to light that the two non-violent movements influenced each other in a significant way. Before World

War II, African-American influence on black South African ideologies and movements had been substantial, but the use of black America as inspiration and example appears to have tapered off during the post-war years. Before the triumph of the Nationalists in 1948, black American interest in South Africa had been limited and intermittent; the African Methodist Episcopal Church had provided the most important and durable connection when it had established itself in South Africa at the turn of the century. For most African-Americans Africa meant West Africa, but awareness of the white-dominated nation at the tip of the continent increased rapidly after the rise of apartheid showed that South Africa was out of step with a world that seemed at last to be moving towards an acceptance of the principle of racial equality.[3]

Nevertheless, the Defiance Campaign does not seem to have made a great impression on African-Americans. The Council on African Affairs, a group of black radicals who sought to influence American opinion on behalf of decolonization, circulated a petition supporting the Campaign that garnered 3800 signatures – many of which came from white radicals – and $835 in donations; but this appears to be the most significant expression of African-American concern. The campaign was also mentioned in passing in a November 1952 petition to the United Nations on African issues sponsored by 25 organizations, including the NAACP, but the Association's organ *The Crisis*, which commented frequently in 1952 and 1953 on the rise of apartheid, did not provide its readers coverage of the campaign against it. By 1952 black Americans were beginning to notice African developments, especially the first stirring of independence movements in West Africa, but interest was far less intense than would be the case a few years later.[4]

Black Americans might have been more aroused by the Defiance Campaign if it had not occurred at a time when interest in direct action as a possible form of protest in the United States was at a low ebb. Non-violence had been placed on the agenda of civil rights activity during and immediately after World War II with A. Philip Randolph's March on Washington Movement of 1941–5 and the founding and first sit-ins of CORE; but by 1952 McCarthyism and the generally conservative mood in the country had made established black leaders reluctant to endorse actions that opponents of civil rights could describe as radical or subversive; they feared a backlash that would weaken popular support for a legalistic and gradualist reform strategy that was beginning to bear fruit, especially in court decisions affirming the basic constitutional rights of African-Americans. When interest in non-violence revived after the onset of the Montgomery bus boycott in 1955–6, scarcely anyone seems to have thought of invoking the South African precedent.[5]

Montgomery, in turn, does not appear to have inspired in any significant way the dramatic bus boycott that took place in the Johannesburg township

of Alexandria in 1957. Martin Luther King reacted to the Alexandria boycott by expressing his admiration for protesters who had to walk ten or
fifteen miles, noting that those in Montgomery had often been driven to
work, but he did not claim any connection between the two movements. The
Alexandria boycott was a desperate act of resistance to a fare increase, not
a protest against segregation or denial of civil rights, and replicated a similar action in the same township during World War II. At the time when
Martin Luther King and the American non-violent movement was first at-
tracting the attention of the world, the faith of black South Africans in passive resistance was in fact wearing thin. When direct action on a broad front
commenced in the United States in 1960 and 1961, the ANC was in the
process of rejecting non-violence in favour of armed struggle.[6]

The movements were connected historically in one sense, however. Both
were inspired to some extent by the same prototype – Mahatma Gandhi's
use of militant non-violence in the struggle for Indian independence. King
of course made much of the Gandhian example and tried to apply the spirit
and discipline of Satyagraha to non-violent protests in the American South.
The official statements of purpose or philosophy issued by SCLC and SNCC
in the early 1960s were permeated with Gandhian rhetoric and philosophy.
Gandhi was less often invoked explicitly by the Defiance Campaigners, but
their methods, especially their public announcements of where, when, and
by whom laws would be disobeyed and their refusal to make bail in an
effort to 'fill the jails', could have been learned from a Gandhian textbook.[7]

If both movements drew inspiration from the great Indian apostle of non-
violence, they received the message by different routes. Gandhism came to
King and the American movement by way of a radical pacifism that derived
mostly from the left wing of the Protestant social gospel tradition. King's
non-violent antecedents and mentors were from the Christian pacifist FOR
and its anti-segregationist offshoot, CORE. Mainly the creation of white Christian radicals like the Rev. A.J. Muste, this intellectual and spiritual tradition
lacked deep roots in the black community, although it did have some notable black adherents like Bayard Rustin and James Farmer. Nevertheless,
as a recent study has shown, there was a long history of African-American
admiration for Gandhi as a brown man who was fighting for the freedom of
his people from white or European oppression. Black newspapers sometimes
expressed the hope that a Negro Gandhi might someday appear to lead a
non-violent movement against racial oppression in the United States.[8]

Gandhi cast an even longer shadow in South Africa, because he had first
experimented with *Satyagraha* as the leader of the South African Indian
community's struggle for rights as British subjects in the period between
1906 and 1914. The South African Native National Congress had been so
impressed with Gandhi's mobilization of Indians for nonviolent resistance
that they included 'passive action' as one of the methods they proposed to

use in their struggle for African citizenship rights. In 1919, the Congress actually engaged in 'passive action' on the Witwatersrand in an unsuccessful attempt to render the pass laws unenforceable through a mass refusal to obey them, but for the next 30 years this potential weapon lay rusting in the ANC's arsenal as the politics of passing resolutions and petitioning the government prevailed. A politically aroused segment of the Indian minority revived the Gandhian mode of protest in 1946 and 1947 when, with the encouragement of Gandhi and the newly independent Indian government, it engaged in 'passive resistance' against new legislation restricting Indian residential and trading rights. With the triumph of the Nationalists in 1948 and the coming of apartheid, the Indian passive resisters gave up their separate struggle and allied themselves with the ANC. The Defiance Campaign itself was in fact jointly sponsored by the ANC and the South African Indian Congress, and several veterans of earlier Indian passive resistance struggles played conspicuous roles teaching and demonstrating Gandhian non-violent techniques, as well as helping to plan the campaign and participating in its actions.[9]

In neither case, however, does a tracing of the Gandhian legacy provide a full picture of the ideological origins of mass non-violent action. Mass pressure tactics do not require a specifically Gandhian rationale; they may derive simply from a sense that less militant and confrontational tactics have proved fruitless and that it is now time to challenge the oppressor in a more direct and disruptive way. The decision of a group to engage in non-violent direct action usually constitutes a major escalation of resistance, a shift from legally authorized protest by an elite to initiatives that are more threatening and potentially violence-provoking because they involve bringing masses of aggrieved people into the streets. A philosophical or religious commitment to non-violence is not necessary to a choice of boycotts and civil disobedience as vehicles of resistance. In fact groups committed ultimately to a revolutionary overthrow of the existing order often embrace non-violent action as a means of raising consciousness and encouraging the kind of polarization that will make a revolutionary upheaval more likely. In the United States, the Communist Party and its allies had engaged in a variety of non-violent protests against racial discrimination during the 1930s, including the first mass march on Washington.[10]

Communists were excluded from A. Philip Randolph's March on Washington Movement of 1941, but Randolph was clearly influenced by their example in his effort to create an all-black movement for equal rights that would go beyond the customary legalistic methods of the NAACP and use mass action to pressure the government. As a trade unionist, he was also aware of the sit-down strike and other examples of labour militancy that owed nothing to Christianity or pacifism. Neither religious nor a pacifist, he found Gandhi's campaigns attractive because they showed what could be achieved by 'non-violent goodwill direct action'. He represented a way of thinking that could endorse everything Martin Luther King Jr was doing without accepting his non-violent theology. For Randolph and those in the movement who shared his views, it was sufficient that non-violent direct action was a practical means for African Americans to improve their position in society – while violent resistance, however defensible it might be in the abstract, was not in their view a viable option for a racial minority. King himself not only tolerated this viewpoint in his associates but at times came close to embracing it himself, at least to the extent that he came to realize that the effectiveness of non-violence resulted more from its ability to coerce or intimidate the oppressor than from any appeal it made to his conscience or better nature.[11]

In South Africa, non-Gandhian pressures for non-violent mass action came during the 1940s from the young rebels in the ANC Youth League who had grown impatient with the older generation's willingness to work within the system of black 'representation' established by the pre-apartheid white supremacist governments of Prime Ministers J. B. M. Hertzog and Jan Smuts. The Youth Leaguers, among whom were Nelson Mandela, Walter Sisulu and Oliver Tambo, favoured a boycott of segregated political institutions and experimentation with more militant and confrontational methods of protest than the organization had hitherto employed. In 1949, the Youth Leaguers won control of the ANC, and the Programme of Action that was subsequently enacted called for 'immediate and active boycott, strike, civil disobedience, non-cooperation . . .' The spirit of the Youth League and of the Defiance Campaign that was the fruit of its action programme was not based to any significant degree on a belief in the power of love to convert enemies into friends or in the higher morality of non-violence. Indeed the very use of the term 'defiance' suggests that anger more than agape was the emotion being called forth. The campaign, as its chief planner Walter Sisulu and its tactical leader, volunteer-in-chief Nelson Mandela, conceived it, was designed to enable an unarmed and impoverished majority to carry on its struggle against the tyrannical rule of an armed and wealthy minority in a more forceful and effective manner. If non-violent methods failed, there was no firm ideological barrier to prevent the young turks of the ANC from embracing other means of struggle.[12]

But there were still influential older figures in the Congress who were non-violent in principle and not purely out of expediency. Among them was Chief Albert Lutuli whose fervent Methodist Christianity strongly predisposed him against taking up arms and sustained his hopes that oppressors could be redeemed by the sufferings of the oppressed. 'The road to freedom is via the cross' was the memorable last line of the statement he made after the government had dismissed him from his chieftainship because he would not resign from the ANC. The fact that the idealistic Lutuli was elected

President-General of the ANC in 1952 showed that the ANC of the 1950s, like the southern civil rights movement of the 1960s, brought together those who regarded non-violence simply as a tactic and those who viewed it as an ethic.[13]

Besides sharing the ideological ambiguity that seems to be inescapable when non-violence becomes coercive mass action, the two movements tended to view the relationship of non-violence to 'normal' democratic politics in similar ways. Some forms of non-violence are difficult to reconcile with democratic theory because they frankly seek to override or nullify decisions made by a properly constituted majority. But in both of these instances the protesters were denied the right to vote and were therefore able to argue that their employment of extraordinary means of exerting pressures were justified by their lack of access to other forms of political expression. One person-one-vote was a major goal of both movements, and the attainment of it would presumably reduce, if not eliminate entirely, the need for non-violent mass action, especially in South Africa where blacks would then constitute a majority of the electorate. As Chief Lutuli put it in 1952, 'Non-Violent Passive Resistance' is 'a most legitimate and humane political pressure technique for a people denied all effective forms of constitutional striving'.[14] Speaking at the Prayer Pilgrimage to Washington in 1957, King made a litany of the phrase 'Give us the ballot', and promised that if it were done 'we will no longer have to worry the federal government about our basic rights ... We will no longer plead – we will write the proper laws on the books'.[15]

In addition to such similarities of ideology and ethos, the leadership of the two movements came from a similarly-situated social group – what might be described as the educated elite of a subordinate colour caste. Studies of the social composition of the ANC through the 1950s have shown conclusively that the organization was dominated by members of 'an African Bourgeoisie' or 'petty bourgeoisie' that was characterized mainly by educational and professional achievements.[16] Examinations of the origins of the southern civil rights movement have found the spur for militant action in the rise in southern cities and towns of what one historian calls 'a relatively independent black professional class'.[17]

It was a special product of legalized racial segregation that such elites were not – as is often the case under less stringent forms of ethnic or colonial domination – subject to detachment and alienation from their communities by a system of rewards and opportunities that allows a favoured few to move into the lower ranks of the governing institutions established by the dominant group. It might be taken as axiomatic that where race *per se* is the main line of division in a society, as it obviously was in South Africa and the American South, that resistance will take the form of a cross-class movement led by members of the educated middle class. This does not mean, however, that less-educated and working-class blacks made little contribution to whatever success these movements achieved. It was of course the plain folk who sustained the boycotts, often at great personal sacrifice. The point is that these freedom struggles were, and had to be, movements of peoples or communities rather than of social classes.

These similarities in the ideological and social character of the two movements did not preclude significant structural and cultural differences, to say nothing as yet of the obvious contrast of situations. The most significant structural difference between the Defiance Campaign and the non-violent civil rights movement was that the latter grew out a number of local struggles and was sustained by strong organizations and institutions at the community level, whereas the former was for the most part a centrally-planned, from-the-top-down operation. The one area where the Defiance Campaign achieved something like mass involvement was in the cities of the eastern Cape, where, as historian Tom Lodge, has shown, it was able to build on the firm base provided by a recent history of local mobilization and protest activity. But nothing like the network of 'movement centres' that was the source of the American movement existed to buttress non-violent campaigns in South Africa. Where such centres existed in South Africa they were usually tied to labour organization and trade unions; in the United States it was the black churches and black colleges that did most to sustain local activism. Since every southern city had relatively prosperous black churches and many had some kind of higher educational facility for blacks, such an institutional matrix for community protest was widely available, whereas black unions were well-established in only a few places in the South Africa of the 1950s. Furthermore, South African black townships of the 1950s were quite different from southern black urban communities. Their populations, which included a large number of transients and illegal residents, were less socially stable and significantly poorer; there were fewer well-established cultural or religious institutions; there was a proportionately much smaller middle class and relatively little black entrepreneurship or business activity. Efforts were indeed made to establish community associations, but they had much less success than comparable efforts in Montgomery or Birmingham.[18]

Even if the forces opposing each movement had been identical in strength and determination – which of course they were not – there seems little doubt that a centralized movement like the South African one would have been easier to repress than the more decentralized and diffuse American movement. Even before the ANC was outlawed, the government was able to hobble it severely simply by banning or arresting its top leaders. In the American South in the 1950s, the NAACP was rendered ineffectual by state legal harassment that in some states amounted to an outright ban. It was partly to fill the vacuum created by persecution of the NAACP that independent local movements developed. These grass-roots movements were more difficult to suppress by state action, and they flourished in places where the NAACP could no longer show itself. If such strong local communities and institutions had existed in South Africa, the government might have faced a variety of local actions that would have been much more difficult to counter than the centrally directed campaign of the ANC in 1952. (This in fact is what happened in the 1980s with the rise of the United Democratic Front, which was a federation of the community organizations that had sprung up the 1970s and early 1980s.) When, during the mid-1950s, the Congress attempted to assume the leadership of local struggles over housing or transportation, it fell short of effectively adjusting its methods and organizational style to accommodate grass-roots initiatives. The ANC supported the Alexandria bus boycott of 1957 and helped it roll back a fare increase, but it failed to turn this spontaneous expression of community grievances into a durable township organization commited to broader objectives. In the later stages of the civil rights movement, SCLC was sometimes accused of coopting local campaigns and undercutting local initiatives. But its great successes in Birmingham and Selma were the product of a skilful coordination of local, regional, and national perspectives. SCLC's genius was that it could channel and harness community energies and initiatives to make them serve the cause of national civil rights reform.[19]

Besides differing structurally, the two campaigns also diverged in the less tangible realm of movement culture and ethos. As the special prominence of ministers and churches in the American movement strongly suggests, religious belief and emotion directly inspired and animated the Afro-American protesters to an extent that could not be paralleled in South Africa. The charisma of King as prophet/saint of the movement was instrumental in making it a moral and religious crusade rather than merely the self-interested action of a social group. The opposition of large numbers of black churches and churchmen to non-violent direct action belies any notion that African-American Christianity necessarily or automatically sanctions militant protest, but King's creative interpretation and application of the gospel showed that it had the capacity to do so. The South African struggle, unlike the American, did not produce a Gandhi-like figure who could inspire the masses by persuading them that non-violent protest was God's will. There was a reservoir of religious belief and practice that might have been tapped – it surfaced at times in local actions that featured prayer and hymn-singing. But the ANC leadership was composed of highly educated men who had gone to mission schools and whose religious beliefs had little connection with those of the masses of Africans, especially those who were members of the independent 'zionist' churches that served a large proportion of urbanized Africans. The rival PAC formed in 1959 made a greater effort to draw the independent churches into the struggle, but it did not have time to accomplish much before it was banned in 1960. What King did that no South African leader was able to do was to weave together the black folk Christianity that was his own cultural heritage with the Gandhian conception of non-violent resistance to empower a cause that both inspired its followers and disarmed the opposition of many whites. Hence the non-violence of the American movement had a soul-stirring quality, both for its practitioners and for many white observers, that the more obviously conditional and pragmatic civil disobedience character-izing the Defiance Campaign normally failed to project. Of course this reso-nance was in part the result of the extensive and usually sympathetic way that the national press covered the American movement and, by the sixties, of its exposure on national television. The Defiance Campaign by contrast received relatively little attention from the white South African press and was not widely noticed abroad (which is one reason why it did not serve as a model for African-American passive resisters).[20]

The possibly decisive effects of contrasting press or media treatment suggests that the differences in the nature of the movements may tell us less about why they ultimately succeeded or failed than we are likely to learn from examining their external circumstances – what they were up against. The American protesters faced a divided, fragmented and uncertain governmen-tal opposition. The most important division among whites that the move-ment was able to exploit was between northerners who lacked a regional commitment to legalized segregation and southerners who believed that Jim Crow was central to their way of life. The success of the movement stemmed ultimately from its ability to get the federal government on its side and to utilize the US constitution against the outmoded states' rights philosophy of the southern segregationists. When King proclaimed that 'civil disobedience to local laws is civil obedience to national laws', he exploited a tactical advantage the South African resisters did not possess; for they had no alter-native to a direct confrontation with centralized state power. South African black protest leaders had long tried to drive a wedge between British im-perial and South African settler regimes, but the withdrawal of British power and influence beginning as early as 1906 and virtually complete by the 1930s had rendered such hopes illusory. For all practical purposes, South African whites in the 1950s were monolithic in their defence of perpetual white domination. In the United States it was of course federal intervention to overrule state practices of segregation and disfranchisement in the southern states that brought an end to Jim Crow. In South Africa there was no such power to which protesters could appeal against apartheid.[21]

The geopolitical context of the Cold War and decolonization of Africa and Asia also cut in opposite ways, ultimately helping the American move-ment and hindering the South African. In the United States, the competition with the Soviet Union for the 'hearts and minds' of Africans and Asians, especially by the early sixties when several African nations achieved inde-pendence, made legalized segregation a serious international liability for the

Eisenhower, Kennedy and Johnson administrations. As reasons of state were added to other factors working against Jim Crow, the federal government became more susceptible to pressures from the civil rights movement. In South Africa, on the other hand, fears of Communist subversion within the country and of Soviet influence in the newly independent African states of southern and central Africa panicked the white political leadership into pressing ahead with more radical schemes for the 'separate development' and political repression of the black majority. Underlying these contrary assessments of the dangers of black insurgency was the basic difference between a white majority facing a demand for the inclusion of a minority and a white minority conscious that the extension of democratic rights would empower a black majority.

It would be cynical, however, to see nothing in the positive responses of many white Americans to the civil rights movement except self-interested calculations. White America has not been of one mind historically on the place of blacks in the republic. In the North, at least, there was an alternative or oppositional tradition in white racial thought, originating in the antislavery movement, that advocated the public equality of the races and offered a standing challenge – although one that was only intermittently influential – to the deeply rooted white supremacist tradition that was a legacy of African-American slavery. At times, as during Reconstruction and in the mid-1960s, racial liberals became ideologically dominant and were in a position to respond to black demands for civil and political equality with major reforms. (But, being liberals, they had great difficulty in addressing the problem of economic inequality.) In South Africa, by contrast, there was no white liberal tradition that went beyond a benevolent paternalism and no deep reservoir of theoretically colour-blind attitudes toward democratic reform that could be appealed to. Nelson Mandela caught this difference when asked by an American journalist in one of his rare prison interviews during the 1980s why he had not followed the example of Martin Luther King and remained non-violent:

> Mr. Mandela said that conditions in South Africa are "totally different" from conditions in the United States in the 1960s. In the United States, he said, democracy was deeply entrenched, and people struggling then had access to institutions that protected human rights. The white community in the United States was more liberal than whites in South Africa, and public authorities were restrained by law'.[22]

Was it therefore inevitable that a non-violent movement for basic civil rights would succeed in the United States and fail in South Africa? As probable as these outcomes might seem to be, one can imagine things turning out differently. It is arguable that without the astute and inspirational leadership provided by King and others that the struggle for black civil and political equality would have taken much longer. Any claim that the Civil Rights Acts of

1964 and 1965 were inevitable obscures the creative achievements of the liberation movement. For South Africa the argument has been made that the 1961 decision of the ANC to sanction some forms of violence was a mistake; the full potential of non-violent resistance had not been exhausted, and the sabotage campaign that resulted from the decision was itself a disastrous failure that devastated the organization. To support this viewpoint, one could point, as historian Tom Lodge has done, to the relative success of the last mass non-violent action of the 1960s – the three-day stay-at-home of 1961. Lodge has also noted that the one ANC-related organization that was not banned shortly after Sharpeville – the South African Congress of Trade Unions – had a capability for politically motivated strikes that was never fully exploited. Clearly the sabotage campaign that became the centre of resistance activity in the 1960s posed little threat to white domination and turned out very badly for the ANC because it exposed its top leadership to arrest and imprisonment. If non-violence had its inherent limitations as a resistance strategy under the kind of conditions that prevailed in South Africa, it would be hard to establish from its record of achievement in the 1960s and 1970s that the resort to violence, however justifiable in the abstract, represented a more effective method of struggle. Of course the key historical actors, like Nelson Mandela, Walter Sisulu and Oliver Tambo, did not have the benefit of historical hindsight and can scarcely be condemned for trying something different when non-violent resistance had obviously failed to move the regime and had become more and more difficult to undertake.[23]

Although Martin Luther King Jr had shown some awareness of the South African campaigns of the mid-1950s – in 1957 he discussed them with the Rev. Michael Scott when both were in Ghana for the independence celebration – he first indicated a deep and abiding interest in South African developments in 1959 when he wrote to Chief Lutuli to express his admiration for the latter's courage and dignity and to forward a copy of *Stride Toward Freedom*. The Sharpeville massacre in 1960 and the awarding of the Nobel Peace Prize to Lutuli in 1961 for his espousal of non-violent resistance heightened King's interest and prompted him to speak out vigorously against apartheid. In a 1962 address to the NAACP national convention, King exemplified his doctrine of non-violence by referring to Lutuli: 'If I lived in South Africa today, I would join Chief Lithuli [*sic*] as he says to his people, "Break this law. Don't take the unjust pass system where you must have passes. Take them and tear them up and throw them away"'.[24]

King made his fullest statement about South Africa in a speech given in London on 7 December 1964, as he was on route to receiving his own Nobel Peace Prize in Oslo.

In our struggle for freedom and justice in the U.S., which has also been so long and arduous, we feel a powerful sense of identification with those in the far more deadly struggle for freedom in South Africa. We know how Africans there, and their friends of other races, strove for half a century to win their freedom by non violent methods, and we know how this non-violence was met by increasing violence from the state, increasing repression, culminating in the shootings of Sharpeville and all that has happened since . . . even in Mississippi we can organize to register Negro voters, we can speak to the press, we can in short organize people in non-violent action. But in South Africa, even the mildest form of non-violent resistance meets with years of punishment, and leaders over many years have been silenced and imprisoned. We can understand how in that situation people felt so desperate that they turned to other methods, such as sabotage.[25]

Like Mandela two decades later, King was sensitive to differences between the two contexts that would make non-violence more feasible and effective in the American case. But in the same speech he indicated a way that non violence could be brought to bear against apartheid. 'Our responsibility presents us with a unique opportunity', he told his British audience. 'We can join in the one form of non-violent *action* that could bring freedom and justice to South Africa; the action which African leaders have appealed for in a massive movement for economic sanctions.' Almost exactly one year after his London speech, King made another strong appeal for sanctions in an address on behalf of the American Committee on Africa. 'The international potential of non-violence has never been employed', he said. 'Non-violence has been practiced within national borders in India, the U.S. and in regions of Africa with spectacular success. The time has come fully to utilize non-violence through a massive international boycott. . . .'[26]

King, who gave vigorous support to the sanctions movement for the remaining three years of his life, did not of course live to see the anti-apartheid movement come to the verge of success without unleashing the violent revolution that so many observers had believed would be necessary for the otherthrow of white supremacy. It is now possible to argue that the breakthrough that came with the release of Nelson Mandela and the unbanning of the ANC was as much, if not more, the result of international non-violence as the fruit of a strategy of violent resistance inaugurated by the Congress in the 1960s. The apartheid regime was not in fact decisively defeated on the battlefield or driven from power by a domestic insurrection. The armed struggle of the ANC served to remind the world that blacks were determined to be liberated from white oppression, but it was the ethical disapproval of much of humanity that destroyed the morale and self-confidence of South Africa's ruling whites, and the increasingly effective economic sanctions that persuaded its business community and those in the government whom they influenced that apartheid had no future. Of course those sanctions would undoubtedly have been lighter and the disapprobation less sharp if the domestic resistance of the 1980s had not provoked the government into a final desperate effort to suppress dissent by force. But that domestic resistance was primarily a matter of withdrawing cooperation from the regime. Not entirely non-violent, it was predominantly so – a great domestic boycott to parallel the international one. The spirit of Gandhi, long since repudiated by the ANC in exile, was alive and well in the United Democratic Front, the domestic movement that rallied behind the ANC's goal of a non-racial democratic South Africa. In 1989, with the emergence of the Mass Democratic Movement, South Africa once again saw massive non-violent actions against segregation, led this time by clergymen like Allen Boesak and Desmond Tutu – both of whom had been greatly influenced by King and the church-based American Freedom Struggle – and featuring the singing of African-American freedom songs. Non-violence may not have been sufficient to liberate South Africa, but it is no longer possible to deny that it has played a major role in bringing that nation to democracy. It would not be beyond the power of historical analogy to describe the successful anti-apartheid movement as Birmingham and Selma on a world scale.[27]

NOTES

1. The standard historical account of the South African movement of the 1950s can be found in Tom Lodge, *Black Politics in South Africa since 1945* (London, 1983), pp. 33–230. A valuable sociological analysis written at the time is Leo Kuper, *Passive Resistance in South Africa* (London, 1956). Documents relating to the struggle can be found in Thomas Karis and Gwendolen M. Carter (eds), *From Protest to Challenge: A Documentary History of African Politics in South Africa, 1882–1964*, vol 2 and 3 (Stanford, Calif., 1973, 1977).

2. A vast historical literature on the civil rights movement now exists. A good overview is Harvard Sitkoff, *The Struggle for Black Equality, 1952–1980* (New York, 1981). A selection of interpretive essays by some of the most prominent historians of the movement is Charles W. Eagles (ed.), *The Civil Rights Movement in America* (Jackson, Miss., 1986).

3. African-American influence on black political thought in South Africa before the apartheid era is detailed in Peter Walshe, *The Rise of African Nationalism in South Africa: The African National Congress, 1912–1952* (Berkeley, 1971). On the black American religious connection with South Africa, see J. Mutero Chirenje, *Ethiopianism and Afro-Americans in Southern Africa, 1883–1916* (Baton Rouge, 1987), and James T. Campbell, 'Our Fathers, Our Children: The African Methodist Episcopal Church in the United States and South Africa', (unpublished PhD dissertation, Stanford University, 1989). I explore some of these connections in *A Comparative History of Black Ideologies in the United States and South Africa* (New York, 1995).

4. Harold R. Isaacs' study of black Negro opinion on Africa, *The New World of Negro Americans* (New York, 1964), suggests that awareness of Africa increased during the 1950s, but that most of it was focused on West Africa and especially on Kwame Nkrumah and the successful movement for independence in Ghana. My own impression from a variety of sources is that intense interest in South Africa did not develop until after Sharpeville. On the petition of the Council on African Affairs, see Gerald Horne, *Black and Red: W. E. B. Du Bois and the Afro-American Response to the Cold War* (Albany, 1986), p. 185. A review of *The Crisis* for 1952 and 1953 (vols. 59, 60) turned up a number of references to the injustices perpetrated by the government under the banner of apartheid, but the only way readers would have known about the Defiance Campaign was from publication in January 1953 of the text of the petition to the United Nations. See *The Crisis*, 60, p. 38.
5. On the fate of the March on Washington Movement, see especially Paula F. Pfeffer, *A. Philip Randolph, Pioneer of the Civil Rights Movement* (Baton Rouge, 1990), *passim*. The effect of McCarthyism on CORE is described in August Meier and Elliott Rudwick, *CORE: A study in the Civil Rights Movement, 1942–1968* (New York, 1973), pp. 63–71.
6. Interactions between African-American and black South African ideologies and movements are dealt with in some detail in my *Comparative History of Black Ideologies*. On the South African bus boycotts of the mid-fifties, see Lodge, *Black Politics*, 153–87. For King's comments on the South African boycott, see *The Christian Century*, 10 April 1957, p. 447. The one tenuous link I have been able to find between South African non-violence and Montgomery is the reference to the use of Gandhi's methods in South Africa in a November 1955 speech by Harris Wofford that was brought to King's attention at the beginning of the boycott. The speech is printed for the first time in David Garrow (ed.), *We Shall Overcome: The Civil Rights Movement in the 1950's and 60's*, vol.3 (Brooklyn, 1989), 1151–62 (Reference to South Africa on p. 1160).
7. Works which emphasize Gandhi's influence on King include David Levering Lewis, *King: A Biography* (Urbana, 1970); John J. Ansbro, *Martin Luther King, Jr.: The Making of a Mind* (Maryknoll, NY, 1982); and James P. Hanigan, *Martin Luther King, Jr. and the Foundations of Nonviolence* (Lanham, Md., 1984). Taylor Branch argues in *Parting the Waters: America in the King Years, 1954–1963* (New York, 1988), that King modified Gandhi's ideas in the light of Reinhold Niebuhr's critique of them. The Gandhian statements of purpose for SCLC and SNCC can be found in Miller, Rudwick, and Broderick (eds), *Black Protest Thought in the Twentieth Century* (Indianapolis, 1971), pp. 302–8. An examination of non-violence in South Africa which stresses the use of a Gandhian model is Leo Kuper, *Passive Resistance*.
8. See David Garrow, *Bearing the Cross: Martin Luther King, Jr., and the Southern Christian Leadership Conference* (New York, 1986), pp. 66–73, and Adam Fairclough, *To Redeem the Soul of America: The Southern Christian Leadership Conference and Martin Luther, Jr.* (Athens, Ga. 1987), pp. 23–6, for accounts how Glenn Smiley of FOR and Bayard Rustin, one of the founders of CORE, persuaded King to adopt an explicitly Gandhian rationale for the Montgomery bus boycott during its early days. The image of Gandhi in the black American consciousness is ably described in Sudarshan Kapur, *Raising Up a Prophet: The African-American Encounter with Gandhi* (Boston, 1992).
9. On Gandhi in South Africa see Maureen Swan, *Gandhi: The South African Experience* (Johannesburg, 1985). Early ANC interest in non-violence is shown in Karis and Carter, *From Protest to Challenge*, vol. 1, 62, 65–6, 108. There is no

authoritative readily available history of the Indian Passive Resistance Campaign, but much can be learned about it from recent collections of the speeches and writings of its two principal leaders. See Dr Joseph M. Dadoo, *His Speeches, Articles, and Correspondence with Mahatma Gandhi* (Durban, 1991), and *Monty Speaks: Speeches of Dr. G. M. (Monty) Naiker* (Durban, 1991).

10. See Dan T. Carter, *Scottsboro: A Tragedy of the American South* (London, 1973), pp. 248–51 for an account of the Communist Party's 'March on Washington' of 1931 to protest the Scottsboro verdict. For other examples of Communist-led non-violent protest in the 1930s, see Mark Naison, *Communists in Harlem During the Depression* (Urbana, Ill., 1983), *passim*, and Sinclair Drake and Horace R. Cayton, *Black Metropolis: A Study of Negro Life in a Northern City* (New York, 1962), vol. I, 85–8.

11. See Pfeffer, *Randolph*, pp. 45–88 and *passim*. For discussions of the realistic side of King's use of non-violence, see Garrow, *Bearing the Cross*, pp. 273–4, Branch, *Parting the Waters*, pp. 85–7; and Fairclough, *To Redeem the Soul*, pp. 51–3. Garrow argues that King began as a naive Gandhian, but Branch and Fairclough believe that King had always been commited to a practical or realistic conception of nonviolent action.

12. On the ANC Youth League and the Programme of Action, see Walshe, *Rise of African Nationalism*, pp. 349–61, and Karis and Carter *From Protest to Challenge*, vol. 2, 301–39.

13. *Speeches of Albert John Luthuli* (Durban, 1991), pp. 41–4 and *passim*. See also Luthuli, *Let My People Go: An Autobiography* (London, 1962). Despite the spelling that appears in both of these titles, 'Lutuli' is now generally accepted as correct.

14. Carter and Karis (eds), *From Protest to Challenge*, vol. 2, 487.

15. Quoted in Lewis, *King*, p. 93.

16. See Leo Kuper, *An African Bourgoisie: Race, Class, and Politics in South Africa* (New Haven, 1965), pp. 101–3 and *passim*, and Alan Cobley, *Class and Consciousness: The Black Petty Bourgeoisie in South Africa, 1924 to 1950* (New York, 1990).

17. Steven M. Millner, 'The Montgomery Bus Boycott: A Case Study in the Emergence and Career of a Social Movement', in David Garrow (ed.), *The Walking City: The Montgomery Bus Boycott* (Brooklyn, 1989), pp. 512–13.

18. The localized basis for the southern movement is set forth effectively in Aldon D. Morris, *The Origins of the Civil Rights Movement: Black Communities Organizing for Change* (New York, 1984). My view of the South African movement derives principally from Lodge, *Black Politics*. Lodge discusses the peculiarities of the Eastern Cape on pp. 45–60 and *passim*.

19. See Lodge, *Black Politics*, pp. 170–1 on the ANC's failure in Alexandria. My understanding of how SCLC operated is based primarily on Morris, *Origins* and Fairclough, *To Redeem the Soul*.

20. Morris in *Origins* emphasizes the local religious basis of the civil rights movement, but note also the critique of Morris's argument by Clayborne Carson in *Constitutional Commentary* 3, (Summer 1986), 616–21. Carson believes that Morris 'should have discussed the conflicts within the church regarding racial militancy and noted the large number – perhaps a majority – of southern black clergymen who did not become active in the civil rights movement or allow their churches to be used for civil rights meetings.' (620–1). Lodge in *Black Politics* describes the grass roots religiosity of the Defiance Campaign on pp. 43–4 and the PAC's overture to the Independent African Churches on p. 81. The subject of religious influences on the South African protest of the 1950s has not been adequately studied, and generalizations must be made with caution.

21. For an earlier formulation of these contrasts of political context, see George M. Fredrickson, 'The South and South Africa', in *The Arrogance of Race: Perspectives on Slavery, Racism, and Social Inequality* (Middletown, Conn., 1988), pp. 254–69.
22. Sheridan Johns and R. Hunt Davis (eds.), *Mandela, Tambo, and the African National Congress: The Struggle Against Apartheid, 1948–1990* (New York, 1991), pp. 193. (Excerpted from the *Washington Times*, 22 August 1985.)
23. See Lodge, *Black Politics*, pp. 196–9.
24. *Christian Century*, 10 April 1957; Lewis, *King*, p. 259; King quoted in Branch, *Parting the Waters*, p. 599.
25. Martin Luther King Jr, 'Address on South African Independence', London, England, 7 December 1964. Library and Archives of the Martin Luther King, Jr. Center for Nonviolent Change, Atlanta, Ga.
26. Ibid., p. 2; Address of Dr. Martin Luther King on 10 December 1965 for the benefit of the American Committee on Africa, Hunter College, New York City. Martin Luther King, Jr. Center, Library and Archives.
27. Good accounts of recent developments in South Africa are Anthony W. Marx, *Lessons of Struggle: South African Internal Opposition, 1960–1990* (New York, 1992), and Richard Prize, *The Apartheid State in Crisis, 1975–1990* (New York, 1991). An explicit repudiation of 'passive resistance' on behalf of the ANC was made by Oliver Tambo in 1966. (Johns and Davis, *Mandela, Tambo*, p. 134). I learned of the extent to which the UDF represented a revival of Gandhism during the course of an interview in South Africa in July 1993 with Mewa Rambgobin, a leader of the Indian community and former treasurer of the UDF. For him, the domestic protest in South Africa during the 1980s, which featured a boycott of elections and leaders going to jail without paying fines or making bail, was a vindication of some of the non-violent methods that Gandhi had employed in the liberation of India.

Index